Soraya Murray is Associate Professor in the Film and Digital Media Department at the University of California, Santa Cruz (UCSC), where she is also affiliated with the Digital Arts and New Media MFA Program, and the Art + Design: Games + Playable Media Program. She is an interdisciplinary scholar of visual culture, with particular interest in cultural studies, contemporary art, film and video games. Murray holds a PhD in the History of Art and Visual Studies from Cornell University.

'An engaging analysis and an entirely unique contribution to video game and media studies.'

– Jennifer Jenson, York University, Canada

On Video Games

The Visual Politics of Race, Gender and Space

SORAYA MURRAY

BLOOMSBURY ACADEMIC
LONDON • NEW YORK • OXFORD • NEW DELHI • SYDNEY

BLOOMSBURY ACADEMIC
Bloomsbury Publishing Plc
50 Bedford Square, London, WC1B 3DP, UK
1385 Broadway, New York, NY 10018, USA
29 Earlsfort Terrace, Dublin 2, Ireland

BLOOMSBURY, BLOOMSBURY ACADEMIC and the Diana logo
are trademarks of Bloomsbury Publishing Plc

First published in Great Britain by I.B. Tauris 2018
Paperback edition published by Bloomsbury Academic 2021

A catalogue record for this book is available from the British Library.

ISBN: HB: 978-1-7845-3741-8
PB: 978-1-3502-1770-6
ePDF: 978-1-7867-3250-7
eBook: 978-1-7867-2250-8

Printed and bound in Great Britain

To find out more about our authors and books visit
www.bloomsbury.com and sign up for our newsletters.

Contents

Contents

Illustrations

List of Illustrations

List of Illustrations

Cover Imaged on the cover of this book is a painted polymer clay head entitled *Gamer (#1)* by Wilfrid Wood. Part of a series, the 2015 sculpture presents a send-up of a gamer "type" in a playful, almost ethnographic rendering of an adolescent Caucasian boy with an absorbed expression. The boy's mouth hangs open, and his blood-shot blue eyes are half-lidded. Jacked in and tuned out, his look wavers between concentration, an artificial high, and a mystical state of having turned inwards. This satirical image emblematizes the ideological notion of who a gamer is, and a persisting public perception, though this has not been the reality for some time. Part of the project of this book is to broaden the narrow understanding of video games as exclusively the purview of children, entertainment and distraction.

Acknowledgements

My teachers took many forms – professors, colleagues, editors, students, family and friends – across the years. To my Cornell University graduate advisor, Salah Hassan, as well as my committee members Laura Meixner and María Fernández: your highly committed and intellectually progressive thinking, teaching and mentorship indelibly shaped this research.

Salah Hassan provided key opportunities for me to publish writing in *Nka: Journal of Contemporary African Art*. Bonnie Marranca at *PAJ: A Journal of Performance and Art* published my first essay on games, for which I'll always be grateful. Patricia Phillips and Joe Hannan generously supported my research by publishing my work in the College Art Association's *Art Journal*. My gratitude goes out to Richard Dyer for publishing my writing in *Third Text*, and for his scholarship, which has been so influential on my own. My games research was presented at Rochester Institute of Technology, LASER, The Center for Cultural Studies at UCSC, and by invitation of Tirza Latimer at California College of the Art's Graduate Program in Visual and Critical Studies. Earlier forms of my research on *Assassin's Creed III: Liberation* were presented at the Canadian Game Studies Association in Ottawa by invitation of Felan Parker; the History of Gender in Games Symposium in Montréal by invitation of Mia Consalvo and Gabrielle Trépanier-Jobin; and the Queerness and Games Conference in Berkeley by invitation of Bonnie Ruberg and her co-organizers, all in 2015. Texas Tech University's School of Art hosted me in a presentation of this research as well, in 2016. Special thanks go to Joe Arredondo and Kaveh Rafie for their efforts. I would like to thank Nicholas Knouf and Orit Shaer at Wellesley College, and my wonderful co-panelists at *Gaming Futures: Perspectives of Women in Games and Play*: Katherine Isbister, Rayla Heide, Cassie Hoef, Anna Loparev and of course my fellow Cornellian, Claudia Pederson. My gratitude goes out to all of you, for introducing my research to new audiences.

Acknowledgements

I wish to warmly recognize Anna Everett, D. Fox Harrell and Jen Jenson, who graciously agreed to participate in a games panel I organized for the International Symposium on Electronic Art (ISEA) in 2015 – all of whom have since extended their collegiality in many ways. Thanks to Ariel Direse for his invitation to the International Meeting on New Technologies in the Digital Age, at *Ventana Sur* 2013, Buenos Aires, Argentina. Thanks to the ISEA 2011 organizers, Lanfranco Aceti and Ozden Sahin, who invited me to present my research, 'Theorizing New Media in a Global Context', in Istanbul, Turkey. The Chair of that event, Yiannis Colakides, went on to publish that research, as did Arthur and Marilouise Kroker at *CTheory*. In 2016, I organized a panel at the College Art Association Annual Conference, entitled 'The Visual Politics of Play: On The Signifying Practices of Digital Games'. The impressive contributions of panelists Hava Aldouby, Kishonna Gray, Derek Conrad Murray, John Sharp and Dietrich Squinkifer were an inspiration, opening up many new interpretive possibilities for the study of games within the context of art history and visual studies. By the kind invitation of Aaron Trammell, I was able to share and develop some of the ideas in this book at *Extending Play* at Rutgers University in 2016.

Thank you to the Digital Arts and New Media MFA Program, and the Art + Design: Games + Playable Media Program. Thanks, too, to my undergraduate and graduate students, whose enthusiasm for the idea of video games as a cultural form sustained me in pursuing this research, and who have taught me so much. My gratitude goes out to Noah Wardrip-Fruin, Katherine Isbister, Robin Hunicke, Michael Mateas, Neda Atanasoski, Felicity Amaya Schaeffer, Miguel Sicart and my colleagues in the Film and Digital Media Department for their support, mentorship, advice and encouragement at key moments.

This book was significantly supported from its inception through completion by grants from UCSC's Arts Research Institute and UCSC's Committee on Research, as well as the UCSC Arts Dean's Excellence Fund. A portion of my research on *Assassin's Creed III: Liberation* was published in an earlier form in the journal *Kinephanos* (2017), due to the efforts of Gabrielle Trépanier-Jobin. Earlier forms of my work on *Spec Ops: The Line* have appeared in *Gaming Representation: Race, Gender, and Sexuality in Video Games*, thanks to co-editors Jennifer Malkowski and TreaAndrea M.

Acknowledgements

Russworm (Indiana University Press, 2017); *Zones of Control: Perspectives on Wargaming*, eds Pat Harrigan and Matthew G. Kirschenbaum (The MIT Press, 2016); and by kind invitation of B. Ruby Rich at *Film Quarterly* (December 2016).

To Senior Editor Philippa Brewster, and editors Baillie Card, Lisa Goodrum and Madeleine Hamey-Thomas at I.B.Tauris, who so eagerly supported me from the outset: thank you for championing this project. Jesi Khadivi and Janet Reed thoughtfully provided invaluable editing and indexing assistance. A special thank you to Senior Publisher Rebecca Barden and Bloomsbury for their support of this paperback edition. To artist Wilfrid Wood: thank you for generously sharing permission to use your provocative, compelling art as the cover image.

My family, especially my parents, Gerry and Gigi Muhlert, paid great care to my education and my spirit of adventure in the world. Thanks to my ever-supportive sister, Leilah Roche. Finally, I would like to express my affection and appreciation to Derek Conrad Murray, who has been my fierce companion in the foxhole, in this and all my endeavours, from the beginning.

This book is for Grace, Wynnie and Gen.

Introduction: Is the 'Culture' in Game Culture the 'Culture' of Cultural Studies?

[T]he best games are the ones tightly woven around the user's desires, seamless, catering, which seem to be filled with options for those who need to break the levels. Participatory, skill-based, emotional, addictive, often competitive, instinctual, frequently violent, yet at the same time immersive, creative, sharing, rewarding, empowering, and frequently community-building, gaming occupies a critical cultural niche. We must learn how to talk about it.[1]

Mary Flanagan, 'Response', *First Person*

Cultural studies matters because it is about the future, and about some of the work it will take, in the present, to shape the future. It is about understanding the present in the service of the future. By looking at how the contemporary world has been made to be what it is, it attempts to make visible ways in which it can become something else.[2]

Lawrence Grossberg, *Cultural Studies in the Future Tense*

Video Games and the Matter of Culture

This book asks a series of questions about video games, assuming they are not only technological, but also cultural. What do mainstream games made in the socio-political context of a globalized, post-9/11, post-Obama, neoliberal expansionist period tell us about dominant presumptions and anxieties? Or about constructions of power? What do games tell us is normal? What do they suggest should be imaged, and what should not? As complex forms of visual culture, what do they reveal about where we are now? And how do games not only powerfully mirror, but also engender, a certain sense of how the world is – as well as the capacities for our relations within it? These nuanced forms increasingly beckon for sustained engagement by various humanistic disciplines. They constitute a visual culture that is literally everywhere, yet troubling disciplinary inaction and a lack of intellectual engagement persists – seeming to suggest games lie outside legitimate areas of cultural inquiry. This book provides one possible model for understanding video games as visual culture and making progressive intervention into one of the most prevalent, impactful and underestimated forms of image-production of our time.

Video games represent powerful invocations of the lived world in playable form, which offer insights into the core fears, fantasies, hopes and anxieties of a given culture in a specific cultural context. Some games exemplify this quality more than others. This is not disconnected from the degree to which any given game is able – like other forms of cultural expression – to capture the spirit of the moment, to articulate a struggle within culture or to meaningfully intervene in its own discourse or larger histories. Much of this book is the result of a course that I developed over many years, which grew from the base assumptions that games are dominant forms of visual culture and fraught artefacts, filled with complex meanings that reflect and grapple with the most important questions of our times. In a way, my own intellectual inquiry is about the speculative possibility of reading the two epigraphs above alongside each other – and imagining what formation that kind of scholarship could be.

Games are potential sites for negotiating unresolved cultural, social or political frictions – or at least providing powerful and indeed political 'texts' to be thought with, in order to develop a more nuanced relationship to mass culture and its effects. To play video games is to engage with the myths of a constituency whose access, agency and ability to wield the technology allows them to communicate their wishes, fears, dreams – and even identity politics – through a form of interactive entertainment. Games differ from theatre, film or television; but they do operate as expressions of the 'dream life' of a culture, whose playable depths are only beginning to be plumbed.[3]

This approach is not typical for the study of games. In undertaking this endeavour, I start by sketching the terrain in order to better locate the discussion of games as thoroughly cultural, not just technical. First, I outline the usefulness of cultural studies strategies for games, as powerful tools for the analysis of mass culture, but whose study is contested within larger shifts in the value systems of higher education. I show how analysing games as dynamic forms of representation, using the tools of cultural critique, can provide a valuable means by which to better understand video games as culture within the matrix of power and difference. The simple question of identifying positive or negative representations is not what matters here, but rather understanding culture as an ongoing struggle that can be observed in games.

But first, it is important to understand the centrality of the term 'culture' and how much of what cultural studies – as it was originally formulated by British academics – turned around a strategic framing of this term away from its previous definitions. The very definition of culture exemplifies its living, breathing, wriggling, transfiguring shifting qualities. Culture as a term is not singular, but a panoply of things. As the venerated cultural critic and theorist Mieke Bal aptly observed, culture can mean something like the 'best' of a society, which bends toward the elitist. Or it can relate to ways of life, which veers more toward the ethnographic. Bal references the work of Raymond Williams, which was key in the development of cultural studies. Williams identified four ways of thinking about culture: (1) in terms of intellectual, spiritual and aesthetic development; (2) in terms of specific artistic and intellectual activity; (3) in terms of a way of life of a social grouping; and (4) in terms of a signifying system through which certain values are conveyed and maintained.[4] But even these four definitions, she asserts, don't really come close to the 'heterogeneous' dimensions of culture. 'Culture,' Bal argues, 'can transmit dominant values, but it can also be seen as a site of resistance where dominant shared codes may be disrupted or displaced, and where alternative shared codes can be produced.'[5] Understanding culture in this way is instructive for conceptualizing games as sites where 'dominant shared codes' find their form, are communicated, are interrupted, or are resisted and reformulated.

When the term 'game culture' is used, it typically refers to some selective practices and communities around games, or in other words to something that might be specifically referred to as 'player culture' or 'fan culture'. This keeps with a common definition of culture as something that concerns the particular ways of life, attitudes, customs and behaviours of a given social group. However, it is predominately thought of as fundamentally separate from culture at large, or at least, something that in only limited ways portends to anything about a given culture in general. As games scholar Adrienne Shaw puts it, '[popular discourses] still define "video game culture" as something very distinct and very different from mainstream US culture.'[6] But games as culture, and the potential of critical game studies, desperately need an expanded understanding of what 'culture' means for games scholarship and criticism, one that urgently takes into account the intellectual interventions of cultural studies and particularly its crucial visual culture studies component. The utilization of this loaded terminology within the discourse of cultural studies alludes to a history of critical thought that explores the complex intersections between identity, representation, ideology and power. Scratching the surface of these concerns, it becomes clear that the gulf between 'video game culture' and the 'culture' of 'cultural studies' is constructed, illusory and highly intentional, something that will be explored more fully throughout this book.

The military and scientific origins of the technologies used for games, as well as their association with violence in general, pose further barriers to the acceptance of games as culture. Some games, like *America's Army*, are military simulations whose functions are to recruit, train and socialize individuals into militarized thinking.[7] This is inarguable. Sociologists have debated – quite inconclusively – about whether games bear any direct connection to displays of aggressiveness or violence toward others. The most extreme form of this position might even suggest that the individual who plays games with extreme content may lose their ability to discriminate between the lived world and their fantasies. Often, when some violent act occurs that involves a young man, such as a school shooting, there is a rush to explain what happened. If the person played video games, it is sometimes inferred, without any real substantiation, that there is a direct causal link between the games they played and their violent act. Mainstream media regularly insinuates relationships between violent video games and mass shootings, such as the Columbine High School massacre in 1999, Anders Breivik's 2011 Norway massacre and the Sandy Hook Elementary School Shooting in 2012. On the other hand, some scholarship examines games as play-training in subtler forms of violence, such as how racial 'types' are imaged and galvanized through games. For example, scholars Anna Everett and S. Craig Watkins have written on games as 'racial pedagogical zones' or 'RPZs' that normalize particular racial stereotypes to players. This is another kind of 'training', one that does not generate specific violent behaviours, but instead indoctrinates by imparting and persuasively shoring up race-based assumptions.[8] More recently, Shaw articulated this sentiment well when she wrote: 'Media texts provide us with source material for what might be possible, how identities might be constructed, and what worlds we might live in. These are the reasons media representation matters…'[9] It would be a mistake to reduce modern-day video games to military simulations, and players of games to passive receptors of mass media. The origins of games do not necessarily define the limits of their potential. However, they do play a powerful role in the capacity to imagine what might be possible, and how we understand the world and our relations within it.

Games are contradictory objects that invoke both spaces of possibility and extreme capitalist mass cultural production. Although Stuart Hall never significantly focused on video games, many of his critical interventions into mass culture and representation provide useful models for thinking about games as culture. Hall, a charismatic, articulate and highly influential figure, in many ways came to embody cultural studies.[10] He also meaningfully brought race and ethnicity into the discussion. As one scholar noted, 'For him [Hall], culture is not something to simply appreciate, or study; it is also a critical site of social action and interpretation, where power relations are both established and potentially unsettled.'[11] As 'everyday' culture, both games as cultural objects, and gamer culture (subcultures, fandom, etc.) are sites where dominant and subordinate entities struggle for recognition.

Hall's essay 'Encoding/Decoding' enumerated how, in mass culture, messages are sent and received in far more complex ways than previously understood. He noted that mass media image-producers (in this case, Hall was specifically discussing television) were often frustrated that viewers did not necessarily absorb the images according to their intended meaning. Since individual viewers are activated participants in a living culture that is shifting and changing, and because they may have varying relationships to the dominant hegemonic viewpoint, it's natural and inevitable that varying interpretations of the image will result. So if we think of this in terms of video games, the person whose value system aligns with a mainstream perspective will look at a game differently than someone who already has an opposing stance, or who breaks from the normative. It is not hard to imagine that players bring a great deal to games, and that their subject positions, histories and cultural contexts (as well as innumerable other factors) shape what they gather from their played experiences. As his work has so much influence upon my own, I refer to the thought of Stuart Hall throughout this book.

The popular discourse on video games dedicates much energy to insisting that games are unimportant and 'low'. This line of logic denigrates gamers as engaged with trivial child's play and frames games as morally vapid and corrupting of youth.[12] Mounting critiques of the games industry's disproportionately high incidents of workplace chauvinism compared to many other professional spheres have caught the attention of the mainstream press. GamerGate, the harassment campaign against the presence of women and other socially defined minorities in games, which I discuss below, illuminates a bleak image of the state of game culture, in-game representations and the game industry's politics of inclusivity. The debate around GamerGate became so vitriolic at one point that the conventional construction of the 'gamer' as an identity (associated with a particular type of white, male, disengaged or antisocial player) was declared dead by several critics.[13] The negativity and misogyny associated with gamers in the public domain even led some within the games community to personally reject the title. Meanwhile, video games are a massive, pervasive and extremely lucrative economic venture enjoyed by a wide variety of people. According to a 2016 Pew Research Center report on gaming, 49 per cent of American adults now play games and 10 per cent think of themselves as 'gamers'. The split between male and female players is statistically narrowing, with women playing nearly an identical share of games. However, women are less than half as likely to describe themselves as 'gamers' – and most American adults (60 per cent) still think that it is mostly males who play video games.[14] Within the United States, consumers spent $23.5 billion on the game industry in 2015.[15] According to the *Nielsen 360° Gaming Report*, in 2016 'half of the population in the world's industrialized countries now identifies as gamers.'[16] Numbers vary, but the Entertainment Software Association estimates that $71 billion was spent on games globally in 2015.[17] The noted research firm Gartner estimated larger numbers with global video game sales topping $93 billion in 2013, and projected the numbers would climb to $111 billion in 2015.[18]

The gulf between the notion that games are the lowest of low culture and their simultaneous explosive expansion as a global form of visual culture is notable – and therefore the moralistic protestations that accompany their presence should be met with scepticism. I am committed to an ethical engagement with technology in general, and video games as a form of visual culture more specifically. As a part of understanding the worldwide phenomenon of games as a popular form, I see contemporary games as situated in larger cultural histories, events and bodies of representation. But in a broader sense, I am also invested in the stakes of this discussion. What drives the persisting disavowal of games as a legitimate area of critical study within the academy? And what does this say about the ethical investments of visual culture studies, and critical cultural studies more generally, relative to games?

Games in the Academy

Within the university setting, the primary investment has been made in innovating technologies of interactive media. According to the *Princeton*

Review, more than 150 undergraduate and graduate games programs emerged by 2015, most notably: Entertainment Arts & Engineering (EAE) at the University of Utah; Florida Interactive Entertainment Academy, at the University of Central Florida; Southern Methodist University's Guildhall; University of Southern California's GamePipe Laboratory; Rochester Institute of Technology's Interactive Games and Media; Drexel Game Design and the RePlay Lab; The Center for Games and Playable Media at the University of California, Santa Cruz; and NYU's Game Center, among many others.[19] While some of these programs do offer courses on the critical cultural study of games, the overarching focus tends towards technical training and the innovation of game production (such as better AI and expressivity, and other procedural aspects of games). Such programs largely prepare students for the dominant games industry or indie game development and related fields. There is also an interactive fiction and electronic literature focus, with origins in hypertext and literary studies, that importantly champions innovating better narrative, expressivity and richer player-tool communication and interaction. In addition to the above, recent popular and academic writing on games exploits the potential for games to affect positive social transformation, raise awareness of key social problems, expand expressive potentials or make ethical interventions on the level of design, such as the work of Jane McGonigal, Robin Hunicke, D. Fox Harrell, Noah Wardrip-Fruin, Miguel Sicart, Mary Flanagan and Katherine Isbister, among many others.[20]

Game studies is in a molten state of turmoil and transition. At the time of this writing, it is neither a codified 'field' with agreed-upon core texts, nor has it been assimilated into a disciplinary formation that occupies a fixed location in the academic setting. In the United States context, game studies remains bifurcated between the Humanities and Computer Science, with much significant work being completed on improvements in form, while there is less (and very often renegade) scholarship within related disciplines like media studies, literature and communications. Additionally, disciplines like sociology and anthropology have produced some significant interventions into games and game culture. There are several dedicated academic, peer-reviewed journals, such as the online-based *Game Studies: The International Journal of Computer Game Research*[21] and the notable *Games and Culture: A Journal of Interactive Media*.[22] However, much of the most influential writing on games often takes place in games journalism and on the blogs of games critics. Academic essays on games occasionally appear in discipline-specific journals for film, media, studies, art, art history and the like.

There are even fewer books that provide close readings of games as cultural expressions. Steven E. Jones, an English professor who was among the first to publish a book-length analysis of games, uses what he describes as a 'textual studies' approach issuing from his background in literary scholarship to consider the way in which games as culture are 'received' during player engagement. He advocates for an expanded understanding of textual studies approaches, considering games as a legitimate object of study. Calling games 'arguably the most influential form of popular expression and entertainment in today's broader culture', Jones suggests that there are good reasons to move beyond 'cultural and aesthetic prejudices' held by scholars.[23] Jones characterizes the meanings of games as fundamentally socially constructed and enacted, rather than fixed. He writes:

> The meanings of games are not essential or inherent in their form (though form is a crucial determinant), even if we define form as a set of rules and constraints for gameplay, and certainly not in their extractable 'stories' (though the fictive storyworld matters most in games). Rather, they are functions of the larger grid of possibilities built by groups of developers, players, reviewers, critics, and fans in particular times and places and through specific acts of gameplay or discourse about games.[24]

This lack of fixity of games, owed to the often-collaborative nature of their making, reception and interpretation, also bears on their representational orders, which invoke previous forms of media, yet diverge in key ways.

Comparatively few who would fall under the loose category of game studies scholars have taken up the concerns of identity, including race, sex, gender, nation, class or other markers of socially defined difference. However, some of the notable foundational examples of games research that intersect with representation will be covered, including those made by people like Lisa Nakamura, Adrienne Shaw, Anna Anthropy, Jon Dovey and Helen W. Kennedy, Geoff King and Tanya Krzywinska, Jennifer Malkowski and TreaAndrea Russworm, Anna Everett, Justine Cassell and Henry Jenkins, Yasmin B. Kafai et al., Brenda Laurel, Nina Huntemann, Derek A. Burrill and Matthew Thomas Payne, among others.[25]

It is also important to understand the rise of games within their socio-political contexts, and this is something that I model within my analyses. Games are the quintessential visual culture of advanced capitalism. Nick Dyer-Witheford and Greig de Peuter's research is extremely useful for thinking about the tension that the serious study of games faces within disciplines like visual studies. Their *Games of Empire* goes straight to the point of the problem of games. Operating from the assumption that they are global media culture, Dyer-Witheford and de Peuter's writing examines the political, cultural and economic force of games, as well as their potentials.[26] Their analysis springs from the interventions of Michael Hardt and Antonio Negri, who use the term 'Empire' to name the 'emergence of a new planetary regime in which economic, administrative, military and communicative components combine to create a system of power "with no outside".[27] Dyer-Witheford and de Peuter extend Hardt and Negri's characterization of a global system, with all of its dehumanizing bureaucratic dimensions, to a consideration of games in their entire cycle of production and consumption. Their work is important for this book because they make a strongly contextual critique of games as sited within, and reproducing of, a dominant social order. While it is not my intention to specifically focus on a post-Marxist inflected critique of games, Dyer-Witheford and de Peuter's groundbreaking work has been an influence in terms of understanding games within the context of global capitalism and the turn toward neoliberal economic values.

Larger shifts toward neoliberal values in the US economy and in education, introduced in Britain by Prime Minister Margaret Thatcher in the 1970s and by President Ronald Reagan in the US in the mid-1980s, announced an inescapable reality of economic globalization and its free-market demands.[28] Neoliberalism called for economic deregulation and enhanced freedom of the market in order to allow it to self-regulate, with the promise of 'trickle-down' economic results. This also included the reduction of government spending on health, education and other social services and increased policy-making that would shift the onus toward individual responsibility, and increased privatization of services formerly considered part of the public sector.[29]

This neoliberal turn impacted the university in ways that bear upon the perception of games in academia – and therefore their reception by society at large. Among many others, Stanley Fish, Milton Friedman, Sophia McClennen, David Harvey, Henry Giroux, Susan Searls Giroux, Stanley Aronowitz, Jeffrey Williams and Masao Miyoshi have debated the conditions of the university under the duress of neoliberal values.[30] Henry Giroux contends that 'higher education appears to be increasingly decoupling itself from its historical legacy as a crucial public sphere, responsible for both educating students for the workplace and providing them with the modes of critical discourse, interpretation, judgment, imagination, and experiences that deepen and expand democracy.'[31] Characterizing a turn within educational institutions toward neoliberal values within their own systems of evaluation, he continues, 'Unable to legitimate its purpose and meaning according to such important democratic practices and principles, higher education now narrates itself in terms that are more instrumental, commercial, and practical.'[32] The increasing prevalence of these ideas, and their impact on institutions of learning, has had direct influence on the degree to which discussions of identity are viable within the emerging areas of digital media. In characterizing the socio-political context of new media (specifically the burgeoning internet), Lisa Nakamura highlighted neoliberalism's role in casting cyberspace as a colour-blind zone, which she says must be taken into account when considering the inequities of digital racial formations.[33] Alexander Galloway similarly described the 'neoliberal, digirati notion that race must be liberated via an uncoupling from material detail, but also that the logic of race can never be more alive, can never be more purely actualized, than in a computer simulation.'[34] Indeed, the impacts of neoliberal values strongly shape the milieu in which video games have come into their maturity as a medium, as well as the terms by which their analysis has been integrated into the academy.

To be fair, liberal forms of pretension also routinely reject video games – and especially mainstream games – as escapism, militarism, hypercapitalist enterprise and as forms inappropriate to serious consideration. Within spaces of liberal education, it is common to find technological training in

game development, yet from a critical cultural perspective, games themselves are openly thought of as entertainment of the uncultured, as intoler-
able visual forms. Liberal progressiveness often performs a disingenuous
refusal to deal with video games. Further, this dismissiveness takes the
form of overbearing ideological constructions around who plays games,
what games are like and the types of impacts they have on players.[35] These
problems also stand in the way of truly addressing the complexity of these
playable media forms.

I question this prevalent tendency in the academy because critical
neglect contributes to the pernicious image-making practices that are
often common in games through the passive refusal to engage. The values
of liberal spaces often express a kind of moral outrage with the topic, or
tokenized disdain, but with little action following in regard to equitable
change or actual intellectual intervention. Can the games industry truly
be exclusively blamed for its elisions and shoddy representations, its pandering to audiences? Or to some degree, does liberal progressiveness that
refuses to engage with this ubiquitous form also bear some responsibility?

This poses a disciplinary problem for me, because in this moment
of rejection, visual culture studies engages in a politics of respectability,
as opposed to an ethical methodological intervention. Slavoj Žižek discusses this in terms of a 'culturalization of politics' – the turning of tolerance of difference into culture, but without any substantive change. He
writes: 'Political differences, differences conditioned by political inequality,
economic exploitation, and so on, are naturalized and neutralized into cultural differences, different ways of life, which are something given, something that cannot be overcome, but must be merely tolerated.'[36] No real
intervention is made, in other words.

Philosopher Wendy Brown also discusses this in terms of the problem
of liberal institutions creating a bureaucratic web of language and sentiment around antiracism, tolerance, anti-sexism and other markers of tolerance discourse. Put into place are forms of language, such as political
correctness, but the institutional structures persist undisturbed so that
power dynamics do not substantially shift, and nothing changes.[37] Žižek is
even less charitable, saying, 'Today's academic leftist who criticizes capitalist cultural imperialism is in reality horrified at the idea that his field of

study might break down.'[38] He points to the hypocritical nature of tolerance discourse, which performs gestures of a certain politics, but ultimately does not intervene in the root causes of rapacious capitalism, imperialism, inequality and injustice. If we can apply Žižek's insight to the specific scenario of critical game studies within the academy, we could say that truly eliminating capitalist cultural imperialism, for example, means eliminating that which props up a key element that makes academic leftists themselves. Namely, it eradicates the societal, cultural, economic and political elements that contributed to their own coming into being as residents of the ivory tower. Worse, it interrupts a powerful self-definition built on the basis of knowing good culture from bad, high culture from low. Perhaps this rejection is merely sentiment, performed out of habit. But as Žižek says, '[h]abits are thus the very stuff our identities are made of; in them, we enact and thus define what we effectively are as social beings, often in contrast with our perception of what we are. In their very transparency, habits are the medium of social violence.'[39]

This dynamic is also troubling because video games appropriate things like, for example, historical wars and constructions of heroes, turn them into culture, and then render that culture playable. Take, for example, the social media-driven outcry against the tone-deaf Twitter ads for EA Games' *Battlefield 1* (2016), a first-person shooter set in World War I. The insensitive hashtag '#justWWIthings' was used, prompting public criticism, and forcing EA to apologize and pull the campaign.[40] It was an unusual moment of rupture in which playing with the history of WWI overstepped bounds and became obscene. Much is at stake in the image-making practices of playable visual culture because it is in fact just that: a way of playing with culture and playing with politics – potentially without any kind of moral and ethical buy-in. There is perhaps a catharsis, but one that constitutes a mere 'culturalization of politics'. This is why it is so important to take game representations seriously, and to hold their makers more accountable to tell the stories of subjects with more consideration. If, as Dyer-Witheford and de Peuter effectively argued, video games are the product of Western Empire, then it seems odd the degree to which visual and critical studies persists in ignoring them as a serious object of study and site of critical intervention.[41] The real obscenity is not the video game as scholarly subject; rather, it is the liberal progressive inaction that maintains both institutional and cultural inequality.

Ultimately, it is neither my intention to make a thorough critique of the neoliberal turn here, nor to debate the value of a liberal arts education. I mention neoliberalism and how its attendant social, cultural and economic ramifications impacted the university as I passed through its systems, because the turn toward universalism and away from the concerns of multiculturalism have influenced this scholarship. These shifts created a material condition through which the market (advanced capitalism) contributed to the definition of a 'field' or 'area' of games studies as something specific, and likewise erroneously cast other kinds of critical cultural discussions (of race and representation, for example) as less viable. On the other hand, the liberal academy has also engaged in exclusionary practices around critical cultural approaches to games. But plainly, the consideration of games *as culture* is both viable and urgently necessary. Because both mainstream and alternative games issue directly from – or in reaction to – the expansion of capitalist enterprise into all aspects of culture, it is precisely due to their very origins in military technology, mass entertainment and hypercapitalism that we may learn from their expressions.

Which Games?

The games considered within these pages were selected not out of personal preference, but because they contain elements of self-reflectivity, ambiguity, satire or a critical edge. They frequently mobilize contradiction as a vehicle for metaphorical engagement with the lived world. Just as pure fandom would be considered poor selection criteria in older forms of criticism like art and film, the pleasing aesthetics, affirmative quality or popularity of games has not driven my choices. Rather, I've remained interested in particular titles because of how they engaged with an ongoing conversation around games through their form and content, gestured toward a recognized cultural shift of some kind or created ruptures. For the sake of the current work, my focus is on so-called 'AAA' or mainstream industry games, since they most closely resemble the mass culture industry from which ideological representations tend to issue, and because they have such a commanding force within visual culture. All of the video games analyzed are third-person perspective and contain navigable, highly articulated spaces. I have excluded massively multiplayer online games (MMOs) because they fundamentally create the conditions for large numbers of people to interact within a persistent space. While the worlds of these games are equally compelling and teem with fascinating representations, the key aspect of their paradigmatic sociality necessitate psychology and sociology-based approaches that are outside the scope of this project. Driven directly by the idiosyncratic interactions of countless participants, these MMOs are more situational and require a slightly different toolkit. Simply put, single-player, multiplayer and MMO design and gameplay are not the same; their social and representational contexts vary greatly.[42] Therefore, I have avoided drawing comparisons across drastically differing game design paradigms by focusing on single-player experience.

My choice to present analyses of mainstream or what I sometimes call 'dominant' industry games is targeted and deliberate. Video games convey dominant meanings in culture. It naturally follows, then, to focus on games that have mass appeal, and that are constitutive of mainstream ideologies. Ignoring mainstream games on the basis of anti-neoliberal politics trivializes these texts and their effects, and I believe that the faulty idea that video games are unimportant galvanizes their power. This allows them to proceed unchecked in the world as dominant forms of culture, without the same modicum of accountability and critical analysis that even films and theatre bear, limited as it may be.

Games access the public imagination, and in their carefully crafted expressions, they fulfill a persuasive function (as other image-making practices), and they mirror aspects of society within a particular historical moment. Analysing them closely can help us reflect upon and understand the ways culture works on us – something that is otherwise difficult to grasp from within that culture. Such insights may accord us more agency as stakeholders within a given context, in a given time. In order to clearly locate my game analyses, all examples have been drawn from a period between 2008 and 2015 and are widely distributed within a Western context – though not all originating there. Within this chronology, intersecting vectors of the post-Obama era, the neoliberal economic turn and post-9/11 anxieties around rapid demographic shifts toward an increased 'minority' presence within the US bear down upon the object of study. In addition, the Obama re-election period after 2012 heralded a conservative Republican pundit rhetoric that America has 'died' or something is being lost, and fanned the notion that the Islamic Arab world constitutes an axis of evil. Games scholar Nina Huntemann pointedly observes that games after 9/11 have taken on different themes, and seem to invoke new meanings as a result of the traumatic historical moment. She comments, 'A game that came out prior to September 2001 that was about fighting terrorism means something very different in our culture now, just because of the very recent history of the world.'[43] Huntemann notes an increase in the number of games that are militaristic, but also that pre-existing military games are now inevitably viewed through a post-9/11 ideological lens. What Huntemann identifies as a dramatic shift in military games after 9/11 can also be observed in those video games whose contents may not be directly military or war-related. I explore some of these shifts in the following pages.

This critical undertaking is largely inspired by the UK-based cultural studies tradition, which has had a significant influence on my approach to games as objects of study.[44] I would not call what I do strictly cultural studies, given my training and commitment to visual culture studies, as well as the practical reality of a generational divide between those who first undertook the critical project and myself. However, the impact of cultural studies' interventions has made it possible for the object of my study and my intellectual investments to have a place in the academy. Cultural studies allows me to think through games in a particularly useful manner. Cultural studies also made visual culture studies possible, which effectively filled the vacuum of that which art history refused to accept as its purview; namely, the visual analysis of the popular, the everyday, the 'low', material culture and more recently the advanced computational. The next section provides an overview of the intellectual investments of cultural studies, outlining key tenets and challenges, as a way of thinking through the stakes of understanding video games as culture, and why cultural studies is so valuable for games.

On the Importance of Cultural Studies for Game Studies

Although there are now institutional spaces dedicated to it, cultural studies can be properly defined neither as a discipline, nor a field.[45] It is more accurately an interdisciplinary set of affinities with few agreed-upon core texts, multiple formations and a contested history. Cultural studies lacks a codified methodology. Stuart Hall himself wrote of the polymorphous nature of its coming into being:

> Cultural studies has multiple discourses; it has a number of different histories. It is a whole set of formations; it has its own different conjunctures and moments in the past. It included many different kinds of work. I want to insist on that! It always was a set of unstable formations. It was 'centered' only in quotation marks ... It had many trajectories; many people had and have different trajectories through it; it was constructed by a number of different methodologies and theoretical positions, all of them in contention. Theoretical work in the Centre for Contemporary Cultural Studies was more appropriately called theoretical noise. It was accompanied by a great deal of bad feeling, argument, unstable anxieties, and angry silences.[46]

While not a 'discipline', cultural studies utilizes interdisciplinary tools culled from areas like sociology, history, literary theory and political science to think about how the workings of power manifest within culture. Its early founders, like Raymond Williams, Richard Hoggart and Stuart Hall, were interested in looking deeply into the so-called 'popular' aspects of culture as sites where power dynamics played themselves out, and where contestation and resistance might be possible.

There are many excellent anthologies of cultural studies, most notably Lawrence Grossberg, Cary Nelson and Paula Treichler's *Cultural Studies*, Simon During's *The Cultural Studies Reader* and the more recent *Cultural Studies: An Anthology* by Michael Ryan.[47] But even these vary greatly in terms of included texts and foci, which is understandable given that from the beginning, even its originators discouraged distilling their affinities and frictions into a canonical narrative. It is generally agreed that cultural studies emerged in Great Britain in the 1950s, and can be traced back to Richard Hoggart's *The Uses of Literacy* (1957) and Raymond Williams' *Culture and Society 1780–1950* (1958), both of which integrated discussion of the working class in relation to expanded notions of the study of culture. E.P. Thompson's *The Making of the English Working Class* (1963) also considered class in relation to studies of culture. Stuart Hall and Paddy Whannel's *The Popular Arts: A Critical Guide to the Mass Media* (1964) defended and theorized the popular arts as worthy of analysis. Hoggart, Williams, Thompson and Hall were all card-carrying members of the 'New Left', an anti-imperialist, socialist, anti-elitist movement that, among other things, set out to understand the connections between popular culture and socialism. It was their intention to activate an understanding of 'lived' culture (as opposed to high culture), in order to better observe it as a site of power, contestation and potential resistance within society.[48]

Hoggart founded the Centre for Contemporary Cultural Studies (CCCS) in 1964 at the University of Birmingham with the activist mission to analyse the popular and other manifestations of contemporary 'mass' culture.[49] The CCCS constituted a drastic intervention into an elitist academic infrastructure that did not see the whole of lived experience as necessarily worthy of dedicated intellectual attention. It bears noting that some of the earliest known video games had already made their appearance by this time: William Higinbotham's *Tennis for Two* (1958) on the Donner Model 30 analogue computer, which was developed at the Brookhaven National Laboratory, and the digital game *Spacewar!* (1962), designed for the DEC PDP-1 by Steve Russell, Martin Graetz, Wayne Wiitanen and others.

Hall assumed Hoggart's former position as Director, holding the post between 1968 and 1979. Under his tenure, the Centre broadened its considerations to include race, cultures of leisure, feminism and issues in education and welfare.[50] It is in his expansion of understanding the popular through racial, transnational and – by his own description, under some duress – feminism, that Hall's work, as well as the next generation influenced by him, has resonated for my own interdisciplinary work in art and culture. In relating his reflections on the shifting practices of cultural studies, he repeatedly mentions in hyperbolic language the violent effect of feminism's irruption into the CCCS. For example: 'it's not known generally how and where feminism first broke in. I use the metaphor deliberately: As the thief in the night, it broke in; interrupted, made an unseemly noise, seized the time, crapped on the table of cultural studies.'[51] In this, Hall is characteristically frank about the 'gendered nature of power' and the resistances that suddenly sprung up around feminists asserting themselves as the subjects of history, within a context that was politically progressive but male-dominated.[52] The example of feminism shows how that which was to be properly included as a part of cultural studies was continually negotiated, struggled with and re-imagined. It is also clear that the intersectionality ultimately demanded of cultural studies accelerated a painful transition.

There is no shortage of literature on the definition of cultural studies, among these the works of John Storey, Lawrence Grossberg, Graeme Turner, Angela McRobbie and more recently Gilbert B. Rodman.[53] Surveying some of the literature reveals great variations in expectations around political transformation, or the specific role of culture in relation to power. Rodman defines cultural studies in plain and strategically generalized terms:

> Cultural studies is an interlocking set of leftist intellectual and political practices. Its central purpose is twofold: (1) to produce detailed, contextualized analyses of the ways that power and social relations are created, structured, and maintained through culture; and (2) to circulate those analyses in public forums suitable to the tasks of pedagogy, provocation, and political intervention.[54]

Key to Rodman's definition is the notion of political intervention, which has been an ongoing site of debate for cultural studies. These contestations deserve some explanation here, as they are directly relevant to my own project. In the first case, there is the issue of whether it is possible to make any kind of political intervention by intervening in culture. The second is the accusation that by making issues of representation into matters of political intervention, 'actual' sites of 'real' intervention (such as interrogating the worth of capitalism in the first place) become impossible within the scope of the conversation. Simon During, for example, has pointed out how critics of cultural studies contest the idea that culture is politics, or that doing cultural studies in any way affects actual political change.[55] He identifies three particular modes of operation for cultural studies that indicate political ambitions. First, there is the notion that popular culture is itself counter-hegemonic; second, that identity politics may effectively validate certain socially defined minorities; and third, that counter-readings of dominant narratives in representation can provide a political intervention on the level of reception.[56] While these are all possible or even likely, cultural studies initially had more direct political ambitions and subsequently held itself to a narrow view of what constituted authentic, measurable political change. In hindsight, this expectation has proven unreasonable, which has been a drain on the energy around cultural studies for its supporters, and an easy target for criticism by its detractors. In response to this, noted art historian Griselda Pollock explains that cultural studies' primary political impact has been in a 'politics of education' that she sees as organized around challenging formalized disciplines, and contesting the notion of disinterestedness or objective detachment cultivated by traditional educational models. 'It can produce,' Pollock asserts, 'the kind of informed, historically situated reflexivity that is necessary to maintain the possibility of democratic citizenship that is the condition of political change both at the formal level and at the level of alternative groupings.'[57]

Simon During's defining of cultural studies underscores the break with social scientific positivism or 'objectivism' and embrace of the role of the social subject or 'subjectivism'. Rejected, too, was the notion that 'culture' was limited by definition to 'high culture', or as 'the "best that has been thought and said" in a society'.[58] Michael Ryan's definition relies heavily upon the notion of culture as more than entertainment, but as 'the software program of human life. Who controls cultural production is an important issue, therefore, because culture not only reflects reality; it also produces it.'[59] Cultural studies reveals, according to him, the workings of power and control in culture, as well as how resistance is also formed through it, and the fabricated nature of our underlying presumptions of the normal versus the deviant.[60] 'Cultural Studies,' he says, 'places us all in the position of the character in *The Matrix* who is offered a choice between a red pill and a blue pill, waking up to cultural fabrication or staying asleep in the real world.'[61]

Cultural studies' transformation of the very nature of the academy in terms of developing a self-critical awareness around disciplinary endeavours, value systems and exclusivities cannot be overstated. Bal, in her consideration of cultural studies' impact on the academy, writes:

> By challenging methodological dogma, and elitist prejudice and value judgment, it [cultural studies] has been uniquely instrumental in at least making the academic community aware of the conservative nature of its endeavors, if not everywhere forcing it to change. It has, if nothing else, forced the academy to realize its collusion with an elitist white-male politics of exclusion and its subsequent intellectual closure. Everything about cultural studies that makes me not want to say that cultural studies is what I do must be considered as a footnote to this major acknowledgement.[62]

Indeed, the very existence of visual studies as an interdisciplinary methodology, and its academic legitimization in the 1990s, was made possible by cultural studies. In addition to greatly expanding the object of study beyond that considered traditionally viable for the academy, the presence of cultural studies has provided a critical framework for understanding the mainstream as more than trivial. The diffusion of cultural studies' intersectionality within many disciplines likewise makes it possible to approach video games as not only technical, but cultural.

To identify video games as visual culture may seem obvious; however, this actually represents a departure from the current direction of scholarship in games. What is at work in the following chapters is more than merely a close formal reading of an unconventional object of study for visual culture. It is not an attempt to prove that games are profound. Further, what is offered is more than a bait-and-switch scheme to replace a discussion of societal problems with that of 'representations' that displace the urgent issues of economics and politics with that of a struggle over culture. But, as Hall, who described culture as a 'constant battlefield', so well expressed it:[63]

> Popular culture is one of the sites where this struggle for and against a culture of the powerful is engaged: it is also the stake

to be won or lost in that struggle. It is the arena of consent and resistance. It is partly where hegemony arises, and where it is secured. It is not a sphere where socialism, a socialist culture – already fully formed – might be simply 'expressed'. But it is one of the places where socialism might be constituted. That is why 'popular culture' matters. Otherwise to tell you the truth, I don't give a damn about it.[64]

If visual culture is indeed a core site of social engineering, political influence and a potent means by which subjects come to understand their place and possibilities within a given social context, games clearly constitute a site of contestation in the struggle for recognition.[65]

Cultural Studies Meets Game Studies

The relationship between games and culture at large is one that has been contested since the inception of game studies. There have been significant declarative statements made about the importance of games, and I have, among many others, argued for games as worthy of academic attention.[66] In 2001, Espen Aarseth, Editor-In-Chief of *Game Studies*, pinpointed the tug-of-war being waged on this emerging field of research. Locating academia as the chief site of resistance and control, Aarseth comments:

The greatest challenge to computer game studies will no doubt come from within the academic world. Making room for a new field usually means reducing the resources of the existing ones, and the existing fields will also often respond by trying to contain the new field as a subfield. Games are not a kind of cinema, or literature, but colonizing attempts from both these fields have already happened, and no doubt will happen again. And again, until computer game studies emerges as a clearly self-sustained academic field.[67]

As Aarseth suggests, attempts from neighbouring disciplines to subsume what he calls the 'richest cultural genre we have yet seen' will most certainly fall short of fully embracing gaming on its own terms.[68] The pointed language around resource scarcity and colonization from other media suggests a conflicted relation to the presence of outside influences. It is understandable to want games and game studies to reach their full potential as more than mimicry of pre-existing media or academic modes. But the concern with purity is troubling. I see the intersectional, hybrid, errant, post-disciplinary impulse in games as constitutive of the medium in itself – and thoroughly an asset rather than a liability. As such, cultural studies approaches offer just the right tools, not a debasement of 'proper' game studies.

There are notable scholars who are more welcoming of critical analysis for the study of games as a rich cultural genre. Alexander Galloway, in his *Gaming: Essays on Algorithmic Culture* (2006), characterizes games as having achieved mass-culture status for more than two decades while receiving comparatively little critical analysis. Claiming games as a part of his own generation's culture, thereby separating himself from sceptics whose suspicions and aspersions impede their ability to assess them, Galloway differentiates games from other media. He especially underscores the centrality of video games as hinging upon *action*: 'Video games come into being when the machine is powered up and the software is executed; they exist when enacted.'[69] These types of actions are differentiated into four major groups, divided between possible machine acts and player or 'operator' acts. Galloway's discernment of not only action as key, but varying *kinds* of action and agents at play in games, is useful in differentiating games from other media when it comes to understanding their representations. He writes:

> Representation refers to the creation of meaning about the world through images. So far, debates about representation have focused on whether images (or language, or what have you) are a faithful mimetic mirror of reality thereby offering some unmediated truth about the world [...] Games inherit this same debate. But because games are not merely watched but played, they supplement this debate with the phenomenon of action. It is no longer sufficient to talk about the visual or textual representation of meaning. Instead the game theorist must talk about actions, and the physical or game worlds in which they transpire.[70]

By refocusing the site of meaning from representation to action and place, as Galloway suggests above, he seems to favour a phenomenological approach that highlights dynamic conditions and flux, as opposed to a consideration of game meaning through images as fixed, or predetermined.

In 2010, Adrienne Shaw, without directly calling out Galloway's position, expresses concern that the focus on interactivity displaces the importance of representation and ideology:

> The focus on games as highly interactive and audience-dependent texts can lead us to ignore that they are in fact encoded with ideological positions just as any other medium (G. King & Krzywinska, 2006; Leonard, 2006). That is not to say we should ignore the activity of the audience but that we should also look at the dominant meanings encoded in the texts they are playing. As Toby Miller (2005) asserts, media must be studied both in terms of active audiences and dominant ideology, rather than one or the other.[71]

Games are not isolated forms, fundamentally separate from culture and its dominant ideologies. Indeed, I agree with Shaw that '[p]lacing video games within larger cultural discourses is important, as video games themselves are the product of larger cultural contexts.'[72] In fact, the comparative lack of attention to game representations, due to the field's overwhelming focus on technical innovation, has greatly hobbled the representational scope and sophistication of games. Games are concentrated, unfettered and absolute representations that say much about inequitable power relations in culture, but even more about their makers and their attendant value systems. One of Shaw's key assertions is that problems of representation will be remedied neither by simply diversifying the games industry, nor by creating more equitable representations within games themselves. She bluntly characterizes game culture as 'particularly masculine, heterosexual and white' and digital games themselves as 'the least progressive form of media representation, despite being one of the newest mediated forms.'[73] This is a characterization that rings true, in the sense that, with little exception, mainstream games present a vision of the world that is devoid of postmodern, post-structural, post-colonial, feminist or any other critical cultural intervention. While I also agree with Galloway that action is key to the discussion, and game worlds matter, this should not displace the centrality of representation. Hence I refer to games as *playable representations*, as a way of acknowledging the dual elements of action and representation at work in the visual culture of games. This also evokes the term 'playable media' – a term coined by Noah Wardrip-Fruin partly to differentiate commercial games from the alternative use of game technologies by artists and others.[74] I want to acknowledge the importance of his term for the subsequent analyses of games, which I think of as *playable visual culture*.

A seminal figure in understanding games as cultural tools that can engender change, Mary Flanagan historically contextualizes their subversive potentials in her *Critical Play*.[75] Arguing that 'electronic games constitute cultural spaces', Flanagan embraces the notion that in general technologies contain values and politics through their very design. Further, they are influenced by ideology, and their development is shaped by human behaviour.[76] On the values embedded in games as technology, she writes:

> games are simultaneously systems of information, cultural products, and manifestations of cultural practice. On some level, systems such as games must, due to the conditions of their creation, represent cultural norms and biases in their realization. These results can go, and have gone, completely unacknowledged.[77]

Characterized this way, games would seem a natural subject for cultural studies. Interestingly, there are few who have brought cultural studies to a study of video games – though one can argue that there are many whose analyses of games owe much to critical cultural studies' investments. One particularly strong example is Dyer-Witheford and de Peuter's previously mentioned deconstruction of games and their origins, through the organizing structure of Michael Hardt and Antonio Negri's canonical *Empire*.[78] They diverge from existing critical game analysis by focusing on the relations between games and global capital. Tackling the topic from the continuum of effects operating between ideological underpinnings, production and consumption, their formidable intervention models a thorough and detailed political examination of mainstream games. Identifying video games as paradigmatic media of Empire, they suggest – not unlike Flanagan – that games also contain within them the seeds of resistance and subversion.

Shaw has directly grappled with the relation between cultural studies and games. In 'What is Video Game Culture? Cultural Studies and Game Studies', she argues that, 'if video game studies are going to look at games as culture, it must adopt the conflicts and struggles of cultural studies, not just the terms and foci.'[79] Through this, she suggests that rather than thinking of games in relation to particular aspects of culture (she points out learning, thinking, gender, war, and children as examples of critical work undertaken by other scholars), it is necessary to understand games in a more contextual manner. Shaw demands more internal, self-critical analysis within game studies. For example, in understanding games and culture, the focus has largely been on 'game culture' as separate and distinct from dominant culture – as opposed to constituting a part of the mainstream. This distinction has largely 'othered' games within the mainstream and shaped the way it has been studied.[80] In the interests of better assembling a flexible set of tools and methodologies to meet the fluid, conflictual and transdisciplinary nature of this object of study, Shaw suggests that the internal struggles and frictions of cultural studies, as I have described them above, should be embraced by video game studies. For her own part, Shaw interrogates how both popular media and the academy ideologically construct video game play as a separate 'culture' with cohesive and identifiable qualities. These stereotypical notions are pervasive in that they are suffused through dominant media representation, and unverifiable in the sense that they do not adhere to actual statistics, or, as Shaw says, the actual history of games. In example, she identifies several scholars who have studied the exclusion of women's stories from the history of computational culture, which has instead focused on white male genius and 'geek' cultural capital as the mythological basis for gamer identity – and, I would add, in a larger sense, the greater coding of computational technologies as masculine.[81]

Ultimately, Shaw suggests the usefulness and indeed indispensability of those reflexive qualities to be found in cultural studies: 'Cultural studies have been subject to much internal debate and critique, and although game studies have come to draw on the concepts and subjects of cultural studies, it has not taken on the conflicts.'[82] Further, she sees the reductive under-standing of video game culture as meaning certain kinds of people, types of games, and conventional game contexts and uses, as constructs that should be troubled.[83] Shaw's call to action for a cultural studies of games offers generative possibilities and openness for what tools game scholars might bring to their objects of study. The following chapters exemplify the spirit of this call.

Form and/as Identity Politics in Games

What is at stake in identifying games as a form of culture (and more spe-cifically visual culture) is game studies' sense of methodological self-reflec-tion, which is key to its continued vitality. The lack of this quality in earlier disciplines had massive ramifications, and it is through such examples that we can understand the present challenges and possible futures of game studies – and games themselves. One pointed object lesson is the forma-tion of visual studies in relation to its elder discipline, art history. Like cul-tural studies, visual studies (or visual culture studies) rejects notions of 'high' and 'low' in favour of understanding a spectrum of visual culture and visuality, broadly defined, in relation to how a particular culture engages in meaning-making. In a previous essay, I have outlined how visual studies arose largely out of the need created by art history's disciplinary unwilling-ness to integrate new genres, material culture, the popular and the global into its object of study.[84] This is not unrelated to the radical shift toward 'everyday life' as a legitimate element of culture, galvanized by Hoggart, Thompson, Hall, Whannel and others that I have described. Mieke Bal has written of art history and its notorious lack of 'methodological self-reflection', which led to a profound crisis around its object of study, and the subsequent formation of alternative approaches to visual and mate-rial culture.[85] Nicholas Mirzoeff, the noted visual culture theorist, similarly describes how 'visual culture seeks to blend the historical perspective of art history and film studies with the case-specific, intellectually engaged approach characteristic of cultural studies.'[86] This issue has repeatedly sur-faced for art history, as an array of scholars brought the concerns of class struggle, race, feminist revisionism, queer politics and post-colonialism to the table that challenge its Eurocentric origins. Bal's 2003 essay, 'Visual Essentialism and the Object of Visual Culture', as well as the seven published responses to her work, notably struggle with the function of art history and its connectedness to other critical approaches.[87] Visual culture studies, the emergent scholarly discipline, promoted analysis that brought rigorous self-criticality to the table. This radically reconfigured the objective of study not in terms of a pedigreed object, but through a sceptical relationship to the object in its various webs of relation. Pushing away from materiality as the sole basis of the study of art objects, Bal unveils the rootedness of this art historical approach in nineteenth-century positivism, binarisms and ideologies of cultural purity. Meaning, then, does not issue only from the form, but also its context.

In time, the academy has seen the melding of art history with visual studies; many departments now bear both names and support both approaches as a means of ensuring the contemporary relevance of art history, while grounding visual culture in the object to some degree. The presence of identity politics and its impact on art history as a discipline has particularly been much debated. In the wake of this comes the inevitable conclusion that indeed all image production is linked to identity politics, regardless of the status of cultural normativity or alterity represented by its makers. Key to this is the notion that the content of the object of study is irrelevant to this determination; politics need not be foregrounded in the work. Contrary to the false construction of a dualism between form and content, formalist pursuits in artmaking, in short, *are* identity politics.[88] The non-normative artist (one marked with some form of socially defined difference) who is perceived as focused on 'identity' is conceived of as doing 'anthropology' – or some kind of ethnographic testimony, narcissistic self-disclosure or maybe articulating themselves as native informants. While certainly expressive, the identity artist is theorized as not in fact making art:

> The troubling misrecognition of these artists is rooted in an
> inside-outside, or binary-based construction of the relationship
> between identity-based art (minority, noncanonical) and main-
> stream (normative, canonical) production. Specifically, this

construction can be located in the notion that there exists a 'social art' and a 'social art history' that operate externally to traditional output, which is indifferent to such concerns. Using the markers 'social' or 'activist' to describe these intellectual and artistic efforts is misleading, in that they place minority engagements in an inherently peripheral position. Simultaneously, it suggests that the politics of identity is somehow not practiced from within the mainstream [...] [T]here is no such thing as one art-historical or critical methodology that is engaged in identity politics and another that is not. There are only those social identities that are seeking recognition, and those that speak from a fictive normative position. The critique of revisionist efforts from the mainstream is essentially an effort to preserve one's identity politics (the histories and power relations they construct) from the political efforts of the Other.[89]

Following from this earlier research, it is central to understand formalist pursuits in games, and the fixation on the restriction of video game studies to the formal material aspects of games, as a manifestation of identity politics. Representation is in fact a frontline of power relations and domination, within particular spheres of influence, and this is no less true of games than other forms of mass culture and their attendant industries. This is a problem that I will revisit throughout this book in relation to particular games.

Key to this is Marita Sturken's and Lisa Cartwright's notion that visual culture is 'not just a representation of ideologies and power relations but is integral to them'.[90] Describing image culture as a space in which ideologies – sometimes conflicting – are constructed, maintained and naturalized, they underscore the ways that visual culture relates and reinforces value systems. Like cultural studies, visual studies is practiced across disciplines. Despite its association with art history, it has strong applications for image-making practices that are non-traditional to that field, such as the popular and the everyday, mass culture and other so-called 'low' forms of the visual.[91]

But what about the problem of using subjective analysis of mass culture as the evidential research for, well, anything? What may count as evidence? I want to return again to my mention of the narratives and image-making practices of games as a kind of 'dream life' of a culture. I borrow this phrase from Hall, who was speaking in relation not to games, but television narratives. As a response to the question of what can be learned from content analysis, he suggested:

> Every time I watch a popular television narrative like, well say, 'Hill Street Blues' or 'Miami Vice,' with its twinning and coupling of racial masculinities at the center of its story, I have to pinch myself and remind myself that these narratives are not a somewhat distorted reflection of the real state of race relations in American cities.
>
> They are functioning much more as Levi-Strauss tells us myths do. They are myths, which represent in narrative form the resolution of things, which can't be resolved in real life. What they tell us about is about the 'dream life' of a culture. But to gain a privileged access to the dream life of a culture, you had better know how to unlock the complex ways in which narrative plays across real life. Once you look at any of these popular narratives, which constantly in the imagination of a society construct the place, the identities, the experience, the histories of the different peoples who live within it, one is instantly aware of the complexity of the nature of racism itself.[92]

In many ways, conceptualizing the potentialities of game studies is still a work-in-progress of the imagination. It is undoubtedly a failure of the imagination to rigidly limit the legitimate study of games to one disciplinary approach. Games are technical, social, phenomenological, cultural, economic, political and more. And, like cultural studies, games have a place in and across many disciplines; they likewise stretch the limits of the canon in their defiance of conventions.

Being Critical

The work of criticism, which has formerly occupied more established disciplines like theatre, music, art and film, has a long and venerated history. However, critical game studies is still in its formative years. Games scholar, designer and critic Ian Bogost has made important interventions in this conversation, advocating for video games as both persuasive and expressive. In his *Unit Operations: An Approach to Videogame Criticism*, Bogost theorizes and models a comparative criticism of games that brings together literary theory and information technology.[93] His *Persuasive Games: The Expressive Power of Videogames* delineates the computational dimensions of persuasion and situates games within the larger history of rhetoric, a seminal contribution to critical game studies. Setting forth the concept of 'procedural rhetoric', Bogost identifies the specific mechanics of games as persuasive, paying close attention to their use of rule-based representations and interactions.[94] He asserts that video games are distinctive in their rhetorical functions – even from software in general – and unveils how the particular persuasions of video games 'disrupt and change fundamental attitudes and beliefs about the world, leading to potentially significant long-term social change'.[95] By extension, careful scholarly and critical attention to video games as 'expressive cultural artefacts' is vital for the maturing medium, as well as for a knowledgeable user who can become an active arbiter of the image-making practices at play in games.[96] Bogost writes:

> Procedural media like videogames get to the heart of things by mounting arguments about the processes inherent in them. When we create videogames, we are making claims about these processes, which ones we celebrate, which ones we ignore, which ones we want to question. When we play these games, we interrogate those claims, we consider them, incorporate them into our lives, and carry them forward into our future experiences [...] these media influence and change us.[97]

Reasoning that understanding games through their procedural rhetorics helps illuminate the processes within them and their influence on players, Bogost ultimately argues for games to be taken seriously as a medium and then provides one viable methodology for doing so. The procedural for him captures another mode of expressing what it is to be human. Bogost's work does not displace the cultural importance of games. Rather it suggests that, with logics implicit to the form of games, it makes sense to observe how their rule-based systems become persuasive and in fact speak to larger cultural concerns. Following from Bogost, one of the roles of an effective critical cultural approach to games would be to potentially consider things like the implicit rules of gameplay, and the function of core gameplay mechanics, in relation to game narrative and larger cultural contexts.

In addition to the procedural dimensions of games, some scholars champion analysis rooted firmly in the concrete experience of gameplay. Brendan Keogh has emerged as a strong advocate for the importance of close critical analysis in video game criticism that is 'grounded in the phenomenological concerns of videogame play'.[98] In his 'Across Worlds and Bodies: Criticism in the Age of Video Games', Keogh writes about the fraught history of games criticism. He notes the ongoing resistance to criticism within game studies and argues for the importance of close textual readings of games.[99] Seeking to make an intervention that can greatly reformulate video game criticism to be more than what he calls 'game studies formalism' the critic and scholar endeavours to lay out an intellectual foundation and methodology for phenomenological approaches, while also breaking from the presumption that the objective of game studies should be aligned with the commercial aims of perpetual technical innovation. As an extension of this, he refutes the pursuit of 'purity' of medium, characterizing it as similar to a hackneyed form/content debate in the arts that is long outmoded. Throughout Keogh's careful analysis, he reasons that game studies' obsession with purism in their object of study is tantamount to a hegemonic act that excludes certain works, and the experience of playing them, as invalid.[100] Worse, the 'sweeping, authoritative a priori claim as to what a video game is at its core' further polarizes the sphere of games by staking out a territory that centralizes the most validated and further marginalizes the least represented producers and players of games.[101] Instead, Keogh advocates for an implicit understanding of games as bastardized, hybrid and messy: as bricolage. It is this core rejection of formal and disciplinary purity that stands out as a possible detour from the quagmire of past debates that have reduced game studies largely, as Bogost so fittingly captured during his 2009 DiGRA Keynote, to a rumble between two restrictive formalisms: narratology and ludology.[102]

To some degree, Keogh seems to characterize the problems of game studies as transitory. He aligns himself with a younger generation of academically pedigreed 'Western cultural theorists' who see games as cultural artefacts indisputably worthy of critical attention, and whose ascendancy will solve many of the fits and starts of a burgeoning area of study. Keogh concludes by embracing a general 'bottom-up descriptive analysis' and methods that 'account for the phenomenological experience of videogame play', which consider both the player's bodily experience and the game's technological dimensions'.[103] He resists making prescriptive, narrow solutions or staking out a discrete critical territory, except to say that in its current form game studies does not possess the critical vocabulary to properly evaluate individual gamic texts. Keogh's searching, personal and incredibly rich *Killing is Harmless* extends this line of inquiry into practice by generating a phenomenological response to a single game: *Spec Ops: The Line* (2012). This book-length consideration of his experience while playing *The Line* recalls the pioneering phenomenological study of the 1978 Atari 2600 game *Breakout*, entitled *Pilgrim in the Microworld* by David Sudnow, an iconic historical precursor to this specific kind of subjective games writing – although Keogh himself does not mention this in relation to his own work.[104] However, Clara Fernández-Vara makes this connection clear in her *Introduction to Game Analysis*, a lucid introductory guide to possible methodologies of critical writing on games.[105]

Cultivating a critical relationship to the overwhelming, engaging spectacle of this form of visual culture does not automatically accompany gameplay. And while games are most certainly not the same as theatre, film or television, they do remediate these previous forms.[106] As a result, the critical study of these representational practices can be useful in unlocking the cultural meanings that are produced, mirrored and contested through their interactions. Shaw writes: 'Understanding how cultural meanings are communicated and how identities are created takes training. That can be academic training or self-education, but it is not something one can wake up in the morning and know how to do.'[107] As a by-product of the economic, socio-political and academic turn toward the neoliberal, and the subsequent emphasis on enhancing the technical and immersive dimensions of video games, there has been comparatively miniscule engagement with their cultural meanings, relative to previous media. And what little engagement there has been has come from an interested segment of the games criticism writers, like Keogh, who are only now beginning to fully distinguish their serious interpretive engagements from more entertainment oriented industry reviewers who have long dominated the writing about games.

Finally, setting aside the ongoing arguments of games studies regarding the nature of the object of study, and of 'proper' scholarly tools, there are strong practical reasons for games criticism. As with the significance of criticism for pre-existing forms of expression (such as sculpture, painting, installation, performance, film and music), there is an inevitable lifespan to the art, an ephemeral quality, a limit to accessing the intended presentation. The monetary expense of the technology itself, not to mention the learning curve necessary to use it, also limits access. The documentation of a performance often comes to stand in for the thing in itself. Games criticism and critical game studies are extremely significant in relation to the transient nature of the technology and the accelerated, structured obsolescence often built into game devices. It is possible, even likely, that for many iconic games, the critical appraisal and documentation may eventually stand in for the video game itself. Some scholars, like Raiford Guins, argue that the material dimensions of computer games are integral to their historicization.[108] The historical function of the many kinds of game analysis will certainly shape the way in which these complex cultural artefacts will be understood in posterity, and their medium specificities may not always be there to be experienced first-hand. Because, as Guins notes, '[v]ideo games are historically specific *things* in time and place (emphasis added),' their contextual meanings and connotations will also shift over time.[109] Games criticism, like the many critical practices around previous media, can serve as a rich resource of what particular games meant and how they signified within their own moment, which will be key documents in posterity. It is coming into being as an array of critical modes flexible enough to address concerns beyond the commercial to consider form, materiality, context, the phenomenological, the ideological and much more.

GamerGate, Games Criticism and Gender Problems

While critical game studies has been exploring possible modes of inquiry, professional games criticism has itself come under intense scrutiny by members of the games community. In an unexpected turn of events, discussions regarding the role of criticism – more specifically ethics in games journalism – and a burgeoning crisis in rampant misogyny and harassment of women in the games industry converged. This had, in fact, been brewing for some time, as was evidenced by several key moments of rupture that spread across social media platforms like Twitter, Facebook and blogs – eventually spilling over into dominant media outlets. For example, back in 2007, threats of sexual violence and death were made against game developer Kathy Sierra, likely due to her prominent role in an industry dominated by men.[110] In 2010, *Penny Arcade*, a prominent games site known for its satirical extremes, came under scrutiny for posting a series of comic strips that contained rape jokes, and in particular mentioned being 'raped by dickwolves'. When faced with criticism that their expression was offensive and promoted rape culture, *Penny Arcade* responded by denigrating the claim and creating and selling 'Dickwolves' memorabilia, including t-shirts and pennants. In what has been characterized as an iconic moment of the gaming world's endemic culture of hostility toward women and hypermasculinist values, some have cited this incident as having larger ramifications.[111] Among other things, it led to a discussion of the rampant 'rhetoric of sexual violence' in game culture, such as the common verbal/textual sexual hostilities aimed at women during online play, and the vocabulary of 'raping' a player as a commonly used slang term for besting a competitor or overcoming a difficult goal in gameplay.[112]

The 2012 harassment of Anita Sarkeesian, an emerging young feminist media critic, proved a particularly watershed moment in terms of visibility and press coverage of the ongoing culture war around the presence of women and socially defined minorities in games. Sarkeesian started a Kickstarter crowdfunding campaign to support her series of web videos, *Tropes vs. Women in Video Games*. The resulting vitriolic attack on her work and her person included an outpouring of online incitements to rape and kill her.[113] Simultaneously, due to the animosity demonstrated against Sarkeesian, the Kickstarter campaign drew enormous attention and resulted in approximately $160,000 in donations, much more than the initially sought $6000 for a series of five short videos. Though she is one of many targeted women, Sarkeesian, with her *Feminist Frequency* blog and the tremendous media focus on both the enormous funding and the excessive harassment, has come to embody a burgeoning organized feminist critique of games representation – one that pushes back against the stereotypical representation and objectification of women in games.[114]

The harassment campaign known as GamerGate, however, is associated with a young game designer named Zoë Quinn, who created an indie game about living with depression called *Depression Quest* (2013). On 16 August 2014, Quinn was publicly smeared in a blog post on Reddit by a former boyfriend, Eron Gjoni. He alleged that she had sexual relations with several games reviewers during their relationship, most notably a journalist for the games site *Kotaku*. Gjoni accused Quinn of providing sexual favours in exchange for positive reviews of her game, a claim later confirmed as baseless by *Kotaku*.[115] Nevertheless, an organized harassment effort began on 4chan, an image-based, mostly anonymous bulletin board. When Actor Adam Baldwin used the hashtag #GamerGate for the first time on 27 August 2014 in regard to the Quinn corruption conspiracy, the tag quickly spread and has come to stand in for an online movement that alleged a breach of journalistic ethics, ostensibly caused by conflicts of interest between game makers and professional game reviewers. According to Adrienne Shaw and Shira Chess, the 190,000 followers of Baldwin's Twitter feed inevitably contributed to the maelstrom, leading to a broader online movement against so-called feminist 'Social Justice Warriors' or 'SJWs'[116] out to destroy games, which circulated on websites, Reddit subthreads, 4chan and 8chan threads.[117] Concurrently, an intense outpouring of mostly women's personal testimonials outlining their experiences of sexism in games erupted on Twitter under the hashtag #1reasonwhy.[118] This spawned copious debate, including what was configured to be a more 'positive-focused' #1reasontobe hashtag that documented the reasons that women should enter into the industry.[119]

In 2013, noted game designer and developer Brenda Romero resigned as a member of the International Game Developer's Association (IDGA) to protest the act of hiring scantily clad female models as entertainment during a GDC party.[120] In 2014, Josh Mattingly, who founded the independent games blog IndieStatik, came under criticism and was forced to resign after a female developer exposed extremely graphic sexist comments she received from him during a Facebook chat. Game developer Brianna Wu was targeted in 2014 for tweeting a joke about GamerGate supporters and for her comments against the harassment of women in the industry. She wrote in *The Washington Post*:

> They've threatened to rape me. They've threatened to make me choke to death on my husband's severed genitals. They've threatened to murder any children I might have [….]
>
> [...] my Twitter mentions were full of death threats so severe I had to flee my home. They have targeted the financial assets of my company by hacking. They have tried to impersonate me on Twitter. Even as we speak, they are spreading lies to journalists via burner e-mail accounts in an attempt to destroy me professionally.[121]

At the same time that there was a clear and definite personal attack being waged upon particular female game developers and critics such as Sarkeesian, Quinn and Wu, significant vitriol was clustered around an issue of so-called 'ethics in games journalism' and the perception that there is rampant corruption and bias. Wu expressed misgivings about the claim: 'It's a pretext,' she said, during an interview with *The Boston Globe*. 'This is an actual hate group [...] they're upset and threatened by women who are being very outspoken about feminism.'[122] Lisa Nakamura similarly noted: 'Gamergate, showed the world the extent of gaming's misogyny and internal conflicts over death threats made against female gamers, critics, and game developers by a cadre of male gamers.'[123] Leigh Alexander, in a *Time Magazine* article on GamerGate, described the incidents as evidence of 'sharp growing pains' in the industry. Ultimately characterizing the debate as a 'tension between "games as product" and "games as culture"', Alexander astutely gets closer to the core of what I would describe as a politics of identity at play in games that supersedes the notion of games as consumer products.[124]

The extreme malice and unfettered bigotry of those opposed to the presence of difference and critical self-inquiry described above is instructive in terms of understanding the culture of games. Recent games 'culture wars', notably GamerGate, definitively confirm that games traffic in the politics of representation, just as any other form of mass media. For example, retrograde representations of women as hyper-sexualized or passive and dehumanizing racial and queer images pervade products of the mainstream industry. During a 2014 interview Anna Everett characterized the hostility pervasive in game culture online: 'Any cursory survey of user comments on gaming sites easily uncovers troves of racist rants that betray how deep-seated racial antagonisms are among gamers and trolls who occupy popular games' message boards.'[125] Truly, observing these representations of 'others' in games is instructive, because it clearly underscores how issues of difference and power remain at the forefront of the struggles for socially defined minorities. It marks a persisting anxiety around the presence of these constituencies in technological fields, including the games industry, which is now a global, multi-billion-dollar enterprise.

From a perspective of how the popular enacts power relationships, the GamerGater struggle to keep games safe from the 'SJW' issues seeping into and ruining them extends a recognizable argument from history that tends to create a false dualism between an 'activist' group involved in some kind of identity politics (i.e. progressive 'Social Justice Warriors') and a normative group that is not. This places the 'activist' group's work in an inherently segregated position of being marginalized and 'political' – and this becomes the limit of their expressiveness. At the same time, it implicitly constructs the normative group as not 'activist', not 'political' and most importantly not practicing a form of identity politics from within their dominant normative position in the mainstream industry. There is such a sense of unshakable domain over this realm of representation, a very aggressive form of territoriality and identity politics at play that is going unnamed. However, I would like to make it clear that I no longer think it useful to merely point out racism, sexism and homophobia in games with the preconceived notion that these exist within the industry and game culture as a result of ignorance. They exist as a result of essentialism. In this regard, GamerGate can be thought of as a paradigmatic irruption of something that would normally remain pervasive but invisible into public view. The controversy made visible the normally hidden identity politics at play in dominant games. Representation is in fact a frontline of power relations and domination, within particular spheres of influence, and this is no less true of games than other forms of mass culture and their attendant industries.

Games are not isolated formations, fundamentally separated from culture and its dominant ideologies. As forms of media culture that are routinely castigated as one of the most debased and rapaciously capitalistic forms, games have gone largely without serious consideration of representation and the politics of identity. Everett described the persisting resistance to speak on race, gender and identity politics, saying: 'racial and gender assumptions still operate as functional structuring presences underlying too many of games' "procedural rhetorics" and tropes of mastery.'[126] To add to this, the dominant popular rhetoric around games is so negative that there exists a residual stigma around taking them seriously as an object of study.[127] Games are thus engaged in extremely complex and nuanced representational effects while, despite limited interventions – some of which I have mentioned above – we are told again and again that video games and their visual cultures don't matter.

Voices within the industry also engage with issues of gender, sexuality, race and ethnicity. Manveer Heir, a gameplay designer at BioWare Montreal, presented a GDC 2014 talk entitled 'Misogyny, Racism and Homophobia: Where Do Video Games Stand?' during which he laid out the stakes of representation in games and, more importantly, underscored the intersectional nature of this challenge for the industry. 'The way we portray characters matters to the world at large and has reaching effects beyond video games,' Heir said. 'It impacts how people treat each other in real life, and I really think that this matters. And no, it's not just video games that cause this. But we do our part, right?'[128]

The increasing presence and consumer power of women in games is likely connected to an increasing sense that 'something is being lost', a common woe of GamerGate supporters. This sentiment echoes broader anxieties in the United States regarding demographic shifts that project the impending minority status of whites by the year 2041.[129] However, as Lisa Nakamura rightly indicates, 'This is precisely the moment for games scholarship originating from Ethnic Studies, Women's Studies, Queer Studies, Film Studies, and Cultural Studies to intervene in this ongoing conversation, and to strategize about the future of race, gender and digital media.'[130] But I would like to underscore that I operate from the base assumption that *all* games engage in a politics of identity, not just some of them. It should be understood that the perceived neutrality of games, even those that do not purport to deal with issues of identity, traffic in the assumption of a perceived 'universalism' or 'neutrality' that is fictive. It has never been the case that there was a politically neutral or a raceless form of games representation. Rather, there was such a stranglehold on the image-making machine by a small and privileged constituency of producers who possessed the temporary power to displace their own subjectivity as 'universal', when in fact it is shot through with the politics of identity.

In her article 'Why Political Engagement is Critical to Games Journalism', games critic Carolyn Petit writes:

> Games are not politically neutral. Neither are mainstream romantic comedies, or action films, or any novel I've ever read. They may sometimes appear politically neutral if the values they reinforce mesh with the value systems of the larger culture, but our culture is not politically neutral, either, and it is not outside of the role of a critic to comment on or raise questions about the political meanings embedded in the works one evaluates. In fact, it is often impossible to review something apolitically, because to not comment on or challenge the political meanings in a work in your review is to give them your tacit endorsement.[131]

While there are still many detractors to the idea that the role of critical games writing should include discussions of the political or representational, it does seem as though there is a critical mass of interest in games as more than technical, more than form, more than distracting images that don't matter. It is an exciting moment in which a new young generation of games critics and scholars are making identity-based critiques of representation, and beginning to hold both the industry and its ancillary realms (online game communities, games journalism, etc.) to a higher standard.

If anything, cultural studies works for games because it demands criticality – including internal, methodological self-reflexive criticality. It refuses fixed subject positions and disciplinary knowledge as sufficient to grasp and understand the world. Things like 'economic development' and 'technological innovation' largely drive games writing, as opposed to the nebulous ideal of the 'public good'. I understand this 'public good' as the cultivation, among other things, of activated, critical players with discernment who knowingly engage with their own self-fashioning. A burgeoning movement in alternative games exists on the side of this 'public good', which is made possible by the increased accessibility of game design tools and the vacuum created by the mainstream industry's failure to model a meaningful sense of inclusion, or take creative risks with the medium.[132] As I see it, one of the key roles of criticism is critical self-reflection, not only in relation to an identified object of study (such as a particular game) but also a broader, meta-self-criticality that interrogates *how* we think about what we think about.

Cultural studies methodologies, such as they are, remain vital to the maturing medium of games as it comes to terms with its own 'elitist white-male politics of exclusion and its subsequent intellectual closure', to borrow Bal's words. While games – as well as their scholarship and criticism – are deciding what they want to be, the history and development of cultural studies can illuminate the medium's past, present and potential futures.

The artificial separation of 'game culture' from the culture of cultural studies poses an impediment to conversations that are vital for games studies to have in order to be a healthy discourse. The perniciousness of the distance created between 'game culture' and 'culture' in general functions to isolate a discussion of games from their situatedness within culture, and to justify the elisions of certain kinds of conversations that are long overdue. Bogost captures the 'provincialism' of games, writing:

> I don't just mean the old-hat, stereotypical image of gamers as teenage boys in basements engorging Doritos and knocking

41

back Mountain Dew, although clearly that image is still very much in circulation. Rather, I mean games have often maintained a separation from other forms of human culture and creativity. And that they – that we – have actively cultured and supported this separation in order to come into our own."[133]

This insularity as described is simply untenable, particularly in relation to their global circulation. Further, the isolation of game culture from culture at large functions to maintain the false notion that games do not work on you as culture does – that they are not part of that place where dominant values are conveyed and contested, alternatives produced and resistances generated. Is the 'culture' in games culture the 'culture' in cultural studies? The answer to that question is both yes and no. No: it is not conceived of in this way; but Yes: in fact they are one and the same, and we should begin to fully think of them as such.

Looking Ahead

In the chapters that follow, I model close readings of mainstream games, using a cultural studies-based form of analysis. Cultural critiques made by luminaries like Stuart Hall, Richard Dyer, Edward Said and others gain a fresh importance in the face of games as complex representations. Chapter 1 focuses on racial difference, diversity and gender-based bias in the games community. This writing first provides a grounding for the interventions of media scholars who have examined games through the lenses of representation and stereotype. In light of interventions by Lisa Nakamura, Anna Everett, Tara McPherson, David Leonard, Adrienne Shaw and others, it becomes clear how certain 'racio-visual logics' are engendered in games, as in previous media forms.[134] Then, I undertake a close reading of *Assassin's Creed III: Liberation* (2012/14), a game set in colonial America that features a black female lead character who fights slavery. Through a consideration of this figure who becomes a cypher for intersecting concerns of race, gender and sexuality, this chapter teases out the deep and irruptive effects of such a figure in the established and beloved *Assassin's Creed* franchise as paradigmatic of larger industry spasms. Drawing on the interventions of computer scientist and digital media scholar D. Fox Harrell, I unveil how the rule-based systems implemented in *Liberation* codify certain power dynamics that are experienced through play. Finally, building upon Shaw's important intervention on player-character identification and the politics of representation, I consider the relations between inclusivity, the deeper Orientalist adventurer roots of the franchise and the affordances built in to *Liberation*'s core mechanics.

Chapter 2 examines the white normative figure under duress through games that present a crisis in American narratives of progress: *The Last of Us* (2013), set in a melancholic post-apocalyptic US, and *Tomb Raider* (2013), a reboot of the now-classic Lara Croft narrative that recasts the heroine as desperate and far from invincible. This chapter proposes an emerging 'aesthetics of ambivalence' that issues from the emptying out of normative tropes through an almost hysterical repetition. In an analysis that draws together key concepts from critical whiteness studies, as well as more recent eruptions of anxiety in the popular discourse around the demographic shifts in the US away from a white majority, I consider the central figures of the games in question. Drawing additionally from the visual studies of whiteness and heteronormativity in film, specifically the work of Richard Dyer, I consider the potentials for 'making whiteness strange' as a means of wresting it from the normative, and in fact rescuing it from its own unattainable ideals and self-annihilating tendencies.[135] This chapter also considers the critique of the traditional military shooter with its attendant white male super-soldier, as exemplified in *Spec Ops: The Line* (2012). The game overtly attempts to interrupt the jingoistic nature of the typical military tactical shooter, while unravelling white masculinity in its most iconic stereotypical gamic form. Similarly, Lara Croft, the unflappable icon of white female adventurism in games, becomes the heroine in peril. Within the survivalist narrative of *Tomb Raider*, Lara occupies a traumatized form of whiteness. Ultimately, this chapter considers the shifting permutations of whiteness that range from a delineation of universal humanity to a beleaguered construction of victimization. Running the gauntlet between these two configurations, whiteness in games takes a beating within a fraught post-9/11 and post-Obama moment of national transition.

Chapter 3 addresses landscape as ideology in several games for which the playable space becomes a dominant character, with a special focus on *Metal Gear Solid V: The Phantom Pain* (2015). Within its spatial features is a highly ideological rendering of Afghanistan in the mid-1980s, which is the exact, sited historical moment in which the Taliban comes into being – eventually giving rise to al-Qaeda. In this chapter, we see how *The Phantom Pain* becomes an extremely entangled cultural document of post-9/11 anxiety and US involvement during the Soviet–Afghan War and beyond. In the first portion of this chapter, I examine how game space has been constructed within the study of video games. Through a consideration of the writings of Mark J.P. Wolf, Henry Jenkins, Mary Fuller, Sara Humphreys, Matthew Payne and Michael Nitsche, I provide an overview of how the game world is discussed. Then, turning to the scholarship of W.J.T. Mitchell and Leo Marx, the chapter contemplates landscape representation and cultural power from the vantage point of visual studies. Unearthing how the imaging of landscape has long been connected to imperialist expansion, I think through *The Phantom Pain* in terms of how it frames, organizes and makes claims about a specific place. And, in its highly constructed sense of space, place and landscape, I suggest how a game world is necessarily ideological, and proposes a certain set of relations to that territory. I additionally consider the bureaucratic nature of engaging with various spaces, the framing of the game world within the logic of its rationalized use-value and identification of its under-exploited potentials. Drawing together key scholarly considerations of landscape and gamescape, this chapter teases out cultural imperatives hidden within the visual logics of representing so called 'naturalistic' impressions of the land.

Chapter 4 explores urban space in visual representation, with a special focus on the cinematic urban theorization of Nezar AlSayyad, as well as David B. Clarke and Christoph Lindner. Through analyses of the dystopic spaces of *Max Payne 3* (2012) and *Remember Me* (2013), I examine the intersecting vectors of globalization, violence and constructions of otherness in relation to socio-cultural angst around urban sprawl, overpopulation, placelessness and the rise of non-Western nodes in the global network. With an additional consideration of the ethnically ambiguous figure as a cypher for the global entity (e.g. the mixed-race playable character of 'Nilin' in *Remember Me*), this chapter suggests that memory and forgetting are used as metaphors for the disorientation associated with globalization. Looking at the decontextualizing effects of global capitalist flows as undercurrents within these games, I consider their speculative cities in terms of what Manuel Castells has called the 'Fourth World'.[136]

Writing on the continued relevance of cultural studies, Lawrence Grossberg claims that '[c]ultural studies matters because it is about the future, and about some of the work it will take, in the present, to shape the future. It is about understanding the present in the service of the future.'[137] Games are a particularly slippery subject because of their multifarious natures. They are contingent, reflect the social reality of their time, and their interpretations and even textual manifestations may be reshaped by their production/consumption through play. They are also extremely compelling forms of visual culture that generate worlds. These worlds contain powerful representations that may closely resemble the fantasies of one constituency, while annihilating the fantasies of others. Grossberg's future-orientation around the importance of cultural studies intersects with Bogost's articulation of the function of criticism. In his *How To Talk About Video Games*, Bogost writes:

> Criticism is not conducted to improve the work or the medium, or to win over those who otherwise would turn up their noses at it. Nor is it conducted as flash-in-the-pan buying advice, doled out on release day to reverie or disdain, only to be immediately forgotten. Rather, it is conducted to get to the bottom of something, to grasp its form, content, function, meaning, and capacities. To venture so far from the ordinariness of a subject that the terrain underfoot gives way from manicured path to wilderness, so far that the words that we would spin tousle the hair of madness. And then, to preserve that wilderness and its madness, such that both the works and our reflections on them become imbricated with one another and carried forward into the future where others might find them anew.[138]

In the following analyses of games, I model a mode of cultural critique indebted to cultural studies but not bounded by its historical manifestations. And as a visual studies scholar, I bring those critical tools to bear upon what I see as the most significant emergent form of visual culture that I have encountered in my lifetime. I make no claim to objectivity. Rather, self-reflexivity and intersectionality that has been the hallmark of a cultural studies approach can be mobilized in the service of engendering critical agency and discernment – both of which need to be constantly exercised.

Ultimately, my interest lies not in explaining the monetary success of particular games, in defending the presence of alternative games or suggesting in any way that, through this book, the dominant industry will be more 'enlightened' and suddenly generate healthier and more equitable images. I am neither a technophile, nor a technophobe in relation to the presence of video games in the world. I am, however, interested in how particular types of culture (in this case, games as a complex form of visual culture) create and uphold the value systems and hierarchies of one constituency, often at the expense of another. As Mary Flanagan aptly notes, 'gaming occupies a critical cultural niche. We must learn how to talk about it.'[139] The perception that some games are about the politics of identity, while others are not, needs to be dismantled. It makes no difference whether the games contain specific identifiable representations that can be seen to correspond to specific subjectivities – or even whether the makers intend to grapple with issues of representation head-on. Even the refusal to engage with identity is a privilege that only a particular segment of the population is able to sustain, through their perceived normativity. In the here-and-now of the proliferation of games, this book endeavours to illuminate their contextual meaning for today, in the service of shaping the potential of games as culture in the future.

1

Poetics of Form and Politics of Identity; Or, Games as Cultural Palimpsests

A mess is not a pile, which is neatly organized even if situated in an inconvenient place underfoot. A mess is not an elegant thing of a higher order. It is not an intellectual project to be evaluated and risk-managed by waistcoat-clad underwriters. A mess is a strew of inconvenient and sometimes repellent things. It is less an imbroglio of the sort one finds in a painting of Pollock or Picasso, and more the mess one finds in a sculpture of Kienholz. A mess is an accident. A mess is a thing that you find where you don't want it. A mess is the cascade of broken glass on the floor when you miss the alarm clock and catch the water glass. A mess is the heap of hot, unseen dog shit on the stoop, and then on the stoop and the bootsole. A mess is inelegant, a clutter, a shamble, a terror. We recoil at it, yet there it is, and we must deal with it.

Videogames are a mess. A mess we don't need to keep trying to clean up, if it were even possible to do so.[1]

Ian Bogost, 'Videogames are a Mess'

Introduction

Assassin's Creed III: Liberation is a stealth, open-world adventure game about chattel slavery. Ubisoft first developed and published it for the handheld PlayStation Vita in 2012, with a 2014 high-definition re-issue for consoles and PC. Primary game mechanics consist of combat, stealth and navigation. *Liberation* presents a rare example of an exceptional black female figure who foments resistance. Set in colonial America between 1765 and 1777, this third-person historical speculative fiction centres on Aveline de Grandpré, a New Orleans-raised woman of French and African descent. By day, she is a gentlewoman of leisure, born of a former slave and living under the care of her French merchant father (see Figure 1.1). By night, she becomes a freedom fighter whose attacks tip the balance of power in the formulation of the new nation. Her motivations largely centre around her anti-slavery sentiments and in influencing the forces of power in her region toward those ends.

More than merely inserting a woman of colour into the central player-character role, *Liberation* maximizes the use of game mechanics that directly engage this heroine's complex identifications and her fraught black subjectivity in public spaces. It achieves this through an innovative Persona

Figure 1.1 Aveline as lady. *Assassin's Creed III: Liberation* (2012) image provided by Ubisoft, Inc. Created, developed and published by Ubisoft.

System, which allows for the strategic use of guises as key tools to attain game objectives. In the three possible personas of lady, assassin and slave, Aveline negotiates her people's freedom using her magnetism, lethal skills and ability to feign anonymity within the enslaved population. Gameplay is modulated through her subject position as a woman and how she negotiates public space. Three modes of dress indicate the character's varying levels of legitimacy to occupy particular spheres. The player manipulates a body (Aveline) that becomes a site through which history is penetrated, organized and structured into meaning. Time machine-aided information gathering and bird's-eye views of the land from high vantage points to achieve 'synchronization' in the Animus offer privileged, fantastical historical views that one can never conclusively possess. In this, the game is all wish-fulfilment, both beautiful and ungraspable.

As the first black and first female protagonist in the high-profile *Assassin's Creed* franchise, Aveline marks a significant intervention into the overwhelmingly white, hetero-normative male primary playable characters that continue to dominate mainstream games.[2] As the primary playable character, Aveline's multiple identifications as woman and Afro-French-American, and again as what would then be called a product of 'miscegenation', present a case in which the presumed 'normative' gamer (according to the current industry focus) would be asked to assume the role of a socially defined minority with floating significations.

Utilizing an intersectional approach that considers the crosscutting of race, gender and class through the three 'faces' of Aveline, this chapter examines the ways that *Liberation* engages in the politics of identity through its playability. Many reviewers complained that the game superficially addressed the main character's identity through a one-to-one relationship between her costumes and her social functions. In fact, her complex entanglements as a Creole woman informs the narrative in many ways, and comes to define her ambivalence and confusion regarding her past, her family, her mentor and the Assassin Brotherhood to which she pledges allegiance. As a notable departure from the *Assassin's Creed* franchise, Aveline de Grandpré had an irruptive ideological effect on the established series. The unique Persona System engaged to simulate her multiple identity roles can serve as a means to understand the connections between cultural content and core game mechanics. By looking at the game's aesthetic origins, I show how a particularly messy poetics of form begins to reveal itself, as well as a larger politics of identity at play in video games.

The complex narrative of *Assassin's Creed III: Liberation* utilizes a narrative frame within a frame. The game that is played is introduced as a product of a fictitious global corporation named Abstergo Industries, which has innovated the technology to mine genetic memories for their entertainment value. A secret monastic military society named the Templar Order controls the corporation. They prize the pursuit of order and seek to control free will, both for the sake of world peace and to curb the natural brutality of human beings. Their sworn enemies with whom they perpetually battle are the Assassin Order, which values free will and fights to defend it. These conflicting ideologies have resulted in an ongoing covert war between the Assassins and Templars. Through Abstergo's innovation of the 'Animus' device, individuals enter the memories of progenitors and virtually experience their lives. Abstergo's tagline is 'History is our playground.' The life of the Assassin Aveline de Grandpré is one such batch of accessible memories and, according to the narrative, the first extracted for entertainment purposes – but also intended to mould historical memory. Her virtualized life takes place at the end of the French and Indian War in the colonial period just prior to the US War of Independence, also known as the American Revolution (1775–83), during which time the 13 colonies secured sovereignty from Britain.

In an extremely detailed and rich rendering of historic New Orleans, we meet Aveline first as a child (see Figure 1.2). We witness a primal scene of horror for her, in which the young privileged girl is separated from her mother while in the city. Chasing after a loose hen, she becomes lost in the labyrinthine alleyways. Aveline stumbles into a slave auction in progress. She cannot find her way back and is shoved to the ground by an unsympathetic guard. Racial dimensions of this primal scene imply that this is likely the moment of Aveline's coming into awareness of both her own racial difference, and the precariousness of her position. Transitioning to the grown Aveline, we see her awaken in terror from her nightmare of this past memory. This sequence sets the tone for her character as traumatized and driven by the past.

Figure 1.2 Aveline as a child with her mother. *Assassin's Creed III: Liberation* (2012). Created, developed and published by Ubisoft. Screen shot by author.

The prospect of occupying the body of a black female figure – even a fictive one – within America's fraught antebellum history is a provocative move. *Liberation* takes place as a virtual experience provided by a fictive multinational corporation whose research into genetic memory allows players to 'game within the past' using a mysterious device that gives powerful access to ancestral memory. Through positioning one's self 'as' Aveline, the player engages with her story to derive intimate understanding of a past experience, and to give witness to the life of a figure who is 'historical' within the narrative of the game. This establishes a kind of relation whereby one can be said to temporarily virtually occupy the subjectivity of a genetic ancestor. As one reviewer put it:

> *Liberation* takes the sci-fi framework of previous *Assassin's Creed* games a step further by presenting the game itself – the one you're playing – as propaganda software produced by a Templar organization within the *Assassin's Creed* universe. The 'real' history of that universe is twisted in the game in order to portray the Templars as the good guys. So *Liberation* is a virtual representation of a virtual representation of a corrupted retelling of history.[3]

This suggests a self-conscious address of history as subjective and moulded by those in power, through its underscoring of how there is an 'official' telling of history and then some other rogue elements that have been censored or misrepresented. At the same time, the entire act is recuperative in the sense that it has a revisionist function to insert a fictional subject, but one whose particular subjectivity as multiracial, privileged female revolutionary has been broadly neglected. The intermittent irruption of a hacker into the in-game virtual representation, who interjects their voice and reveals 'truths' in the form of alternative outcomes, reinforces this even further.

Through gameplay, we see Aveline's story unfold in her relations with those around her. Her African mother is absent, missing or presumed dead. Her father is Philippe de Grandpré, a wealthy French merchant. He has raised her and has another wife, Aveline's stepmother, Madeleine de L'Isle. Madeleine has educated and brought up Aveline in the home, and the game initially portrays them as having close relations. Fairly quickly, it becomes clear that although Aveline is someone of privilege and status, she is not content to be a gentlewoman of leisure. She spends her nights using her skills as a member of the Assassins, aiding those in need and concealing her actions from her family. Her work begins with mysterious slave disappearances, and from that point the story and the environments through which she moves expand. In the course of the game she travels across several regions that primarily include the Louisiana Bayou and the ruins of the ancient Mayan city of Chichen Itza in the Yucatan, Mexico. Using the device of nested narratives, this title, like other games in the *Assassin's Creed* series, moves across key historical moments, creating speculative fictions against a backdrop of actual events.

As the narrative takes place between the mid-1760s and 1770s, it is important to note that control of New Orleans, the primary setting, shifted from the French to the Spanish. The city is rendered in the sort of detail expected of *Assassin's Creed*, with great attention to the figure's mobility within public space. Like many other open-world games, the spaces offer a breathtaking backdrop with the intent of presenting an authentic rendering of various locales during the time period; however, as with many of these games, there is little motivation to linger and take in these spaces because of the rigidly goal-oriented nature of gameplay. Time limitations, moving targets and the immediacy of the action sequences often limit one's ability to contemplate the shifting light, textures and goings-on of the simulated spaces. Nevertheless, the artful application of architectural and natural forms, environmental sound and award-winning music establishes a grand sense of place. The richly atmospheric subjective experience of moving through the natural terrain of the Louisiana Bayou provides an aesthetic foil to the bustling and orderly New Orleans environs. In the caves set deep beneath the ruins of Chichen Itza, a strong sense of interior verticality gives an overall impression of a parallel world, ancient and distinct from the other environments.

The varied sites presented, the multiple origins of the primary playable character, and even her shifting social roles during gameplay displace the possibility of essentializing Aveline or her story. In my use of the phrase 'politics of identity' I refer specifically to a call that cultural studies theorist Stuart Hall makes for a new 'politics of identity', to be differentiated from conventional 'identity politics', which is associated with essentializing notions of the subject.[4] Gesturing toward political identities that are not 'founded on the notion of some absolute, integral self', he embraces instead a tripartite strategy of a politics of difference, of self-reflexivity and of contingency.[5] Scholar James Procter has interpreted each of these elements as: (1) a rejection of binaries and an understanding of difference as existing within both the group and within individual identity; (2) an understanding that all subjects speak from a specific position; and (3) an understanding that those positions we do take are contextual and may shift in different circumstances.[6] This represents a decidedly anti-essentialist turn in Hall's later work that breaks with absolutisms around group solidarity. And in relation to analyses of games representations it provides a far more flexible framework for intersectional approaches in keeping with the messy object of study.

Aveline stands as a strikingly intersectional figure in the history of game protagonists. Critical race theorist Kimberlé Crenshaw popularized the notion of intersectionality, unpacking the ways in which race and gender bear down on the lives of Black women, and the necessity of a more holistic approach to their experiences. Acknowledging the multidimensionality of women of colour, Crenshaw noted that her 'focus on the intersections of race and gender only highlights the need to account for multiple grounds of identity when considering how the social world is constructed.'[7] 'Through an awareness of intersectionality,' Crenshaw writes, 'we can better acknowledge and ground the differences among us and negotiate the means by which these differences will find expression in constructing group politics.'[8] My use of the term 'intersectional' is influenced by this theoretical rejection of an identity politics of essentializing categories, instead embracing multiple identity markers and discursive power relations that may simultaneously be at play in the subject. When considering the representational politics of Aveline as an intersectional construction, she occupies a rare position as a character whose subjectivity – as a woman of colour of a particular class and sexuality – is directly manifested and continually re-instantiated to the player through game mechanics.

For the consideration of such an intersectional figure as Aveline, this anti-essentialist position helps to formulate an interpretation that is flexible enough to meet her fluid identity. When referring to 'ideology', I refer to Hall's usage during a discussion of racist ideologies in media as meaning 'those images, concepts and premises which provide the frameworks through which we represent, interpret, understand and "make sense" of some aspect of social existence.'[9] Per Hall's thinking, ideologies are not isolated concepts; rather they are connected by chains of meaning. Likewise, ideologies are not driven by individual intention, but shift as part of a collective process. They may seem natural, but are in fact highly constructed. And, according to Hall's definition, ideologies construct a place for subjects from which to perceive themselves as speaking truths, in a way that feels so authentic to themselves and their experience that they take it for their own – although it actually arises from larger discourses and forces at play.[10]

Hall and many before him have effectively made the argument that mass culture and the popular are worthy of study, and offer insight into the dreams and fears of a given culture (see Introduction). As one scholar said of Hall, 'For him, culture is not something to simply appreciate, or study; it is also a critical site of social action and interpretation, where power relations are both established and potentially unsettled.'[11] Games do function on the level of myth, and as machines that produce power relations, both reifying dominant values in their preferred readings, and, presenting the possibility for oppositional interpretations and moments of rupture. However, the predominant analyses of games to date have been formal and technical in nature, and there is comparatively little address of games from a cultural studies or visual culture studies perspective. Thinking through this specific game also affords possible intellectual frameworks for a more general critical cultural approach that can guide an understanding of games as more than technical – as *visual culture* – and certainly as one of the most impactful forms to have been witnessed in the twenty-first century.

A Digital Politics of Identity

There have been some significant interventions into racial and cultural representations in games, and issues around stereotyping, such as the works of Anna Everett, Lisa Nakamura, Dean Chan and David Leonard.[12] Regarding issues of gender, Adrienne Shaw's work – which I will further discuss – has made important contributions to the study of games, and there has been groundbreaking scholarship done by Derek Burrill, Geoff King and Tanya Krzywinska, Justine Cassell and Henry Jenkins, Yasmin B. Kafai, Karrie Heeter, T.L. Taylor, Kishonna Gray, Jill Denner and Jennifer Y. Sun, among others.

Despite the current overwhelming focus on the technical aspects of games, several established scholars and critics have argued for the importance of considering racial representation in new media in general, and games more specifically. Hall wrote of media as 'not only a powerful source of ideas about race. They are also one place where these ideas are articulated, worked on, transformed and elaborated.'[13] The concerns of race, racism, representation and stereotype have been present in the consideration of video games, although they largely come from areas outside of academic game studies. Media scholars Anna Everett and S. Craig Watkins make an important early intervention into how race intersects with game culture and the games industry and, through their consideration of games as 'racial pedagogical zones', unpack how some games impart highly problematic tropes around race and ethnicity to young players.[14] Media and technology theorist Alexander Galloway likewise asserts that the 'contemporary format of animation, both cinematic and gamic, is one of the most important sites today where racial coding is worked out in mass culture.'[15]

David Leonard reflects on the racial ideologies present in games as early as 2006. He asks: 'How can one truly understand fantasy, violence, gender roles, plot, narrative, game playability, virtual realities (all common within the current literature), and the like without examining race, racism, and/ or racial stratification – simply put, one cannot.'[16] Outlining the egregious examples of blatant racial and gender-based stereotyping, Leonard calls for an intersectional approach to the analysis of games. It is clear that from early on there was a strong sense of the impact that games have on their players and how potently they can shape lived world perceptions of 'others'. As games representations grow ever more complex, the demand for intersectionality remains more important than ever.

Aveline's appearance as a fiction within her own historical context, as well as the time in which *Liberation* was released, both influence how the politics of identity operates in this game. Speaking more generally of advanced computation and its relation to history, Tara McPherson calls for the desegregating of technological histories from socio-political histories, since they mutually reinforce one another.[17] '[I]f digital computing underwrites today's information economy and is the central technology of post-World War II America,' McPherson reasons, 'these technologized ways of seeing/knowing took shape in a world also struggling with shifting knowledges about and representations of race.'[18] Though her scholarship does not address video games in particular, their representational logics must also be understood contextually, since they are computational forms. This will become important for understanding the cultural significance of Aveline de Grandpré since, as a departure from the white male protagonist, she emerges against the backdrop of the critical mess of a growing harassment campaign against women and socially defined minorities, namely GamerGate. Likewise, Ian Shaw and Joanne Sharp argue that games are forms of 'social irrealism' that place real world questions of humanity's future in the context of imaginary landscapes. They assert that the fictional worlds of games nevertheless engage social commentary and create the immersive spaces that allow players to grapple with lived political imaginations.[19] Within an American context, the centrality of race for 'political imaginations' is indisputable. This resonated within the public sphere on a daily basis during the time of writing this research, as shown in the increased media attention focused on the racial disparity wrought through the brutal mistreatment of black male bodies by the police.[20] This cannot be thought of as discontinuous with the origins of race-based inequity and the subjugation of bodies within the history of the United States, imaged in *Liberation* through the playable representation of slavery. Indeed, Alex Amancio, Creative Director from *Assassin's Creed: Unity*, said of the original *Assassin's Creed*:

> When *AC 1* was released, it was right around the Iraq War. Truthfully, it's a combination of two things: serendipity and when we pick a setting, current topics seep into our choices and we try to reinforce that. It influences our creativity and it finds its way into the game. Any piece of art – if you look at *Catcher in the Rye*, Salinger having those pages with him when he was fighting the Nazis, that experience seeped into the work whether he wanted it to or not. In the same way – to a lesser level – I think it seeps into *Assassin's Creed* whether we want it to or not.[21]

This comment suggests a tremendous awareness of and engagement with the situatedness of *Assassin's Creed* in the present, and how historical or quasi-historical narratives may map themselves onto an engagement with myth that constitutes the brand.

The shaping of political imaginations around race (and all forms of difference) indeed occurs powerfully in playable media, and demands critical tools suited to a digital politics of identity. One of the most important interventions into race and digital space has been the work of Lisa Nakamura. In her thoughts on the intricacies of race and the internet, Nakamura concludes that the mediation of images has shifted due to computational and communications technologies, and subsequently the attendant experience of the image has changed, too. Building upon the research of Mark Poster, Nicholas Mirzoeff and others, Nakamura discusses how the internet as a discrete visual technology, along with the neoliberal socio-political moment of the 1990s from which it arises, engendered a particular set of racial formations, or 'racio-visual logic'. At the same time, studies of the internet have, in Nakamura's characterization, 'emphasized the technology of image making as well as the technology of its reception but have failed to consider its racio-visual logic' as a constitutive element.[22] She underscores the ways in which utopian visionaries championed the internet as a democratizing, colour-blind space where race could be neutralized or elided altogether.[23] Through her careful analysis of paradigmatic examples of digital media production by socially defined minorities on the internet, Nakamura highlights the ways in which self-imaging and self-authoring strategies have engendered new modes of expression. Thinking through socially defined minorities' reception and use of new technologies as a means of representation in the face of a neoliberal turn that attempts to dematerialize race, Nakamura identifies their awareness and activation of their own cultural capital within the internet's racio-visual logic as a site of optimism. While games do depart from the intended focus of her observations, it is useful for thinking about the ways that racio-visual logics are sited within particular contexts and technologies. Those variables are both ever-present, though unfixed in the sense that they are constantly being negotiated. And, no less important, her assertions expose a set of relations between users, makers, authors and consumers of digital visual culture that somewhat destabilizes fixed power relations.[24]

Specifically in relation to playable media, Adrienne Shaw's significant intervention into game culture, *Gaming at the Edge: Sexuality and Gender at the Margins of Gamer Culture*, considers the politics of representation, largely from the perspective of gamers' identification and dis-identification with their onscreen characters. She studies those who play – and who may or may not self-identify as 'gamers' – in relation to the kinds of preconceived and often hackneyed notions around the politics of representation. Shaw asks potent questions about how the politics of representation may be explored in new ways in relation to games. How can intersectional and hybrid forms of identity be accounted for without falling back on forms of minority bean-counting that ultimately marginalize groups into niche markets?[25]

Importantly, Shaw's work provides qualitative evidence of the ways that players, as collaborators in the production and consumption of games as culture, relate to those texts in unexpected ways. By her own account, her research yielded unexpected results in terms of how players think about the characters they guide and otherwise engage with. As it turns out, it is not a simple matter of demanding more reflections of themselves or more equitable representations. The scholar's findings suggest that games scholarship and criticism generally adopt a flawed approach to analysing representation in relation to games. Shaw proposes that instead of continuing to make the pervasive argument that there should be certain kinds of representations in games because they 'matter', we should embrace the reality that they *do not* matter as much as previously believed.[26] Yes, we can project ourselves into all kinds of identities as players, and yes it is true that the relationship between player and player-character is much more fluid. Following Shaw, we should argue that diversity should exist in games for the betterment and expanded potentials of play, as opposed to hammering away at the industry using the blunt instrument of a 'moral obligation' to be inclusive and pluralistic because this ultimately only reifies the binary and hierarchal relations between the 'norm' and the peripheral. Her research further suggests that socially defined minorities should not be expected to demand representation or educate the dominant group about their alterity, since it both: (1) creates problematic 'niche' markets, effectively ghettoizing groups into identified, separated, fixed constituencies; and (2) presumes those marginalized groups are statistically more preoccupied with seeing themselves represented than they actually are.[27] Shaw pragmatically does not displace the need to make allowances for commercial interests in relation to the knotty problem of representation, while also endeavouring to shift the argument toward greater expectations of the social responsibility of makers, as opposed to the obligation of marginalized audiences to perform the labour of demanding change.[28]

How can Shaw's findings be reconciled with the example of *Assassin's Creed III: Liberation*? This particular game will likely be most remembered for how its primary player-character blatantly intervened into the now well-known and exhausted presence of the white male protagonist. And *Liberation* will remain significant for having done so during a particularly contentious moment for games, since it was initially released during the very public and ongoing harassment of Anita Sarkeesian for her feminist criticism of mainstream games that began in 2012. The subsequent full-blown harassment campaign of GamerGate in 2014 coincided with *Liberation*'s HD re-release. The game therefore became a flashpoint for a public conversation that spilled over from the insular games community into mainstream media, and which drew attention to the dearth of equity in representation, both within games and in the larger games industry.

Rather than focusing on the need for corrective representations of socially defined minorities in games, I am interested in how a politics of identity speaks to the complex renegotiations at work in a game such as *Liberation*. How does Aveline's nebulous claim to cultural 'authenticity' or 'purity' inform the ways in which this primary playable character is understood within the framework of her representation as a hybrid, errant and ambivalent character? Most central will be the importance placed on the creole subject as a key formation that can help push against the tendencies toward racial, national and ethnic essentialisms. Through an examination of the creole, the polyglot, the global cosmopolitan, the figure that falls between categories, we can gain insight into the carefully constructed social identity that Aveline occupies at the centre of the game (see Figure 1.3).

As the playable aspects of any game constitute protocols for engagement, core mechanics of gameplay must be unpacked for their ideological underpinnings. In *Liberation,* an unusual protagonist in the hero role productively exaggerates the fact that all games are cultural palimpsests.

Figure 1.3 Aveline as assassin. *Assassin's Creed III: Liberation* (2012) image provided by Ubisoft, Inc. Created, developed and published by Ubisoft.

Matthew Thomas Payne's work on post-9/11 military games has similarly described games in this way, saying, 'video games are modern day palimpsests; they are interactive records that possess layers upon layers of creative practices and that contain – like the faint and hidden writing on ancient parchment – earlier iterations of code, mechanics, and cultural beliefs about citizenship, patriotism, sacrifice and government power.'[29] In terms of *Liberation*, the list of cultural beliefs easily extends to include gender, race, sexuality, class and a host of other considerations. Aveline's presence strains the limits of this game and the context it creates, in such a way as to be useful for thinking about what Ian Bogost described in the epigraph above as the complicated nature of video games.[30] Through *Assassin's Creed III: Liberation*, the inherent messiness of the politics of identity within all games as cultural manifestations comes into sharp focus. But where did this messy palimpsest of a gamic vision originate?

The Poetics of Form in *Liberation*

Liberation was developed by Ubisoft Sofia and co-written by Jill Murray and Richard Farrese, who jointly won an award for Outstanding Achievement in Videogame Writing from the Writer's Guild of America. Ubisoft Sofia is a Bulgarian subsidiary of the French video game company, Ubisoft, which is the third-largest independent publisher of games globally. With over 9,000 employees and 30 studios on six continents, Ubisoft in many ways epitomizes the influence of economic globalization on the production of mass culture in terms of its multinational distribution of its production, as well as its highly successful global consumption.[31] As developers of iconic titles such as *Assassin's Creed*, *Far Cry*, *Watch Dogs* and *Prince of Persia*, Ubisoft locates itself centrally in the 'hero business', manufacturing interactive games that place the player in the position of an exceptional individual, the vast majority of whom have been constructed as heterosexual white male protagonists.

Upon its release, the game received middling reviews, with a Metacritic score of 70/100. Typical responses included: complaints of glitches, lack of technical inventiveness and narrative superficiality. Many were frustrated by the game's inability to capitalize upon the tri-costume mechanic or fully

61

capture the sprawling vastness of the *Assassin's Creed* franchise in a hand-held format.[32] However, many lauded its presentation of a female assassin, and found Aveline herself to be compelling – though some complained that her unique positionality was underexploited in the gameplay.

To date there are nine main instalments of *Assassin's Creed,* with more than a dozen other releases. It bears mentioning that the original *Assassin's Creed* (2007) owes much to the swashbuckling vision of *Prince of Persia,* whose creator Jordan Mechner described as 'a game inspired by movies' (see Figure 1.4). During a presentation about the connection between *Prince of Persia* and cinema, Mechner described the direct influence of early filmic versions of stories from *The Arabian Nights,* such as *The Thief of Bagdad* (1924) starring Douglas Fairbanks. The original action sequences for the swordfights in the first *Prince of Persia* were lifted directly from those by Errol Flynn and others in the *Adventures of Robin Hood* film from 1938, using a rudimentary rotoscoping technique.[33] Two members of Ubisoft's *Assassin's Creed* development team, main writer Corey May and animation director Khai Nguyen, were also on the *Prince of Persia: Sands of Time* (2003) series team that migrated the game from 2D to 3D format and integrated mechanics inspired by parkour, which are prominent in all *Assassin's Creed* instalments.[34] Additionally, *Assassin's Creed* was originally envisioned by game designer Patrice Désilets as *Prince of Persia: Assassin* and would have featured the prince's bodyguard as the central playable character. Eventually it evolved into its own title, but the connective tissue runs deep between these two titles.

The ties between *Assassin's Creed* and its origins in *Prince of Persia*'s Orientalist narratives influence the form of *Liberation.* The spectral presence of the swashbuckler and fantasy of adventure against an exotic backdrop looms heavily in the game's core mechanics of navigation, stealth and combat.[35] The presence of Aveline as a heroine can be read against the typical scenario of the Orientalist fantasy of 'saving the princess' employed by Mechner in *Prince of Persia,* and inspired by innumerable previous iterations of otherness around the Islamic world, which are connected to perceptions of the Middle East. The noted Palestinian American academic and political activist Edward Said, in his *Orientalism,* utilized a comparative literary approach to fully unpack the West's nineteenth and twentieth-century

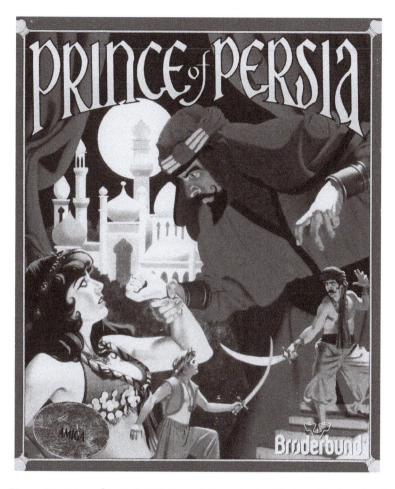

Figure 1.4 *Prince of Persia* (1989). Game designer Jordan Mechner, developed and published by Brøderbund Software, Inc. Cover art used for Amiga.

stereotypical vision of the 'Orient' and the purposes this served in bolstering Western colonial policies.[36] Like Stuart Hall, Said was committed to cultural critique, but from a post-colonial perspective that interrogated cultural representations of the strategically exoticized 'other'. He traced the deployment of extremely potent fantasy and stereotype around Islamic society in various textual practices, and how the 'Orient' operated as a foil for the West and irreducibly alien – with forceful ramifications. Rather than dismissing stereotypes that return unendingly, such as tropes around the inherent cruelty and barbarism of the Middle East (especially in terms of dominating women), and visual signifiers like minarets, bazaars, harems, deserts, belly dancers, beady-eyed swarthy enemies and scimitars, Said says we should understand them within the machinations of empire. As Said himself wrote, 'To believe that the Orient was created – or, as I call it, "Orientalized" – and to believe that such things happen simply as a necessity of the imagination, is to be disingenuous. The relationship between the Occident and Orient is a relationship of power, of domination, of varying degrees of a complex hegemony...'[37] Said contended that the persistence of these narratives in itself evidenced the degree to which they were central to galvanizing the West's power on a global scale:

> One ought never to assume that the structure of Orientalism is nothing more than a structure of lies or of myths which, were the truth about them to be told, would simply blow away. I myself believe that Orientalism is more particularly valuable as a sign of European-Atlantic power over the Orient than it is a veridic discourse about the Orient [...] Nevertheless, what we must respect and try to grasp is the sheer knitted-together strength of Orientalist discourse, its very close ties to the enabling socio-economic and political institutions, and its redoubtable durability. After all, any system of ideas that can remain unchanged as teachable wisdom (in academies, books, congresses, universities, foreign-service institutes) from the period of Ernest Renan in the late 1840s until the present in the United States must be something more formidable than a mere collection of lies. Orientalism, therefore, is not an airy European fantasy about the Orient, but a created body of theory and practice in which, for many generations, there has been a considerable material investment.[38]

Consider that, if one were to apply Said's assertion to persisting tropes that perpetually resurface (sometimes to the extreme) in games, we must try to understand them not as outmoded ideas that, once outed, lose their potency. Rather than seeing games as reflecting the world as it is, we had better conceive of them as operating within the matrices of power, and as recreating the object of representation in a *desired* and highly buttressed form.

The connection between Said's scholarship and specific representations of Islamic society and Arab people in games has been excellently studied by Vit Šisler in his scholarly work on digital stereotyping. In his 'Digital Arabs: Representation in Video Games', Šisler examines how the Muslim or the Arab has been constructed as Other, consistent with the findings of Said, in order to collapse a complex constellation of disparate identities into stereotypes of terrorists and hostiles. He argues that the Middle East is a favourite setting in both quasi-historical and modern games. Contemporary settings tend to present Arabs or Muslims in schematized ways, creating a visual shorthand between modes of dress, skin colour and terror acts or extremism. Conflict usually defines gameplay in this case, while diverse cultures from the region are often flattened into one unsympathetic monolithic enemy.[39] Following Said's characterization, games set in the fantastical Middle East often imagine the Orient as timeless, exotic, naive and fundamentally contradictory to modernity. 'Since video games are usually produced with their consumer base in mind', Šisler contends, 'they tend to incorporate and reflect the general imaginations of the Middle East prevalent among the Western public, as well as the audience's expectations of particular genres.' He continues, 'Moreover, the highly competitive nature of the game market, together with high production costs, reinforces the iteration of proved and successful patterns in game genres and content.'[40] In his theorization, Šisler traces a clear line, through Said, that follows the connectedness between the popularization of the cultural representation of Islamic and Arab societies in games and the Western imperial policies that inform and sustain them.

I do not intend to infer anything about the individual creator or team's perspectives during their development of the *Prince of Persia* or *Assassin's Creed* series. Nor do I seek to make presumptions regarding their intentionality. Instead, what I assert here engages the extremely durable myths and fantasies that are inevitably expressed in the language of the cultures that birthed them. Myths and heroic stories have been core to all cultures since the beginning, and have been expressed through various media, but it is in video games that we find the opportunity to engage with them in playable form.[41] Said characterizes Orientalism as 'shot through with doctrines of European superiority, various kinds of racism, imperialism and the like, dogmatic views of "the Oriental" as a kind of ideal and unchanging abstraction". This does exist beneath the surface of *Liberation*, albeit more in its poetics, than the narrative and setting.[42] By 'poetics', I mean the perceptible elements of a gamic text – and how they converge to bring about particular aesthetic and expressive effects for the player. This corresponds to new media scholar Lisbeth Klastrup's definition of poetics as it relates to virtual worlds:

> *A poetics of virtual worlds deals with: the systematic study of virtual worlds as virtual worlds. It deals with the question 'What is a virtual world?' and with all possible questions derived from it, such as: How is a virtual world an aesthetic form of expression? What are the forms and kinds of virtual worlds? What is the nature of one world genre or trend? What is the system of a particular developer's 'art' and 'means of expression'? How is a story constructed? What are the specific aspects of instances of virtual worlds? How are they constituted? How do virtual worlds embody 'non-fictional' phenomena?* (italics in original)[43]

Klastrup goes on to describe a kind of 'worldness' created through the manifestation of these elements together in a given virtual world, arguing that '[a] general poetics of virtual worlds should then try to describe what influences the emergence of "worldness" and how this worldness is related to the presence of multiple users in the world and the properties of computer-mediated "interactive" texts as such.'[44] The notion of a poetics of games clearly applies to what I would describe as a focus on those aesthetic formations and complex cultural signifying that together contribute to the world-making of a game and its affective experience.

Now, in the case of *Liberation*, it is a kind of princess who possesses the sword, and she does the saving, rather than being saved. This breaks with the damsel-in-distress trope and places the female figure at the centre of the narrative in an activated, heroic role. However, a significant dimension of the game's poetics issues from its core mechanics: the aforementioned combat, stealth and navigation. The manner in which our protagonist moves through environments with fluid maximum efficiency and command evinces a particular kind of relation to place. The covertness of her movements and the clandestine meetings suggest, among other things, access to an insider's knowledge of the machinations of power at play in her environment, and perhaps a modicum of influence in this regard.

Aveline's combat methods – largely consisting of sword fighting and various kinds of hand-to-hand combat – invoke the beloved swashbuckler through her distinctive fighting stances and dramatic swordplay, her strong, prototypical 'chivalric' desire to rescue others and defend ideals (i.e., freedom) and her particular brand of sprawling adventure. These components invoke deeply seated cultural narratives that closely connect to the history of European imperial expansion and the attendant value systems that would justify and legitimate ambitious exploitation. Together, these elements signify what lies beneath the story of Aveline, namely the vestigial presence of the decidedly gendered swashbuckler and Orientalist fantasy, which are predicated upon a notion of adventure that Hall described as 'synonymous with the demonstration of the moral, social and physical mastery of the colonizers over the colonized'.[45] In other words, while the game's narrative of liberation and its exceptional heroine of colour break with the dominant reading of the swashbuckler figure and Orientalist fantasy, its poetics retain the eroded, fragmented, accumulated gestures that recall a cultural history of European empire (see Figure 1.5).

Figure 1.5 Aveline fights. *Assassin's Creed III: Liberation* (2012) image provided by Ubisoft, Inc. Created, developed and published by Ubisoft.

Aveline as Queered, Creole, Intersectional

Atop this already sedimentary foundation rests another complicated construction, in the form of the game's heroine. The character of Aveline de Grandpré – along with the persona mechanics – are fairly universally considered to be the primary innovations of the game. Aveline is young, fetching and an agitator against slavery, due to her self-awareness of her own tricky subject position as the daughter of a former African slave. Her heroic actions seek to tilt history in the direction of liberation and she shares her revolutionary logics with friends and foes in intermittent dialogues. Given the outcomes of history, she is clearly configured as a hero. In the binary of Templars versus Assassins, which map onto a dualism between total control and total freedom, respectively, she is a zealot for liberty.

Her skin colour, which is a deep golden hue, reflects her creolized origins and clearly marks her as being of mixed origin during a time when there would be a social stigma attached to this. Aveline is not the first mixed-race character in the *Assassin's Creed* franchise. In *Assassin's Creed III*, the primary character Connor (also known as Ratonhnhaké:ton) is half Mohawk and half British. He lives during the same colonial American period as Aveline, and their paths cross briefly in the course of her story. It should be noted that this character is described as 'black' by innumerable reviewers, as a part of their observation that she breaks the white-male-protagonist trope.[46] However, online comments beneath many of these reviews suggested that some players do not consider Aveline to be authentically black, due to her mixed-race status. This concern with racial purity clearly intends to break identification with the character by disqualifying Aveline from a grouping the commentator feels would be of legitimating value to those who laud her presence. In other words, she is a figure whose blackness is 'queered' in the sense that she stands outside the normative construction, generating friction against hetero-patriarchal values, such as is theorized in the work of interdisciplinary art history and visual studies scholar Derek Conrad Murray.[47] Interestingly, this becomes even further complicated by inferences about her sexual status, which I subsequently discuss.

Jill Murray, one of the writers at Ubisoft Montreal, and co-writer of *Liberation*, has spoken about the development of Aveline and strategies for effectively writing for diverse characters. In a talk entitled 'Diverse Game Characters: Write Them Now!', Murray examined strategies regarding writing motivations, setting, voice, research and gameplay to define character, the mobilization of particular mechanics in games and the importance of creating greater sensitivity to diversity within the game design team.[48] Responding directly to the claims made by Evan Narcisse that *Liberation* specifically reiterated certain kinds of racially oriented tropes, such as the Back-to-Africa movement, the slave vendetta narrative, the tragic mulatto and the Uncle Tom, Murray insisted that these were not consciously built into the design, and as she came onto the project after the inception of Aveline as a character, 'there was no time for a cultural studies course or to learn about the entire history of African American film and literature.'[49] According to her, the team was more focused on getting the context right, so that they would properly understand the rule of law by imposed by the shifting colonial presences of France and Spain within the Louisiana region during the time. The emotional core of the story, informed by slave narratives that Murray researched, reveals itself most directly in the diary pages of Jeanne, Aveline's mother. In these scraps of narrative that are discovered throughout the game, Jeanne chronicles her experience of being a *placée* under the regulation of the *Code Noir*, a French legal document that regulated slavery in the French territories.[50] As these articulations are subsumed somewhat beneath the primary narrative, they feel secondary, although they provide great insight into the absent mother around whom so much of Aveline's identity circulates. Murray spoke of how Aveline's subjectivity inspired the Bulgarian designers to make unique game mechanic adjustments to suit her conditions. These were reflected in her clothing options, and the corresponding skills and limitations accorded to each.

Reviewers generally accepted the character of Aveline as a positive step in games and a complex representation. Critic Evan Narcisse's assessment suggests that the game was successful in its rendering of an empathetic and relatable, albeit unexpected, hero:

Aveline may be a nearly superhuman assassin, but she's still cut off from her history in a very raw way. You feel that void in this title. By putting you in a game where you play through the sometimes painful push-and-pull of gender and racial identity in American history, *Liberation* takes a potentially polarizing risk. It pays off, though, and this *Assassin's Creed* is better off for casting a broader net.[51]

It is true that Aveline is a complex character, rendered in a manner that takes into account her race, gender and class status. These are configured as integral in the game mechanics, particularly in regard to her own spatial mobility, skills and abilities.

BioWare Montreal's Manveer Heir, an outspoken advocate of inclusivity in games from within the industry, similarly pointed to the game as an exemplar of a step forward in pushing the centrality of a character's identity from the narrative to the mechanics level:

That *Liberation* uses race so prominently, not just for narrative reasons but for actual game design reasons, is extremely exciting and wonderful to see, to me. The player can get a sense of what racial passing is and means, and how it works. [...] Playing *Liberation*, you begin to understand what advantages you have as a proper lady, but also what is expected of you and your place in the world. And when you pass as a slave, you start to better understand how subhuman you are considered by others due to your surroundings and treatment.[52]

The complicated question of the character's ability to pass as other 'personas' is literalized in the three forms of clothing as signifiers of caste. However, larger themes of passing, contingency, the rejection of binaries and the function of context for identity are referenced throughout the game. Late in the narrative, Aveline attends a ball at the governor's mansion, clothed in her 'lady' guise. As she mingles in order to gain information, she is addressed by a male guest, a stranger: 'Señorita, give us your name, that we may know how to address the fairest woman at the ball.' To which his acquaintance quips: 'Fair? I think not. But still, your complexion is beguiling.' After some chatter, a young woman loudly gossips,

Figure 1.6 Aveline as lady, engaging in charming and bribing. *Assassin's Creed III: Liberation* (2012). Created, developed and published by Ubisoft. Screen shot by author.

'...and her complexion! Of course, she is a dear friend of the family, but her mother... it is shocking!' Gathered up here in this brief verbal interaction are character developments around Aveline as both having a degree of social mobility granted by her father's pedigree, while being marked by her skin colour, which evidences her mother's African origins (see Figure 1.6). The non-playable character's reduction of Aveline to her race is a simulation of a social identity that is violently mapped onto the subject.

This experience of being racially marked as a socially defined other is captured well by Frantz Fanon in his devastating account of feeling his own complex identity shattered and ideologically reconstituted as black through the fearful look and stigmatizing utterance of a child: 'Look, a Negro...!' For Hall, the Caribbean represents the primal scene of a tragedy in the matrix of which the negotiations between what he termed *présence africaine*, *présence européenne* and *présence américaine* are in a constant state of productive transformation. The process of creolization refers to the brutal interaction of culturally different populations as they have occurred in different parts of the world in which the system of plantation-organized society. *Créolité*, on the other hand, is the 'fact of belonging to an original human entity which comes out of these processes in due time.[53] For the character of Aveline, her creolization marks her contingency, rather than a fixed or monolithic identity. It issues from a dynamic set of circumstances wrought by turbulent history and a relational condition of transformation.[54] One could more accurately link her contingent, contextualized and multifaceted identity to Paul Gilroy's notion of a 'black Atlantic' with its syncretic relations to Africa, Europe, the Caribbean and the West.[55] Key as well is her immersion in and witnessing of a new nation in the process of asserting its global modernity, exactly through its mobilization of great masses of enslaved black bodies, following Gilroy's now-canonical argument that slavery was at the centre of the drive toward modernity. It is against this backdrop that Aveline's own creolized identity as part African, part French, born in Louisiana and traverser of the Caribbean and Gulf of Mexico regions comes into focus.

Aveline's capacity to pass from one class status to another, through her use of ingenuity and the manipulation of costuming as a tactic, points to a kind of intersectionality being expressed in the game. But its more immediate reference also invokes the complexity of race in early American history, and even more specifically the figure of the ex-slave Harriet Tubman (c.1822–1913), a freedom fighter, Union spy, abolitionist and iconic 'conductor' of the Underground Railroad. In her lifetime, she became the first woman in American history to lead an armed expedition during the Civil War as a scout. Tubman does not appear in *Liberation*, as some other historical icons in the *Assassin's Creed* series have. The game's timeframe (1760s–70s) pre-dates Tubman's birth. However, Aveline's strategic use of clothing – such as her 'blending in' to the slave population – invokes the memory of this figure, who was known for utilizing various disguises and misdirection to evade captors (see Figure 1.7). In one oft-repeated anecdote, Tubman had to conceal her identity in order to enter into a county where a former master would likely recognize her. Wearing a large bonnet to cover her face, Tubman carried two live chickens whose legs were tied with string. When the former master passed nearby, Tubman pulled the strings and the chickens escaped and made a scene, causing a distraction. As one historian wrote, 'Harriet was nearly always prepared with a change of costume or

Figure 1.7 Aveline blending in as a slave through her mode of dress. *Assassin's Creed III: Liberation* (2012). Created, developed and published by Ubisoft. Screen shot by author.

some other diversion.'[56] The misdirection using fowl is – perhaps coincidentally – echoed in Aveline's childhood traumatic moment of chasing after a stray chicken and thereby being separated from her mother. Privilege was in fact largely dependent not only upon race, but one's class. Tubman exploited this, posing as a slave, an old woman and even donning a Union soldier's coat and rifle during her army scouting. In keeping with the image presented in *Liberation*, it is important to remember that not all black people were slaves during pre-Independence times; in fact, significant numbers of them were not. The first Africans in what would become America arrived as explorers and servants, as well as a labour force. Free black people had more mobility, and some were privileged and themselves owned slaves.[57]

Cued through clever in-game dialogue, Aveline's sexual identity is similarly contingent and plays on clothing as a metaphor for gender construction. Aveline's sexual status might be presumed heterosexual on the basis of the game mechanic of 'charm' that she exclusively directs towards male targets and the repeated verbal references to her beauty uttered by male non-player-characters. However, interestingly, this matter is markedly understated in the game context. There is a strong sense that she and her childhood friend, Gérald Blanc, are close, and that he has feelings for her. Reviewer Evan Narcisse mentions this, and suggests that it may be a thematic nod to the 'social impropriety' and prohibitions around their potential interracial union.[58] Early in the game, for example, Aveline's father admonishes her: 'I do fear you are more like your father than is fit for a lady…' He then indicates that Blanc has requested her assistance at the family warehouse, to which Aveline's stepmother Madeline comments: 'Is that all he has to offer? I should think for all his attention, he would request your [Aveline's] hand.' Aveline replies: 'All the same, it's the work that interests me.' Later, in another cutscene, Gérald broaches the subject of his affection for her, and Aveline deftly pivots from the subject, while not pushing him entirely away.

The inference within the cutscene suggests Aveline's preoccupation with the urgent matters at hand. However, one critic takes the interpretation further, proposing that Aveline's character may be a paradigmatic example of how some games are slowly integrating indirect references to LGBT subjectivities. In Aveline's reappearance as a part of the PlayStation exclusive DLC for *Assassin's Creed IV: Black Flag* (2013, Ubisoft Montreal for Ubisoft), buried content as well as encoded dialogue led game critic Jagger Gravning to point out the notable ways in which sexuality operated around her. He mentions the figure of Aveline among several others, such as Lara Croft in the *Tomb Raider* reboot, whose significations were ambiguous enough to create the space for possible queer readings.[59] The markers identified by Gravning as signalling Aveline as queer-identified included her Assassin's clothing, a modified male costume. Also, combatants in pursuit sometimes refer to Aveline by a male pronoun, calling out: 'He's getting away!' or 'He's trying to shake us!' And, in discoverable recordings documenting the experiences of the subject who accesses Aveline's genetic memories, we learn that person is male. All three of these elements point, for Gravning, to a potentially transgender narrative. But most important, and highlighted by Gravning, is a section of dialogue between Aveline and a revolutionary slave figure and potential Brotherhood recruit, Patience Gibbs, that overtly plays with innuendo during their initial meeting:

PATIENCE: 'What is it you want, if not my charm?'

AVELINE: 'Only you. Charmless.'

PATIENCE (STEPPING CLOSER):   'Is it a game of flats you fancy then?'

AVELINE: 'A friend sent me. Connor. He will offer you safety and training.'

PATIENCE: (STEPPING EVEN CLOSER) 'Mademoiselle, if you get my charm back, you can take me as your game pullet.'

Uttered as repartee, this eighteenth-century dialogue makes reference to lesbian sex (in the term 'flats') and a young prostitute or sexually forward girl (with 'game pullet').[60] Importantly, Aveline does not display a phobic response to Patience's coy remarks, though it is less certain whether she is receptive (see Figure 1.8). As Gravning puts it, 'ideas of gender fluidity and homosexuality constantly surround the character Aveline. Yet she neither confirms nor denies a specific orientation.'[61] It is in keeping with Aveline's character, in fact, that the fluidity that defines her own shifting identifications may also extend to all dimensions of herself. She continually re-orients herself as per context and necessity. Perhaps, in the roles of assassin, spy and freedom fighter, Aveline's sexuality would just be

Figure 1.8 Aveline and Patience Gibbs. *Assassin's Creed IV: Black Flag* (2013). Created, developed and published by Ubisoft. Screen shot by author.

another tool in her arsenal (not unlike James Bond or the Blaxploitation hero, who uses sex to get what he wants). There isn't enough specificity to say for certain. But, in Aveline there is a strong sense of becoming, and queer potentiality in the sense of departing radically from normative gender role expectations on many levels. While some of these schematic references are ultimately inconclusive, these allusions at least disrupt the automatic presumption of Aveline's sexual preferences and interior life, opening up the possibility of other readings.

Playability and Phantasms

One of the key problems in representing difference in games relates to its translation into algorithms, whose underlying functions ideologically configure these distinctions as fixed and immutable. Alex Galloway critiques the software algorithms used to model race and class as 'often essentialist in nature, paralleling certain offline retrograde notions of naturally or physiologically determined and unchangeable human races'.[62] Galloway interrogates the ways in which games like *World of Warcraft* and *StarCraft* map particular racial qualities onto machinic behaviours that shape gameplay. The result is that, despite a game's use of fantasy species such as elves, trolls and gnomes, it 'assigns from without certain identifiable traits to distinct classes of entities and then builds complex machineries for explaining and maintaining the natural imperviousness of it all'.[63] Digital media scholar and computer scientist D. Fox Harrell makes an important intervention into this problem, through his theoretical considerations of creative expression, cultural analysis and computational systems. His mobilization of the key concept of 'phantasmal media' vitally unpacks ways in which cultural worldviews can be built into computing systems. A 'phantasm' – a term with origins in cognitive science – is a blend of a cultural idea and sensory imagination that may fluctuate from one societal context to another but which, within a given societal frame, seems implicit and immediately perceived. Highly suggestive and not conscious knowledge, these phantasms, like ideology, are persistent, tacit and largely invisible. Through theorization as well as the development of computational models that take into account the interstices of cultural phenomena at the code level, Harrell intervenes in the ways in which user representations can and sometimes do make use of phantasms that stereotype or codify power dynamics through the rule-based systems and data structures from which they are constructed.

Phantasmal Media, therefore, is about understanding computational media in terms of cultural meanings. It functions as a manual for thinking through systematized methods for theorizing what Harrell calls 'cultural computing'. And it articulates methods for devising systems of computational expression that more accurately reflect the subtle and unexpected functioning of identity-based elements such as social stigma, inclusion and exclusion, interpersonal relations, non-verbal cues, gender, race, sex, ethnicity, fashion, metaphorical expression and relative social station or class. The larger, overarching aim would be to create models of these systems that are more complex and able to computationally account for the subtle goings-on of cultural meanings as they come into being.

Harrell's work emphasizes the conceptualization of a worldview in computing systems and the importance of expressivity, two key areas that are often insufficiently addressed in computing. As he himself attests, some in the field dismiss these concerns as fundamentally outside the aims and values of computing.[64] 'It is imperative,' Harrell indicates, 'to reflect on the cultural values built into the computer-laden society we are building.'[65] Describing his critical interests in broadening the expressive range of computation, Harrell expands the expressivity of computations tools, so that, for example, games with gender options can engage in more meaningful impacts than simple changes in character skins and pronouns. How can we think more intelligently about the meaningful narrative shifts and interactive opportunities that come from a more nuanced understanding of a character's subtle elements of identity? Insisting on more dynamically generated interactions on the basis of these more fluid elements, Harrell argues that this would lead to a more nuanced reflection of the complexity of the world. For him, this is not a simple call for political correctness in the cultural meanings conveyed through digital media, but a way to model an intersectional approach to social identity in the very medium of computational form.

Harrell's important intervention provides disciplinary language and theorization that illuminates how worldviews are built into the data infrastructure of computational systems. It opens up many possibilities for understanding computational systems as machines for thinking about the construction of socio-cultural values into apparently empirical systems. This research can help enliven an understanding of the Persona System built into *Liberation*, which modulates the degree to which Aveline can move, unencumbered, through the game space. The gameplay dictates which persona can be used for each mission. Dressing chambers dot the city to provide adequate access to changes of garb. Missions provide didactic instruction about which persona to occupy, and it is highly unlikely to be able to complete a mission without the proper guise. The Lady guise is a corseted gown with lace and a brimmed hat, which comes in an assortment of colours, with a default green colour. It renders Aveline most persuasive and influential to in-game characters, enabling her to more readily extract information and manipulate the outcomes she wishes with words rather than weapons. In this costume she additionally possesses the skills to bribe and 'charm' male guards, and has less notoriety. However, it is impossible to jump, climb or sprint, and is generally the weakest in combat, as there is limited availability of weaponry. The Slave persona is simplified, also relatively weak in combat with limited access to weaponry and tools. Its primary advantage is that is allows the character to free run, and also grants Aveline the anonymity that allows her to disappear into the local slave population, crowds or other groups. The third persona, the Assassin, renders Aveline persistently 'notorious', which limits her anonymity. However, in this guise she may also free run and climb, and it allows her to execute a 'chain kill', which is a manoeuvre that more efficiently dispatches with up to three enemies when fighting against larger groups. Jill Murray described to me that, in her mind, Aveline felt most authentically herself as an assassin, on the rooftops (see Figure 1.9).[66]

But how do these three possible personas manifest differences in gameplay experience? For example, in the first sequence, a short mission entitled 'Taking Care of Business' requires Aveline to investigate a missing shipment from the family business. In the guise of a lady, she bribes the ship's guards, then 'charms' the lecherous Captain Carlos Dominguez, in order to

Figure 1.9 Aveline above New Orleans. *Assassin's Creed III: Liberation* (2012) image provided by Ubisoft, Inc. Created, developed and published by Ubisoft.

gather intel on the whereabouts of the missing cargo. When it is revealed that the goods have been hidden in two warehouses, Aveline must charm at least one guard in order to locate them. While the Lady guise limits her freedom of mobility – which can be palpably sensed in the more lumbering movements of the character in her burdensome gown and petticoat – only this persona can utilize the charm function. In sequence four, in the mission entitled 'The Secret of the Cenote', Aveline, garbed as a slave, is in Chichen Itza in a cave system beneath the ancient Mayan ruins. There, Aveline must navigate underground cave ponds and the extreme verticality of the caverns to find an artefact that contains a prophecy. The mobility required would be impossible in the Lady guise, and the previous investigations have necessitated that Aveline blend in with the slave population that makes up the nearby community and dig site (see Figure 1.10). The limited weaponry of this guise is acceptable, since most of the game activity consists of navigation. Aveline runs and climbs with ease, and as the environment is friendly to the semi-freed slaves, this cover allows her to move freely within the local population. She does not need to coordinate a rebellion or concern herself with the disempowerment that comes with the signifiers of being a slave. Because the more powerful Assassin guise would

Figure 1.10 Aveline as slave investigating at Chichen Itza. *Assassin's Creed III: Liberation* (2012). Created, developed and published by Ubisoft. Screen shot by author.

generate a spike in her status as 'notorious' and thereby call attention to her investigations, it is not an option for the mission.

In sequence eight, in a mission entitled 'A Fool's Errand', Aveline travels to contact a fellow brother of the Assassins, Connor. As he is aware of her true identity, notoriety is not a concern, so there is no need for her to mask herself as Lady or Slave (see Figure 1.11). With her maximum mobility as an Assassin, and arsenal of weapons, she is best equipped to navigate the wintery terrain and locate her next mark, an officer who possesses knowledge of the identity of a key enemy. Like the cavern sequences, navigation of the space as 'Lady' would be impossible due to the necessary leaps and climbs, and she is well-served by the additional armour that her assassin garb provides. Throughout, the selection of persona is closely tied to the specific demands of each mission, and gestures toward the relative mobility and access afforded to the guise Aveline must adopt. The effect is at times tedious in terms of the obstacles it throws up around gameplay. However, within the logic of the game, it serves as a means to generate a series of player insights about the fluidity of identity and the politics of context, as it bears down on Aveline's racially marked body.

Figure 1.11 Aveline meets Connor. *Assassin's Creed III: Liberation* (2012). Created, developed and published by Ubisoft. Screen shot by author.

Although Harrell does not specifically discuss *Liberation*, his scholarship is useful for understanding how the Persona System mobilizes the affordances of each mode, to bring more meaningful attention to the complexities of identity embodied in Aveline. Playable engagement simulates internal self-inquiry around these various constructions. In other words, power relationships between playable and non-playable characters are determined by the game mechanics, which (as Harrell theorizes) embody particular cultural meanings in the game's system of computational expression. This is constantly reinforced to players, who must strategize around Aveline's varying possible social roles within her in-game historical moment, in order to successfully navigate the game.

'History is Our Playground'[67]

Whether it is appropriate to render fraught historical eras into playable form is not a new question. Particularly in relationship to the popular game settings of historical conflicts such as World War II, for which there are innumerable gamic representations, the question arises as to whether an entertainment form of representation is in poor taste. Is it disrespectful to those conflicts not to have a more deferential position? Does the very form of a game preclude the possibility of a serious stance toward the content presented? Many games contain presentations of actual historical footage intercut into gameplay, or presented as cutscenes or transitional imagery to lend legitimacy, pathos and gravity to the game. Tanine Allison, among others, has examined this phenomenon in relation to games about World War II, concluding that the primary import of tropes in games borrowed from the image-production around World War II reveal more about present-day sentiments toward current military conflicts, than necessarily disclosing much about the past.[68]

Evan Narcisse, a game critic who has shown a dedicated, long-term commitment to analysing racial representation in games, has written extensively on *Liberation*, addressing various aspects of the game, including questions around the effective capture of 'blackness' in its representational tropes, the unpopular casting of a non-black actress to voice and do motion capture for the lead character and the overall success of the character development.[69] Speaking on a similar problem of looking at history through game-play, Narcisse wrote about *Assassin's Creed IV: Freedom Cry DLC*[70] (2014), in which a player occupies the role of Adéwalé, who stirs revolution in the Caribbean. Adéwalé is himself a former slave and first mate on the Jackdaw, captained by Edward Kenway, a primary figure from *Assassin's Creed IV: Black Flag* (2013). Narcisse grappled with the quandary of a playable version of a history of slavery:

> While I played, I kept asking myself if *Freedom Cry* cheapens the historical horrors of the Triangle Trade to use them in an entertainment like this. For me, it doesn't. The chattel slavery of millions of black people from the 16th to 19th Century is one of the most heinous things in human history. But that doesn't mean that it should be out-of-bounds as source material for pop culture creations.[71]

One of the questions that arises with Aveline is her position as an 'exceptional' black character, someone whose unique position and skills set her apart from the typical. Her fighting skills, her heightened resourcefulness, as well as her preternatural abilities for synchronization with the surrounding environment, render her unique from those people of colour around her, who the game largely configures as elevated victims, with the exception of her mentor, Agaté. Surely, she is not invincible, and not even impervious to the attacks of others. The narrative is configured as anti-oppression, anti-colonial and as one that validates the defence of freedom against all those who would oppose it.

What is presented in *Liberation* is certainly a historical fiction, in the mode of action adventure. But the concept of accessing and perceiving history as it actually happened (so that one may know one's heritage, authentic history or uncover truth) runs deep in the storyline – and is wonderfully explored throughout the game. Aveline discovers her origins in more ways than one: rooting out the truth of her disappeared mother's role, revealing the complex agendas on the part of colonial forces of France and Spain in the Louisiana region while slogging through the muck of a coming independence and fraught nation-formation. How this delving takes place presents an interesting set of problems. What does it mean for a player to fictitiously re-enact painful and sometimes extremely bloody parts of American history as a form of play?

When thinking through this question of a 'proper' representation of America's history of slavery, it is useful to take into account other such manifestations of visual culture around the time of the game's release. *Lincoln* (2012), Steven Spielberg's reverential portrait focusing on the historical events leading up to the passing of the 13th Amendment, which secured emancipation, was released the same year as *Liberation*. Also that year, *Abraham Lincoln: Vampire Hunter*, a Timur Bekmambetov film, reimagines the Civil War between the American North and South as a fantasy action horror featuring literal blood-sucking Confederates who use slavery to provide labour and a food supply to what they hope will become the first vampire nation. The film depicts Lincoln as an axe-wielding, covert assassin of the undead enemies of American freedom. Quentin Tarantino's *Django Unchained* (2012) tells the story of a freed slave-turned-bounty hunter. In the director's trademark fashion, *Django* brings vendetta fantasy, buddy-film tropes and satire to the table.

In its irreverent treatment of the subject through the genre form, *Django* drastically broke with the tradition of deferential earnestness toward America's history of slavery present in examples like the television miniseries *Roots* (1977) and Spielberg's *Amistad* (1997). Director Steve McQueen's Oscar-winning *12 Years a Slave* (2013) provides a polar opposite treatment of the slave trade to *Django*. Based upon the autobiography of Solomon Northup, it takes the form of a reverent period drama. For some, the more bludgeoning, mischievous treatments of a most shameful part of American history as imaged in *Django* may be offensive, especially in the cases where history is made fantasy, or where levity, satire or iconoclasm is brought to the discussion. However, it could be argued that films like *Django Unchained* and *Abraham Lincoln: Vampire Hunter* did better critical work in terms of interrogating a mandated relationship of deference demanded of the history of American slavery, and cracked open new possibilities for contending with that difficult historical moment.

Whichever position one might take in regard to the proper representation of history, the timeliness of *Liberation*'s release within the larger scheme of mainstream visual culture must be noted. It is interesting to consider that, given the relative paucity of the historical American slave narrative in mainstream cinema, so many films of this nature would be released in such a short timespan. This certainly relates to the obvious historical impact of the election and re-election of America's first black president, in 2008 and 2012 respectively. A parallel can also be drawn between President Barack Obama's highly debated biracial status and Aveline's construction as a similar figure who defies easy categorization according to racial logics in the United States that connect a legible form of blackness to the presumption of a particular experience.

One critic on a prominent site for game reviews lamented the lost opportunity of presenting such a unique protagonist, but then not taking advantage of the thorny issues in American history that drive both Aveline's identity and the narrative:

> Aveline is a rare sight in video games: an empowered female protagonist whose mixed ethnic background touches on powerful, resonant historical themes. She's the product of two completely different worlds: her father is a wealthy white trader, and her mother is an African slave brought to America by way of Haiti. After her mother mysteriously disappears when Aveline is still

a small child, she is taken in by her father and raised in a society that will likely never fully embrace her[...]

[...] Ultimately, *Liberation* feels like a game that isn't sure of its own identity. Does it want to be a handheld game with a quick, punchy story suited to those playing it on the go, or does it want to take on an ambitious narrative and explore one of the darkest periods in American history? In the end, I feel like *Liberation* tries to do both and suffers for it.[72]

Adrienne Shaw weighed in on this particular issue in regard to *Assassin's Creed III*, of which *Liberation's* narrative is a spin-off. Remarking on the problems of contextualizing gamic fictions in historical realism, she writes:

> The critique of realism here is not on the quality of the research or design, but rather that the focus on realism actually belies the fact that what the game reflects is a particular perspective on history that was assumed to be interesting to anticipated players. This is evident in the downloadable add-on 'Tyranny of King Washington' where, as Ratohnhaké:ton in an alternate world, the player battles alongside his people and still living mother to free the land from a maniacal George Washington. In a game invested in historical detail, this anti-colonial revenge fantasy is simply not an option as the main game. Only in a hyperfictional add-on can there be a reimagined history where Native Americans could be victorious. Even then, the end result of the story is that things are returned to a normal and America stands as it always has.
>
> That is the tyranny of realism that games focused too much on questions of accuracy, rather than emancipatory possibility, must struggle to overcome. It is also indicative of the way imagined audiences over-determine the stories companies are willing to tell. If we can only imagine new ways of viewing what has been, we never get a chance to imagine what might be.[73]

Shaw's point is well-taken, and it is clear in *Liberation* as well that all fictive elements of the game operate within the scope of actual historical outcomes. That is to say, whatever speculative elements there are, the game does not ultimately offer a different unfolding of history. Rather, all outcomes reaffirm history as having an inevitable progression that persists with its results, even within the fantasy realm and time of the game. One can say, at most, that it recuperates obliterated subjectivities and offers 'hyperfictional' asides that provide the catharsis of an alternative outcome or emission of some quashed truth. At the same time, the game renders history as malleable, subjectivized and elusive. Within the larger meta-narrative of the past being controlled by an entity (Templar Order) with interests in how its narratives are related, the rhetorical device of a machine constructed for virtually re-living that past in playable form reveals a very real struggle for history.

Conclusion: Embracing the Mess

In a *New York Times* review of the high-definition reboot of *Assassin's Creed III: Liberation*, critic Chris Suellentrop lauded the developer's efforts, while cynically pointing to the game's poorer quality compared to other *Assassin's Creed* titles with larger budgets and larger development teams. He also noted that developers marginalized what he described as 'the greatest black heroine in the history of video games' to the PS Vita, which is a handheld console.[74] And it does feel like a cautious manoeuvre to test the waters before releasing it for PlayStation, Xbox and PC. His assessment is damning of the industry for its embarrassingly retrograde track record around diversity and inclusion:

> *Assassin's Creed: Liberation* is not the only, or even the best, game with a nonwhite protagonist. For that, you would probably have to look at one of the *Grand Theft Auto* games or Minority Media's *Papo & Yo*. But that a game as mediocre as *Liberation* feels like a revelation should serve as a rebuke for an industry that styles itself as the art form of the 21st century, even as its labor force and its characters too often look like a parody of the 20th, or the 19th.[75]

In considering the playable representations of games, it is important to mine and fully understand the phantasmal aspects of culture that are at play. This is impossible without a contextual understanding of the object of study in relation to the milieu from which its representations and signifying practices arise. If it is true that, as Jill Murray suggests, Aveline is most

Figure 1.12 Aveline performs Assassin's 'Leap of Faith' from a rooftop. *Assassin's Creed III: Liberation* (2012) image provided by Ubisoft, Inc. Created, developed and published by Ubisoft.

herself while leaping from rooftops in her Assassin's guise, then it is in this gender-non-conforming mode that the game presents the most possibility of complex agency, through its mechanics (see Figure 1.12). Aveline and her personae do model a more diverse and multi-layered game protagonist, crosscutting issues of race, class and gender – and in her second iteration, fluid sexuality. The game mechanics, in this case the Persona System, function to engender self-inquiry in the player regarding the complexities of social mobility at the many intersections of Aveline. This is achieved through the specific affordances and limitations of each persona. In a larger sense, it is important to account for how a politics of identity is expressed, not only through the manifestation of the exceptional figure of Aveline, but in the very form of the game's playability. On the level of poetics – or all that constitutes a game's 'worldliness', as Klastrup put it, ethical questions must be asked about the messy forms that chatter deep beneath the surfaces of our games.

2

Aesthetics of Ambivalence and Whiteness in Crisis

How a group is represented, presented over again in cultural forms, how an image of a member of a group is taken as representative of that group, how that group is represented in the sense of spoken for and on behalf of (whether they represent, speak for themselves or not), these all have to do with how members of groups see themselves and others like themselves, how they see their place in society, their right to the rights a society claims to ensure its citizens. Equally representation, representativeness, representing have to do also with how others see members of a group and their place and rights, others who have the power to affect that place and those rights. How we are seen determines in part how we are treated; how we treat others is based on how we see them; such seeing comes from representation.[1]

Richard Dyer, *The Matter of Images*

Introduction

Chapter 2 examines constructions of the normative white figure under duress and, particularly, an amassing crisis in relation to crumbling dominant Western narratives of progress. In the course of this chapter, I trace the emergence of an 'aesthetics of ambivalence' that has emerged as a political response to the exhausted masculine types that have populated mainstream games. The primary game in question, *The Last of Us* (2013) by Naughty Dog, portrays a melancholic vision of a post-apocalyptic United States. But in order to more fully unpack ideologies around representations of whiteness in crisis and a discernable aesthetic turn toward ruin as the backdrop for these representations, I also discuss two other iconic games: *Spec Ops: The Line* (2012) and *Tomb Raider* (2013), both of which feature victimized white protagonists in hostile circumstances. *The Last of Us* takes place two decades after an outbreak of an airborne fungal pandemic. As the fungus spreads in their brains and slowly takes over their bodies, the infected are rendered progressively more deformed and rabid. Scrappy factions of survivors operate in desperation, set against a horrific backdrop of civilization gone feral. In this game, the future is sublime and bleak and terrorizing, and it won't be over quickly. Spectacular inside-outside spaces within the ruins of a once-high-capitalist culture are imaged as repurposed by humans and largely reabsorbed by nature (see Figure 2.1). Much of what was once considered so precious is now

Figure 2.1 Joel and Ellie in the remains of civilization. *The Last of Us* (2013) image provided by Sony Interactive Entertainment America LLC. ©Sony Interactive Entertainment America LLC. Created and developed by Naughty Dog LLC.

useless, while the simplest scavenged tools (bricks, bottles, alcohol) can mean the difference between life and death. *The Last of Us*, as one high-quality example in a plentiful survival-horror genre, taps into the popularity of zombie and pandemic apocalypse narratives in films like *28 Days Later* (Danny Boyle, 2002), *Planet Terror* (Robert Rodriguez and Quentin Tarantino, 2007), *The Road* (John Hillcoat, 2009), *Zombieland* (Ruben Fleischer, 2009), *The Book of Eli* (Albert Hughes and Allen Hughes, 2010), and *World War Z* (Marc Forster, 2013). Even more recent and somewhat less directly 'apocalyptic' narratives like the highly successful reboots *Rise of the Planet of the Apes* (Rupert Wyatt, 2011), *Dawn of the Planet of the Apes* (Matt Reeves, 2014) and *War for the Planet of the Apes* (Matt Reeves, 2017) create similar scenarios of whiteness in ruins. Other narratives, like that of the blockbuster spy-action movie franchise *Mission Impossible: Ghost Protocol* (Brad Bird, 2011), eschew the epidemic model but create the conditions for the white hero to become a victim/underdog through spoiled master plans, personal failings, faulty technologies and disavowal from the power structure.

Widely acclaimed as a masterpiece, *The Last of Us* strongly provokes discussion of the ethical quandaries arising around the cost of survival, such as has been explored in the popular television series *The Walking Dead* (AMC, 2010–). The greater collective fear of contagion – of being overrun, overwhelmed, colonized – and the complex fixation on the extreme survivalist scenario all resonate in a cultural moment when there is so much global restructuring, competition and transformation underway. In keeping with the rapid pace of change, the infected have gotten faster as well.

This chapter undertakes close textual analyses of each of these games, as mass culture artefacts that are powerful representations of social groupings, in this case, an embattled so-called 'majority'. The centrepiece of this examination, *The Last of Us,* has become iconic as a beleaguered, mournful magnum opus. It reflects a cultural moment of anxiety in the United States as an embattled superpower under the dual pressures of economic globalization and environmental catastrophe. I have also chosen two other highly successful AAA games: *Spec Ops: The Line* (2012) and *Tomb Raider* (2013). Both games thematically resonate with the turn that *The Last of Us* epitomizes. The paradoxical *Spec Ops: The Line* has become famous (or notorious, depending upon one's position) for upending the conventional military shooter genre. The white, heteronormative male protagonist begins the game as an icon of masculine prowess, a super-soldier on a mission, who purports to be a conventional hero onto which a player may map themselves. Yet hours of gameplay purposefully test and manipulate the player's identification with this character, over time becoming unnatural and strained, and eventually utterly estranged, as the clichéd 'hero' character gradually metamorphoses into a psychopath. My second example, the cinematic survival action-adventure *Tomb Raider* (2013), reconfigures its iconic white female protagonist Lara Croft from her indomitable super-archaeologist-adventurer status into a much more vulnerable figure, surely capable but clearly imperilled. I am keen to read this narrative and its representations in an intersectional manner alongside *The Last of Us* and *The Line* for several reasons. Certainly, there are conspicuous parallels in terms of seeking to interrupt the conventional hero image, which is an ongoing theme of this book. But Lara Croft is also almost universally discussed in terms of gender, which greatly overburdens readings of the character for obvious reasons. But, the intervention of considering the revamped Croft through an analysis of whiteness opens up new possible interpretations for the *Tomb Raider* heroine, as well as for an aesthetics of ambivalence that seems to mark some of the most iconic titles in mainstream games today. And like both *Spec Ops: The Line* and *The Last of Us*, *Tomb Raider* has a narrative of loss, disempowerment or disadvantage – of things going horribly wrong. A tension exists between the figure and a hostile, brutal or unrelenting environment. In short, this chapter scrutinizes a moment of self-consciousness in regard to the interruption of heroic protagonists, as exemplified by these three dominant games that so strongly feature beleaguered forms of whiteness.

In the following pages, I paint an image of the complex representations in *The Last of Us*, making connections to other forms of mass culture and considering its key iconographies, its makers and socio-political context. Then, I consider theoretical connections and comparisons to the other aforementioned games, in the interest of articulating how form, representation and affective qualities within each of these games engender a particularly ambivalent, embattled form of whiteness. This will necessitate theoretical examination of whiteness as a construct. I largely focus on constructions of whiteness in visual culture as theorized by film theorist Richard Dyer, alongside critical whiteness studies scholars like sociologist Ruth Frankenberg and others. Through detailed formal analysis and careful attention to these paradigmatic examples, this chapter critically deconstructs the 'normative' invisibility of whiteness and how it functions within mainstream games, particularly at a critical historical juncture in which whiteness is in crisis. This chapter asks: within the cultural context of their development and release, how do these mainstream games represent whiteness? How is whiteness seen in them? And what does this tell us about the prevailing sentiments in a fraught cultural moment in which power dynamics are shifting? This should not be confused with unilateral statements (that I would never make) regarding a group of people that one might collectively call 'white'. And this does not have to do with presumptions of what individuals within that group might be thinking. This has everything to do with *systemic* issues of representation and cultural construction – and the observation of visual politics at play – as it relates to an ideological construction of whiteness. Such seeing, as Dyer argues in the epigraph, comes from representation, and this chapter concerns itself with what is seen within dominant games.

We can begin once again by underscoring the importance of thinking about games as meaning-producing practices.[2] Games engage in a politics of identity through their inclusions and omissions, their complex constructions and their highly manufactured totalities. It is important to consider that, when examining any game, its images are all entirely intentional – and 'images', once again, encompass visual, aural and textual elements in the broadest sense. While photography's presumptive realism has come under question in recent years due the manipulability of the image, there is still a sense that the photographic image to some degree connects to something that existed and was captured by the camera. With digital imagery and simulations, one has no such expectation of its connectedness to any kind of realism. As Marita Sturken and Lisa Cartwright explain, in the shift from the photographic to the digital image, relations to the referent have shifted:

> an image generated exclusively by computer graphics software
> can be made to appear to be a photograph of actual objects,

places, or people, when in fact it is a simulation, that is, it does not represent something in the real world. There is no expectation, in digital imaging, of the camera 'having been there' to document something that really happened, which we see here and now in the image. Digital simulations of photographs imitate photographs of real phenomena using mathematical formulas translated into visual coordinates that approximate photographic conventions of space. The difference resides in the fact that the process of producing a digital image does not require that the referent (the actual object, person, or place) is present or even that the referent exists.[3]

So, to an even greater degree than photographic representation, the images produced in games are completely and thoroughly constructed and intentional. Even if they are highly naturalistic and display extreme photographic realism, they are not documents of something that has occurred, and was recorded. Rather, they are refined, totalizing visions that are collaboratively developed using software in order to produce a series of effects. This is not to suggest that unintended interpretations of the image are impossible; however, it is key to understand that their visual cultures are purposeful and highly calibrated. Digital media theorist Wendy Hui Kyong Chun even goes so far as to discuss software in general as 'a functional analog to ideology', calling computers with their software and hardware 'ideology machines'. She declares: 'They fulfill almost every formal definition of ideology we have, from ideology as false consciousness (as portrayed in *The Matrix*) to Louis Althusser's definition of ideology as "a 'representation' of the imaginary relation of individuals to their real conditions of existence."'[4] According to Chun, the form of software as medium engages in 'the very effort of making something intangible visible, while at the same time rendering the visible (such as the machine) invisible.'[5] However, the software theorist simultaneously acknowledges that the analogy between ideology and software must be understood in all its complexity – the 'onion-like' nature of software, while analogous to ideology, also has connections to the critique of power that all ideology necessarily contains.[6] 'By interrogating software and the visual knowledge it perpetuates,' she posits, 'we can move beyond the so-called crisis in indexicality toward understanding the new ways in which visual knowledge is being transformed and perpetuated, not simply displaced or rendered obsolete.'[7]

Fully comprehending this highly constructed and intentional, apparently indexical nature of games as software, while also appreciating the complexity and multi-layered dimensions of them as both ideology and ideological critique, renders the analysis of games incredibly insightful in terms of what they *seem* to make visible, and what they purport to hide. Rather than assuming the visual culture of games to be a more naïve form of image-making that lacks the presumed sophistication of filmmaking, art or theatre, I consider them as complex, fully formed visual media equally suited to nuanced ideological deconstruction. Video games convey themselves through the images resulting from the action of the software, but also, as D. Fox Harrell has similarly asserted, through the ways in which their software systems themselves contain social values. As he writes, 'All technical systems are cultural systems.'[8] As the current investigation focuses on the visual culture of games and their ideological formulations, I will not deconstruct the specific software systems that have gone into their construction, and Harrell has already excellently done so. However, it is useful to consider the playable aspects of these representations – both their affordances and their limitations – in relation to the worlds they image for their players. Harrell's work sets forth affirmative strategies for thinking about how computational systems can better serve human needs and values. As a computer scientist, his research and in-depth consideration of the cultural phantasms that exist within computing systems is invaluable.[9] I would assert, on the basis of Harrell's interventions, that the software systems of games already serve human needs – yet they serve some humans' needs more than others. That is to say, mainstream games as software systems tend to prop up the values of dominant culture, by creating fields of possibilities circumscribed by particular value systems and world views. Other visions become difficult to image within the scope of a game as a computational system, or are even altogether annihilated. While, like Gerald Voorhees, I agree there is always transformational potential in the 'agonistic incitement of an economy of motivations, desires, discourses and signs provided by player and game', the worlds of games and the contexts that produce them strongly impact how players receive messages from the games they play.[10]

Cultural Context: Whiteness in Crisis, Racial Violence and Games

When an act of violence occurs in the United States, especially when perpetuated by a young white male, it is quite commonplace that the mass media casually mention video games – even in cases where there has been no evidence that the perpetrator actually played them. As I write, the United States has suffered a blunt force national trauma in the form of a racially motivated mass killing in an historic black church. On Wednesday, 17 June 2015, just after 8:00pm, a young man described as Caucasian, clean-cut and in his early twenties entered the Emanuel African Methodist Episcopal Church in Charleston (also known as 'Mother Emanuel'), South Carolina, one of the most historically significant churches in the nation and celebrated as a core site for the revolutionary uplift of African Americans since its founding in 1816. After sitting with a prayer group that included Senator Clementa Pinckney (also a pastor) for almost an hour in the church basement, the young man pulled a gun from his waist pack and killed nine African-Americans, including the senator. Three others survived. A suspect, Dylann Roof, was identified and apprehended within 48 hours and, almost immediately, information surfaced in the form of testimonials from acquaintances, as well as from survivors, that he had verbalized his desire to start a race war.[11] Photographs gleaned from the Facebook page of the accused contained Roof wearing a jacket with flag patches of the former white-controlled Rhodesia, current-day Zimbabwe, as well as the apartheid-era South African flag. Then, a website called 'The Last Rhodesian', purchased under Roof's name, was discovered, containing 60 photos of the young man waving the Confederate flag, which is associated with the US antebellum period and also the secessionist and white power movements in the South. In an essay in *The Atlantic*, one journalist summarized the flag as 'created by an army raised to kill in defense of slavery, revived by a movement that killed in defense of segregation, and now flaunted by a man who killed nine innocents in defense of white supremacy'.[12] There were images of Roof visiting plantations, confederate museums and cemeteries, of displaying his handgun, and defacing the national flag in various manners including burning, spitting and trampling. An extended manifesto declared a belief in white supremacy, a tirade of bigotry outlining how various races eroded the dominance of whiteness around the world, his disdain for race mixing and his coming into a racial awareness that his 'superior' white race is losing ground. The manifesto ended by explicating his target, Mother Emanuel, as follows:

> I have no choice. I am not in the position to, alone, go into the ghetto and fight. I chose Charleston because it is most historic city in my state, and at one time had the highest ratio of blacks to Whites in the country. We have no skinheads, no real KKK, no one doing anything but talking on the internet. Well someone has to have the bravery to take it to the real world, and I guess that has to be me.[13]

By Sunday, 21 June, a news story broke indicating that several prominent politicians including Republican presidential nominees had accepted campaign donations from Earl P. Holt III, leader of a right-wing Council of Conservative Citizens and known white supremacist, whose website was cited by Roof as an inspiration for his radicalization.[14]

Video games repeatedly surfaced as a cause, among the many commentators in the first few days of the massacre's news reportage, even though no official connection has been drawn between the accused and games. Of particular note was a mention by Martin Luther King III, son of the slain civil rights leader, who commented on the Charleston church massacre on CNN:

> When you have kids playing video games all day long, when you have some of our cartoons [having] violence in them. When you have movies that are violent, it is no wonder that our society is violent. We've created and accepted a culture of violence. We must find a way to create a culture of nonviolence.[15]

It bears mentioning that this racially motivated act of killing, which was immediately identified as a hate crime – an act with many precedents in terms of a long and determinedly pre-video game history of racial violence against African-Americans in the United States – was unquestioningly and unequivocally linked to games, and by such a notable public figure.[16] This is problematic on many levels, not the least of which is that it suggests a dimension of influence, moral corruption and brainwashing endemic to the medium that has not been conclusively verified by study. But the grim coincidence of this rhetoric's resurgence is nonetheless relevant within the context of a white-supremacist act of violence, when considering constructions of whiteness in this embattled medium.

Unlike King, I do not wish to suggest a literal connection between video games and enacted violence. Nor do I believe that the three games in question have a white supremacist agenda. However, I do want to underscore the relationship between the overblown language of Roof's 'Last Rhodesian' manifesto that contained multiple references to the loss of white power in the supremacist sense, and a more general perception of a decline in the dominance of whiteness around the world.

This violence occurred within a long history of a 'disturbing epidemic of angry white boys and young men participating in the burning of black churches and the murder of their schoolmates around the country' outlined by critical whiteness studies scholar Ruth Frankenberg.[17] Identifying these acts as an extension of fears, Frankenberg identifies several false presumptions used to argue that white dominance in US society has become destabilized: civil rights gains, a government that fails to see whites as the new 'oppressed' group, and 'overcorrection' resulting in reverse-racism and unfair gains by non-whites. Indeed, a strong ideological bent in US visual culture configures whiteness – and more specifically the white male protagonist – as *victim* rather than hero.[18] Richard Dyer colourfully sends up these overblown white fears as they manifest themselves in visual culture: 'in the future, what with the teeming hordes and the remorseless march of affirmative action, we [whites] shall be the niggers.'[19] The games in question tap into the kinds of deep-seated anxieties that scholars like Dyer and Frankenberg outline as an extension of a larger cultural malaise. That is to say, in the following discussion of whiteness in relation to the games in question, it should be understood that I see whiteness not as 'invisible' or 'empty' or normative, but as occurring within the context of a dominant culture that is in fact intensely aware of whiteness, and an entertainment industry that is likewise tuned in to what will resonate with the dominant market.

The Last of Us

The Last of Us presents a scenario steeped in loss, melancholia and an aesthetics of ambivalence. It tells the story of Joel, a white working man and single parent, and his pale, slight, blonde daughter, Sarah, with whom he has a close relationship (see Figure 2.2). It is clear that Joel has long strenuous workdays and is under duress. He is not well-off and the game clearly represents him as doing his best despite the odds. Initially playing in the third person as 'Sarah', players wander the domestic space and learn from contextual clues and secondary characters that their Austin neighbourhood is in turmoil, and in fact the problem goes far beyond their location, having spread to both national coasts. An aggressive infection is spreading that renders those who contract it violent. In the aftermath of a car accident that occurs in the chaos, the player character role switches to Joel, as he tries, unsuccessfully, to protect his injured daughter from the pandemonium ensuing. A soldier who has been ordered to execute the potentially infected mistakenly shoots Sarah, and she dies in Joel's arms. Even though all this happens in the dark of night, her skin and hair give off a soft glow.

Figure 2.2 Joel and his daughter, Sarah, in better times. *The Last of Us* (2013) ©Sony Interactive Entertainment America LLC. Created and developed by Naughty Dog LLC. Screen shot by author.

In the aftermath of these events, the player is reintroduced to the primary playable character, Joel, some 20 years later. He is now a smuggler, and a much more dishevelled, worn-down figure to whom far too much has happened. We find him in a post-apocalyptic Boston that is a crumbling police state. The 'new normal' is a daily existence of scavenging and desperation, barter and bribery, limited resources and survivalism. Alongside a female companion named Tess, who initially acts as a guide for the player through the perils of the militarized zones and quarantined areas, Joel grimly traverses the environs. As an action adventure survival-horror game, stealth, puzzle-solving and effective utilization of the environment are key, but the game also uses a crafting system that allows for the development of weapons from found objects, in addition to guns and other arms. Killing is a core mechanic, although it is framed mostly as grim and necessary for survival, rather than spectacularized and heroic. While it is immediately clear that Joel is resourceful and jaded enough to address his circumstances pragmatically, he (as the playable character) is clearly traumatized and endangered. His look and manner are consistent with mainstream representations of a 'heartland' American male: presumed straight, Caucasian, shortish dark hair and beard, assertive carriage, able-bodied and wearing a Western shirt and jeans. He doesn't talk much, and is acerbic when he does.

Soon after a series of scenarios that function largely as in-game tutorials on controller usage, and to relay content that contextualizes the aftermath Joel lives in, we meet Ellie (see Figure 2.3). She is 14 years old, and a precocious, dark-haired, wide-eyed vulnerable young white teenager who predictably invokes the memory of his lost daughter, Sarah. Ellie externalizes Joel's seriously compromised sense of hope. Protected by a revolutionary militia called 'The Fireflies', who mysteriously deem her important, Ellie becomes the precious cargo Joel and his partner Tess are enlisted to smuggle safely away from the Boston quarantine zone. Tess is lost soon after, and the remaining gameplay mostly consists of Joel's odyssey to ferry the young Ellie to safety while trying to fully understand her significance to the militia. Along the way, Joel and Ellie grow close as they face tremendous peril, hardship, loss, failures and ethical quandaries.

Figure 2.3 Ellie. *The Last of Us* (2013) ©Sony Interactive Entertainment America LLC. Created and developed by Naughty Dog LLC. Screen shot by author.

In addition to the post-apocalyptic United States backdrop, to which I will return, key to this narrative are the 'infected' themselves. These are humans whose brains and eventually whole bodies have been overtaken by a horrific mutation of the Cordyceps fungus, which slowly transforms them into something uncontainable, violent and monstrous. Unlike the typical zombie narrative, there are four distinct phases of the infection and therefore a variety of types of infected: Runners, Stalkers, Clickers and Bloaters. Runners still retain some human characteristics and seem as though they are simply rabid and unable to control their impulses toward aggression. However, they are relatively easy to fend off except if they are able to overwhelm a player in very large groups. Stalkers demonstrate a more profound fungal infection and are known for hiding and sneak attacks; they are quick and deadly. Clickers are stronger than the previous two forms. As they are more thoroughly infected, they take on a more mutated, horrific form, and possess the power of echolocation. Their nickname derives from the sounds they make in order to orient themselves in space. Clickers are difficult to kill, and even blasting off huge chunks of the fungus may not impair them. The fourth category of infected humans, Bloaters, are the most fearsome due to

Figure 2.4 Joel aims at a Bloater. *The Last of Us* (2013) image provided by Sony Interactive Entertainment America LLC. ©Sony Interactive Entertainment America LLC. Created and developed by Naughty Dog LLC.

their imposing stature and resilience when under attack (see Figure 2.4). Bulbous fungal growths cover their entire bodies like a kind of armour plating. Little of their human form remains. To be caught in their grip means instant death. Bloaters function completely on aggressive instinct, and are able to lob infectious clumps at the player-character. Even after a Bloater dies, the fungus continues to grow and spores are released from their decomposing bodies. I cannot underscore enough the psychological revulsion these creatures engender: they at once conjure uncontrollability and phobias around communicable disease. They stimulate such dread, disgust, panic and horror that it was common to read that the intensity of the overall affective experience made players take frequent breaks to collect themselves.[20] Unlike the survival-horror genre conventions, the violence enacted within the game was observed as 'heavy, consequential and necessary'.[21] In my own playthrough of the game, it seemed that the affective dimensions of the game were established not merely through horror, but the interplay between horror and the melancholic. More specifically, these affective dimensions emanated from the ideological construction of whiteness as ineffectual, as characters stumble about in the ruins of a patriarchal

Figure 2.5 Joel fights a cannibal. *The Last of Us* (2013) image provided by Sony Interactive Entertainment America LLC. ©Sony Interactive Entertainment America LLC. Created and developed by Naughty Dog LLC.

order that is defunct and deathly. Faced with overwhelming odds, as well as the imminent threat of both the infected and the human (see Figure 2.5), Joel is forced to repeatedly place his own body between this overwhelming terror and the innocent Ellie, and he does so grudgingly. It is the binary opposition between whiteness and radical otherness – and particularly the repeated trauma narrative of declining white masculinity – that comes to the fore and reconfigures Joel as victim.[22]

The critical response to the game was overwhelmingly positive. *The Last of Us* received a Metacritic score of 95 out of 100 for both its PlayStation 3 and 'remastered' PlayStation 4 iterations. It was considered landmark for its effective AI, photorealism and character development. Many lauded it as the last great game of its console generation. *The Last of Us* was proclaimed by many notable game review sites to be a perfect game, and along with its remaster, a 'masterpiece' of its generation.[23] A melancholic and poignant score by Academy Award-winning composer Gustavo Santaolalla, combined with the strong storyline and unrelenting scenarios, make for a great deal of pathos and affective engagement during play. Many critics described the affectively taxing nature of the game, describing it as 'both emotionally exciting and physically exhausting'.[24] While there were some complaints that the game ultimately failed to outstrip the male-oriented narrative, many others hailed the game for its complex representation of several female characters, including Ellie.[25] The scholarly response focused thus far more on the construction of the relations between the natural world and human beings in the game, as well as ethical decisions that the game refuses to let players skirt – though it engenders internal self-reflection through the difficulties encountered.[26]

Critical Whiteness Studies and Whiteness After 9/11

My use of the term 'whiteness' is not one of simple classification of skin colour, but a term that has come to define a much more phantasmagoric position that takes into account ideological dimensions of meaning ascribed to this complex construction. Whiteness studies, or 'critical whiteness studies', arose from post-colonial and post-modern theory made popular in the 1970s and 1980s, with a strong surge in the US in the 1990s. As Tyler Stallings summarized this moment, 'vocabularies and strategies had developed based on the notion that forcing the dominant culture to recognize itself – to *name* itself, when for so long it had claimed to have no name – was the first step toward dismantling it.'[27] Ruth Frankenberg, in her *White Women, Race Matters*, outlines three key facets of whiteness: 'First, whiteness is a location of structural advantage, of race privilege. Second, it is a "standpoint," a place from which white people look at ourselves, at others, and at a society. Third, "whiteness" refers to a set of cultural practices that are usually unmarked and unnamed.'[28] She goes on to discuss the ways in which naming whiteness displaces its 'structured invisibility', reconnecting it to complex histories of colonialism, imperialism and assimilation; it productively racializes whiteness; and it opens up possibilities for antiracist whiteness.[29] There are many and disparate approaches to critical whiteness studies, most of which are associated with Frankenberg's delineations, but which also study other dimensions of the subject such as white privilege,[30] the stratification of various groups according to race and its effects, ontological questions of whiteness, and the connections between race and power.[31] Some see the study of whiteness and white privilege as a topic that has become dated in a purportedly 'post-racial' Obama era. Denaturalizing the normative position of whiteness is extremely useful for unpacking dominant representations in games.[32] While there are numerous intellectual resources in many established disciplines that engage with whiteness, I focus primarily on interventions in visual culture, as well as a uniquely post-9/11, and subsequent post-Obama moment of anxiety in which the stability of white heteronormative patriarchy is threatened.[33]

Whiteness just isn't what it used to be in America. The white majority has waned in the United States and, along with it, value systems have shifted. This has been taken up in the popular media, as well. For example, Hua Hsu in his article 'The End of White America?' reports:

> According to an August 2008 report by the U.S. Census Bureau, those groups currently categorized as racial minorities – blacks and Hispanics, East Asians and South Asians – will account for a majority of the U.S. population by the year 2042. Among Americans under the age of 18, this shift is projected to take place in 2023, which means that every child born in the United States from here on out will belong to the first post-white generation.[34]

The perception that something has changed in terms of the eroding of white dominance has become a site of intense racial anxiety.

The World Trade Center bombings in New York on 11 September 2001, referred to as '9/11', complicated this sense of white racial anxiety further by traumatizing the public imaginary of white America through, according to Thomas Ross, the ideological configuration of the victims of 9/11 as white fire fighters and white Wall Street business people caught in the towers.[35] Of course, the reality was much more diverse – especially given the international melting pot of New York. Nevertheless, there emerged a strong binary opposition between white 'heartland' (i.e., straight and Christian) authentic American families and Arab-looking (i.e., Muslim) men, whose resemblance to the hijackers of the doomed planes instilled a new fear into the hearts of white America. The mass media incessantly covered the losses of families that conformed to the flag-flying, white picket-fenced, heartland ideal that came to stand in for all victims of the tragedy. Images of the Twin Towers collapsing were looped on the news, while pre-existing images of the towers were scrubbed from popular culture so as to avoid distressing Americans while the nation healed. If there was any doubt about the global attack on an American 'way of life', this event was politically managed to effect an absolute nationalist, jingoistic sentiment that has religious, cultural and racial overtones.[36]

In summarizing the psychic damage wrought by 9/11, Ross suggests:

> The White man at the dawn of the twenty-first century faces all the commonly shared perils of his fellow citizens, the lingering horror of 9/11, the uncertain contours of the War on Terror, but also and uniquely, he faces the knowledge that an America that he has always thought of as essentially his seems to be slipping away in an increasingly multi-racial America.[37]

This perspective is similarly supported and enhanced by Frankenberg, who in the same year wrote 'Cracks in the Façade: Whiteness and the Construction of 9/11', which connects the nomenclature around this event with ideological connections to whiteness and 'narratives of innocence, goodness, Godliness and strength'.[38] Ultimately calling attention to how 'alongside national self-importance, a sense of entitlement and the actuality of US military and economic might, is a brittle and fragile sense of nationhood which easily senses danger everywhere', Frankenberg entreats readers to honour the dead by not imbricating them in false narratives of whiteness and Americanness.[39] Hsu similarly describes demographic shifts in the nation and the subsequent fear of what Pat Buchanan has called 'Third World America'.[40] Calling attention to an increased expectation of diversity in entertainment, advertising and the presence of high-profile success stories such as Will Smith's Hollywood success as an A-list leading man, Tiger Woods' dominance in golf, Sean Combs' entrepreneurial empire in the music industry and the general global impact of hip-hop, the author points to the profound sense held by some white Americans that they are 'losing control' of the institutions that were once theirs.

Notable, as well, are the ways in which these kinds of conversations repeat themselves in times of duress. For example, the fear of a 'Third World America' echo debates that took place in California around Proposition 209 in 1996, which argued for the elimination of affirmative action programs in state institutions.[41] Over the course of the debates that took place around this proposition, whiteness became constructed as a form of victimhood that, according to some whiteness scholars, 'was repeatedly used as a threat in this campaign'.[42] In the introduction to their anthology on whiteness, editors Birgit Brander Rasmussen, Irene J. Nexica, Eric Klinenberg and Matt Wray described the political manipulation as follows:

> The image of 'angry white men' – the men supposedly left behind as women and people of color advanced – was called upon in many debates over affirmative action and made occasional appearances in campaign advertisements and journalistic stories. This figure was both a sign of the putative loser of affirmative action programs and an implicit suggestion that white men around the state were seething with outrage, perhaps even preparing to use violence to defend their interests. Identifying men who were angry and increasingly unhappy, the term signified and promoted a white backlash against civil rights gains of the 1960s. It served as an effective means of configuring people of color (and, to a lesser extent, white women) as an oppressive group and angry white men as a group who could, would, and should revolt.[43]

This is complicated by the fact that whiteness, in an American context, has shifting associations that fluctuate between: a racial categorization, an ideology of power relations, a Western term of normativity, an 'empty' signifier for lack of authenticity or ethnicity, a marker of violence and terror for some, and an extension of an institutionalized and pernicious form of categorization installed during European colonial and imperialist expansion.[44] This is shored up through visual culture, of which games are now a part, and it is through analysis of these forms of dominant culture that insight can be gained.

Insofar as visual culture is concerned, Richard Dyer's *White* is most urgent for this discussion, though the author never specifically addresses video games. Surveying a broad array of Western image-making practices such as photography, cinema and print media, Dyer presents a clear-eyed assessment of images that purport to present 'nonparticular' (i.e., white) identities by underscoring their particularities and addressing the underlying presumptions that accompany their imaging.[45] This text is key for my own analysis of the three games in question, although, given their playable dimensions, I expand upon Dyer's innovations in constructive ways for the medium.

Dyer unpacks the normative and 'invisible' nature of whiteness in both representation and the ways in which the visual is spoken of. While the film scholar clearly identifies that 'the privilege of being white in white culture is not to be subjected to stereotyping in relation to one's whiteness,' he also points out the contradiction that this perceived sense of being the normative, betrays a persistent and underlying fixation with whiteness.[46] Dyer writes on the representation of whiteness and heteronormativity:

> Women, ethnic minorities, gay people and so on are not the only ones to be social groupings; everyone belongs to social groupings; indeed, we all belong in many groupings, often antagonistic to one another or at the least implying very different accesses to power. The groupings that have tended not to get addresses in 'images of' work, however, are those with the most access to power: men, whites, heterosexuals, the able-bodied [...] This must not imply, however, an equivalence between such images and those of women and other oppressed groupings. The project of making normality strange and thus ultimately decentering it must not seem to say that this has already taken place, that now masculinity, whiteness, heterosexuality and able-bodiedness are just images of identity alongside all others [...] As in all issues of representation, we must not leave the matter of power out of account any more than the matter of representation itself.[47]

The non-particular status of white identity as normal or universal identity is often perceived of as unthinking or oblivious in its usage. However, importantly, in his book-length examination of whiteness, Dyer does not let those engaged in so-called 'normative' representation off the hook. Rather than excusing them on the basis of ignorance, he points instead to the self-consciousness of these representations:

> most of the time white people speak about nothing but white people, it's just that we couch it in terms of 'people' in general. Research – into books, museums, the press, advertising, films, television, software – repeatedly shows that in Western representation whites are overwhelmingly and disproportionately predominant, have the central and elaborated roles, and above all are placed as the norm, the ordinary, the standard.[48]

He discusses whiteness in terms of its tremendous instability, the fluidity with which certain ethnic groups like Jews and the Irish may have held different positions in terms of the colour hierarchy, as a means to police the privileges whiteness affords.[49] Pulling away from a discussion of whiteness as 'white ethnicity', and certainly not white nationalism, he instead deconstructs whiteness itself and conceives of how it can be possible to go about 'making whiteness strange'.[50] Covering a history of the term – in accordance with several cited venerated scholars including Winthrop Jordan and Martin Bernal – Dyer finds the modern origination of the term 'white' to be connected to the American colonies, and deeply imbricated in the Christian tradition.[51] It is all innocence, purity, cleanliness, beauty and ultimately a form of absence. Of course, as he further explains, these are not without their underside: 'the lure of the ideal is also, often imperceptibly, haunted by misgiving, even anxiety. Not only is whiteness as absence impossible, it is not wholly desirable. To relinquish dirt and stains, corporeality and thingness, is also to relinquish both the pleasures of the flesh and the reproduction upon which whiteness as radical power depends.'[52] Interestingly enough, the logical outcome of the ideal of whiteness is ultimately unattainable and self-annihilating.

The Last of Us and Imperiled Whiteness

The impossible, imperilled position of whiteness is embodied in Joel, the bedraggled protagonist and primary playable character of *The Last of Us*.

He is self-consciously normal and 'everyman' in his manifestation, possessing neither superhuman powers nor the skills of a supersoldier. He is vulnerable, emotionally shut-down and compromised, definitively an anti-hero. At some point in the narrative, his young partner, Ellie, takes on the protector/provider role after he is seriously injured. Several extended analyses of this game utilize a feminist approach that variously interprets the game as either propping up gender norms or displaying a sense of mourning toward the loss of heteronormative unity.[53] Commentators observed that this game presented a paradigmatic example of the 'dadification' of video games, or in other words an emerging thematic trend toward paternal relations between a primary male character and a younger female character who needs protection.[54] Joel is in many ways a cypher for the so-called American average hardworking man, come to the end of his rope and emptied out of his inherent value in a society that has changed around him. Dyer's examination of this male everyman type is best exemplified in his analysis of the 1993 crime drama directed by Joel Schumacher, *Falling Down*, which describes the events in the day of an 'ordinary' middle-class man (to be read as *white* man) who finds himself at war with the 'everyday world' (to be read as the increasingly diverse world) and descends in to a nihilistic meltdown after losing his job, his family and his sense of purpose.[55] In the case of this film, it is exactly the main character's ordinariness through which the anxieties around the endangered nature of the white man comes into focus: '*Falling Down*'s success may derive from its expression of the state of play in the contemporary construction of whiteness, between a renewedly respectable supremacism, the old everything and nothing-in-particular hegemony and the fear of an annihilation that will be the realisation of our [whites'] emptiness.'[56] Importantly, the *Falling Down* model of white masculinity ideologically melds ordinariness and a constructed alterity, something which *The Last of Us* repeats to excellent effect. Dyer ultimately summarizes the film as 'an allegory of the death of the white man, or at any rate, the white man as endangered species'.[57] Teetering at the mouth of this gaping emptiness, Joel of *The Last of Us* demonstrates a similar disorientation, but it comes in the form of a deathward-looking melancholia that is staved off by the purpose of protecting Ellie against a hostile environment.

There are many meaningful essays on the connection between photographic/filmic technologies as media of 'light', the visual culture of the luminous white woman, and the white man's muscles as depicted in cinema. However, for the sake of this analysis, the connection Dyer draws between whiteness and melancholia or death at the end of empire interests me most. Deconstructing the ideological roles of white women and white men in the imaging of European imperialism, he asserts that man embodies colonial expansion within many of these narratives. Likewise, white women specifically embody the fall of empire by complicating the scenario with sexuality and heterosexual duty that interrupts the fundamentally masculine and homosocial relations taking place. White women constitute a sexual drain on the male imperializing spirit, and possess the potential to betray white men through their relations with non-white men. And they demonstrate a conscience around empire that generally weakens the will.[58] In his enumeration of these tropes in relation to his specific televisual object of study (the 1984 British TV series *The Jewel in the Crown*), Dyer uses descriptors like 'ineffectiveness', 'lethargy', 'desolation' and 'nondoing' to capture the affective qualities of whiteness – specifically white female positionality – at the end of empire.

In the case of *The Last of Us*, this is exemplified in the glowing white, blonde Sarah (daughter of Joel), whose life is lost in the game's inciting incident. The ineffectual role Joel played in protecting his child is presumably the origin of his bitterness, and this psychology becomes transferred onto Ellie, a surrogate young white girl. Although Ellie has more agency, Joel repeatedly refuses to permit her a weapon, and persistently adopts a protectorate role. In one scene, for example, Joel comes across a bow and Ellie asks to use it, proclaiming, 'I'm a pretty good shot with that thing.' Joel responds, 'How 'bout we just leave this kind of stuff to me.' Ellie protests: 'Well, we could both be armed. Cover each other.' Joel admonishes her: 'I don't think so.' Given that it would be fairly difficult to shoot oneself using a bow and arrow, it is more likely that Joel wants to spare Ellie the traumatizing experience of killing. The various fatherly shielding gestures enacted during gameplay emphasize this (see Figure 2.6). For example, when crouched together in a cover position, Ellie often nestles under Joel's arm. Similarly, while standing, he protectively places an arm across her body

Figure 2.6 Joel protects Ellie. *The Last of Us* (2013) image provided by Sony Interactive Entertainment America LLC. ©Sony Interactive Entertainment America LLC. Created and developed by Naughty Dog LLC.

like a barrier against harm. She is also represented as physically diminutive next to his strong stature. She represents purity, cleanliness of spirit, a normative sense of beauty. Joel's reticence for Ellie to have the agency to kill (by possessing a weapon) throughout the narrative strongly signals his desire to preserve that innocence. Eventually this dynamic shifts, but it comes late in the game and only when it is clear that Joel cannot complete objectives singlehandedly.

Describing the specific role of white women in the colonialist fiction, Dyer asserts that they:

> voice a liberal critique of empire and are in part to blame for its decline. Because of their social marginality and because, when they do do anything, they do harm, the only honorable position for them, the only really white position, is that of doing nothing. Because they are creatures of conscience this is a source of agony. Yet it is an exquisite agony [...] Women take the blame, and provide the spectacle of moral suffering, for the loss of empire. For this, they are rewarded with a possibility that already matches their condition of narrative existence: nothing.[59]

In an uncanny reflection of this very conundrum, Ellie's character, who is born into the post-pandemic space, moves about within the flickering embers of Western culture as an embodiment of innocence – that is, in the absence of her actual usefulness as an agent of society's redemption and cure, she is instead ideologically over-determined as an externalization of conscience, as Joel's last grasp of his own humanity, and as a youthful figure who symbolizes the very possibility of a future. For much of the game, he is configured as protector, and she occupies the role of a resourceful kid who needs defending. Her expressions of wonder the first time that she walks in the woods, or sees an old record shop, point to a sense of discovery and a freshness in her perspective that Joel lacks. Yet, increasingly she constitutes a liability for Joel, in that she causes him to deviate from a self-serving routine that has kept him alive. Gameplay reveals that her role is ultimately to do nothing. And of course, true to Dyer's characterization, she ultimately saves nothing. In this case, Joel shares the blame for the downfall of culture through his refusal to allow Ellie's brain matter to be harvested in the pursuit of a cure. While she is unveiled as a kind of sacrificial lamb, this actual role goes unfulfilled, due in no small part to Joel's unwillingness to let go of her. There is an argument to be made, as well, for the connectedness between the imaging of the ruins of empire and the female figure. According to Dyer, the female figure often operates as the embodiment of a critique, while being configured as the cause of the downfall itself. Joel is, after all, imperilled by his growing attachment to a girl who holds the keys to humanity's survival – and who will force him to face insurmountable odds. The ethics of Joel's decision sparked much debate.

This is connected, as well, to the notion of a crumbling phallocentric order that is embodied in the ruins within which the primary player characters move. Spaces of play, as simulated civilizations, become symbolic extensions of the patriarchal law; only, in this case, that civilization is completely broken. And, as a by-product of the system's having become compromised, other orders become possible. Even the mundane act of imagining other possible uses of the objects strewn about in the destroyed landscape invites new ways of thinking about what the space should be. Describing architectural structures and urban planning as symbolic 'monuments of a masculine dominated society' Evan Watts argues that their ruin is a 'space that offers freedom from the same gender-oppressive institutions that once permeated them, and thus sites of empowerment'.[60] Watts analyses this through several games, most notably the remains of the underwater city of Rapture in *BioShock* (2007), arguing that in a larger sense, even though the new social order arising from the game is 'horrific' and dystopian, it at least reveals the heteronormative order to be socially constructed and therefore malleable. He identifies the relationship between ruined physical structures and social structures that exist in various media, and in games as well, the frustrated ' "masculine" satisfaction accompanying gameplay mechanics of dominating one's environment using violence and aggression'.[61]

This holds true for *The Last of Us* as well. In the first case, the violence is almost always desperate and off-balance. Beyond scripting and the story's arc, this is also deeply embedded in the game mechanics. With the jerry-rigged weapons and need to constantly scavenge around for anything that will help, one does not feel the power of fetishized weaponry, technological dominance or masterful kills. As a construction, Joel configures whiteness as fundamentally desperate and in crisis. As one critic observed: 'Because of the do-it-yourself crafting system, Joel never felt too strong or overpowered. I had just enough supplies to make what I needed in almost any given situation [...] but the nerves start kicking in when you know your supplies are running out.'[62] The scrounging, in other words, is neither glamorous nor glorious. Protracted scenarios of scavenging for anything at all that will aid the characters in their survival, heightens the sense of desperation fundamental to the experience of gameplay.

Scavenging in the game is key to a critique of failed capitalism, which is also an extension of the critique of a white hetero-patriarchal order that is now in ruins. One of the key characteristics of hypercapitalism is the splitting of objects from their literal use-value. Advanced capitalism invests objects with meaning that may be thoroughly detached from their actual usefulness. The survivalist scenario presented in *The Last of Us* reinvests objects with their practical function, against a backdrop where the ruins of hypercapitalism possess little value except as they may be repurposed. In the second case, as I will show, the militarized male supersoldier trope is frustrated. Rather than enhancing normal human capabilities, in *The Last of Us* one always feels the limitations of too little ammunition, not enough places to hide, the fallibility of the body, the necessity of collaborative effort and the vulnerability of everyone involved.

One possible reading of the *Last of Us*, as an extension of the apocalyptic narrative of contagion or zombies, is that the foe (virus/undead attacker) represents the externalization of an inner threat by making it into a targeted enemy that can be identified, isolated and destroyed. For example, in speaking about the role of the infected in another massive franchise, *Resident Evil*, media and culture studies scholar Derek Burrill writes:

> In *Resident Evil*, the true antagonist is the virus. The virus is an oft-used nemesis in videogames from similar genres (such as *Parasite Eve* or *Syphon Filter*), as the virus serves as an internal threat, playing on general cultural fears of HIV, Ebola, and other physical dangers, while it also manifests itself as an external threat in the form of some infected physical presence. This enables the player to overcome representations of internalized struggle and weakness through virtualized, external physical destruction and violence.[63]

This suggestion of the transfer of an internal or nebulous fear into an object that can be isolated, controlled or ultimately killed is made within a larger discussion of the performance of masculinity. However what is enacted again and again in *The Last of Us* – as a kind of technology that is engaged with – is a traumatized, frustrated white masculinity. Keith Stuart of the *Guardian* made several insightful observations about the genre, most notably that a heroic sense of masculinity is off-balance in these games:

> there's no coincidence in the sudden onslaught of dystopian fiction, which has affected movies and literature as well as games. We've seen these spikes before and they usually reflect and explore wider sociopolitical fears. The rush of '50s sci-fi flicks about mutated insects and invading aliens came out of post-war fears about the atom bomb and communist revolution; and the slasher films of the seventies processed the global economic downturn, the collapse of the patriarchal nuclear family and the rise of feminism's second wave. Our current obsession with zombies and failed utopias is arguably driven by the gristly meat of 24-hour news coverage: fears of pan-global diseases

like avian flu, the over-population of the Earth, the financial collapse of 2008 and mass uprisings like the Arab Spring. Our sense of certainty has been decimated over the last five years – the world is once again a weird, unpredictable and violent place. Video games are reflecting this. But they are reflecting it through a very particular prism.[64]

Attenuating the analysis to consider how this is manifested in games about the zombie-apocalypse, Stuart picks up the thread of the dystopian representation as it is played out in a flurry of high-profile games like *Bioshock Infinite*, *The Walking Dead*, *State of Decay* and *The Last of Us*. While the scenarios themselves might have continuity with the history of these types of narratives, the protagonists are compromised, flawed and decidedly unheroic:

In the past, these characters tended to be assured action heroes; men fighting for a just cause against irredeemably evil enemies. But in current titles that is all getting muddied. Lee [*The Walking Dead*], Booker [*Bioshock Infinite*] and Joel [*The Last of Us*] are damaged men, victims of the violence they have perpetrated on others. Lee has killed his wife's lover and ruined his own life in the process; Booker has been destroyed by his involvement in murderous military campaigns, Joel has had to become a sociopath to survive 20 years in a devastated America. These guys aren't heroes like Master Chief or Marcus Fenix; they're scarred, vulnerable fuck-ups, barely functioning as reasoning adults anymore.[65]

One scholar went even further, describing the nature of the aforementioned representations as tantamount to visualizing the end of heteronormativity. Gerald Voorhees writes of the *The Last of Us*:

trauma and loss are the most frequently recurring ideas. Death colors the tenor of the game and defines the most poignant moments of the narrative: Sarah bleeding out in Joel's arms, Tess in a pool of blood on the capitol floor, Bill's lover hanging from a ceiling fan, Sam and the two bullets from Henry's gun, Joel's incapacitation at the university campus, David stealing the last shreds of Ellie's faith in humanity, and of course, the world that died during the open credits and the dream of resurrecting that world that died with Marlene's final plea to Joel.

But it's the death of heteronormativity, heroic masculinity in Joel's case and heterosexism in Ellie's, that some players and commentators can't seem to get over.[66]

The latter part of this observation relates to additional downloadable content, called *The Last of Us: Left Behind*, released in 2014. It contains additional narrative around Ellie, and depicts a same-sex kiss between her and another young female survivor, Riley. Many hailed this moment as a 'breakthrough' for its deviation from heteronormativity that is especially pronounced in game representation.[67]

It is true that trauma and loss are foregrounded in the game, as Voorhees describes. However, what is also at work is Dyer's theory of 'white death': that is to say, that whiteness has associations with 'deathliness'[68] and that whiteness is ultimately configured as being dead and bringing death, something that the film theorist goes on to explicate through his interpretation of the zombie film.[69] There is a palpable sense in which the configuration of whiteness as purity, otherworldliness, a certain rigidity of body and pallor begins – for Dyer – to approach the horizon of death as the absolute expression of whiteness. Through his interpretation of 'startling images of white people as the dead devouring the dead' it becomes clear that, on an ideological level, whiteness as death results in a kind of inevitable, almost hysterical catharsis linked to finally capitulating to the horrors of its own making – something that Dyer identifies as the apotheosis of whiteness itself: 'to be destroyed by your own kind'.[70] While misery is at the forefront, more central is the notion of whiteness as endangered and fundamentally unsustainable, albeit through its own complex machinations.

In the game, this is relayed in all the ways that Voorhees has described. But, it is also self-contained in the very character of Ellie, the white female, who is at once the embodiment of innocence to be protected, the bearer of the moral suffering for the way things have become and the unwitting cause of the decline of (American) empire. This is illustrated through the final catharsis of the game in which Joel learns of Ellie's true importance from the Fireflies leader, Marlene. Ellie's purpose, as someone immune to the fungus, is to submit to an invasive brain matter-harvesting that would provide key samples necessary to developing a vaccine. Her function, in other words, is to die. This is relayed in a cut-scene in which Marlene (who, according to the narrative, values Ellie) attempts to convince Joel of her moral position. However, after all that he and Ellie have been through, Joel is strongly bonded to the girl; so he opts to save her.

What follows is extensive combat in which an injured Joel takes on the Fireflies, in a maze-like defunct medical facility, while locating a sedated Ellie and snatching her from the operating table before it is too late. In an upending of all that Joel and Ellie strived for throughout their travails, our anti-hero must kill everyone who knows of Ellie in order to liberate her from the burden of her responsibility to humanity. In terms of actual playability, the player has no choice but to pursue this killing if they wish to continue playing the game. No ethical option to save or not save Ellie is offered. The prototypical last stand that Joel engages in, with the limp Ellie in his arms, is bitter (see Figure 2.7). It evokes the vulnerable body of Joel's dying daughter, and this is confirmed when he calls Ellie 'Baby Girl' – a term of endearment he once reserved for his own child. It also generates ethical questions in the player regarding the pyrrhic victory of saving Ellie

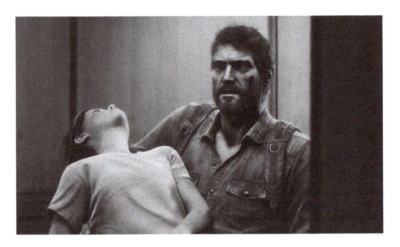

Figure 2.7 Joel attempts to save Ellie. *The Last of Us* (2013) ©Sony Interactive Entertainment America LLC. Created and developed by Naughty Dog LLC. Screen shot by author.

at the cost of a possible cure. While the player must be goal-oriented in their efficient killing of the Fireflies, the context of this bloodbath suggests that it is highly problematic, and forecloses the possibility of heroism on behalf of humanity. One may be a hero only to Ellie, and only nebulously so. After preserving her from immediate physical harm, in a conventional shooter/action sequence that culminates with killing Marlene, Joel and Ellie escape. In a cut-scene, the player sees Joel and Ellie returning to a small community of uninfected, where it is presumed that they hope to live. Ellie asks one last time whether it is really true that the Fireflies militia has stopped searching for a cure, and therefore it is no longer necessary for her to sacrifice herself to this cause. While it may be true that her brain matter may not result in a cure (we learn from a found doctor's recording that past attempts have not been successful) it is patently untrue that the doctors no longer want to use her to create a vaccine. Although it is unclear whether Ellie believes Joel, she acquiesces to his declaration that he speaks the truth. Thus, the dying of the world is symbolically sealed in a lie that Joel tells Ellie, out of his weakness for her.

Voorhees locates the difficulty players have in negotiating the value of Joel's choice as one that issues from the player's own relative attachment to normative heroic masculinity.[71] He suggests that the degree to which the player has a melancholic response to the decision made is directly connected to their perception that his heroic American masculinity is compromised by his irrational choice made on the basis of weakness, sentimentality and selfishness. A much healthier 'mournful' response is one through which the player can see Joel as 'flawed but redeemable'[72] in the face of highly problematic forms of American maleness. In both cases, the presumption is that there is an erosion of the normative, to which a player will undoubtedly have a strong response. This is likely to be at play to some degree. However, I am less interested in the debate around the difficult ending, than how the representation of Joel and Ellie – as iterations of desperate whiteness set against ruin and abolished social structures – resonated so strongly with audiences (see Figure 2.8). This suggests a response not only to the individual narrative of the game, but the conditions or socio-political moment within which that kind of narrative would be understood as impactful. The most notable of these in US culture was

Figure 2.8 Joel and Ellie in Salt Lake City. *The Last of Us* (2013) image provided by Sony Interactive Entertainment America LLC. ©Sony Interactive Entertainment America LLC. Created and developed by Naughty Dog LLC.

the re-election of President Barack Obama in 2012, which drew a dramatically more negative response from Republicans than his first election four years prior. Among the reactions associated with the news of re-election were notable paroxysms of anxiety from major right-wing public figures like Rush Limbaugh, Ted Nugent, Ann Coulter, Bill O'Reilly, Donald Trump and many others, who declared that traditional America had 'died', that they had to take back the nation, or strive to make America 'great' again.[73] Numerous YouTube videos documenting Republican emotional meltdowns were circulated. Several reported murders and attempted murders were associated with perpetrators who specifically named the cause as distress over the re-election of Obama. There was a small riot on the campus of The University of Mississippi, located in a strongly Republican state whose flag still contains the Confederate battle emblem. What was evidenced was a strong anxiety around the future of the United States, one that carries with it a racialized encoding of what in the nation was perceived as being lost. Tropes around imperilled white masculinity in games clearly reflect this tension. What was as play was a response to a perceived shift in power within the nation, evidenced in the displays of grief and profound anxiety, but also communicated in forms of visual culture like *The Last of Us*.

Spec Ops: The Line and the White Hero Interrupted

The connection between white masculinity, ruin and abolished social structures is starkly presented in another major title released approximately a year before *The Last of Us* and a few months before President Obama's re-election, entitled *Spec Ops: The Line* (2012).[74] While there are many possible examples of such themes, *The Line* is notable for the way in which it mobilizes core mechanics of gameplay, as well as a self-conscious frustrating of military shooter genre conventions, to interrupt player expectations and engender ethical self-inquiry around the masculinized force represented. Designed by Yager Development and published by 2K Games, *The Line* received solid though less than stellar reviews compared to *The Last of Us*,[75] but was critically heralded for its unique interventions into player-character identification and the ethical conversation it seemed to stir in players.[76] Among its many innovations, the most important of these was the strategic use of both narrative elements and the core game mechanic of shooting to strain the relationship between player and the playable character.

In the primary role of Captain Martin Walker, the player of this third-person shooter must guide a small team of Delta Force operators (Adams and Lugo) into present-day Dubai, which, in this parallel reality, has been destroyed by a series of mega-sandstorms (see Figure 2.9).[77] In the guise of the stereotypically rendered white male protagonist super-soldier, the player must navigate the phantasmagoric space of an abandoned Arab metropolis that has been swallowed up by the elements, in order to find the origin of a distress signal from a highly decorated and beloved Army Colonel, John Konrad, and his missing 'Damned 33rd' battalion. While the mission seems simple, once within the ruins of the city a great number of challenges face the team: overwhelming natural elements, desperate refugees and the perils of a defunct urban space. Early parts of the game seem

Figure 2.9 Walker and his team enter Dubai. *Spec Ops: The Line* (2012) developed by Yager Development and published by 2K Games. Screen shot by author.

jingoistic. A smart-mouthed band of brothers and the militarized violence that it seems to celebrate set the tone. All the myths about the 'good' and 'justified' American militarized humanitarian vision seem to hold true. As the game progresses, it begins to call into question the construction of such a character – as well as a player's presumptive identification with him.

Reviewers described *The Line* as the *Apocalypse Now* of video games for the many similarities it bore to Francis Ford Coppola's film from 1979.[78] While the setting of the game is the modern-day Arab world, not Vietnam War-era Cambodia, both the gamic and filmic narratives create the conditions for a white American normative male character to traverse a hostile space that takes an increasing mental toll, until the figure finally unravels. Walt Williams, the Lead Developer of *The Line*, indicated that Joseph Conrad's 1899 anti-colonialist novella *Heart of Darkness* constituted a primary source material for the game.[79] The same novella inspired the psychedelic anti-war vision of Coppola's *Apocalypse Now*, and so the connectedness between these three texts that illustrate the mental deterioration of a normative figure under the duress of increasingly hellish conditions makes symbolic sense. In the film's narrative, which is set during the Second Indochina War, an emotionally damaged US Army

Captain and Special Operations officer named Willard is assigned a mission to pursue and terminate a highly decorated Special Forces Colonel, Walter E. Kurtz, who has become a madman. The journey Willard undertakes into the remote jungle by river from Vietnam into Cambodia reveals increasingly intense visions of horror, as he travels deeper and deeper into a heart of darkness. That the game would be described, therefore, as an *Apocalypse Now* narrative suggests an anti-war sentiment generated through the deeper associations with the two earlier texts, as well as the game's own story.

It is reasonable to make this claim, given the strongly inferred relationship between Coppola's dominating anti-war vision and the game's resonant thematic elements of traveling into a new (Arab) 'heart of darkness'. And Williams did reveal the team's intention to thematically broach the war-is-hell conversation that has long existed in literature, theatre, cinema and television, stating, 'we wanted to make a game in our medium that spoke to the truth of war just like every other medium had done.'[80] But the game feels much more intentionally focused on critiquing the jingoistic military shooter than making a larger statement about current military interventions in the Arab world. In an interview on *IGN*, a major site for games and entertainment news, Williams described the ways in which the game was designed to grate against the player on an emotional level:

> 'We wanted that sense that the game was physically opposing you,' says Williams. 'Not simply as a simulation, but also as the game itself.' Williams refers to the loading screens, which eventually stop giving gameplay tips and start reminding you of the mistakes you've made and the damage they've caused. Death as well as progress rub salt in your wounds.[81]

Constructing an opposition between player and game demonstrates a self-consciousness toward military shooter genre norms, which typically lack much self-criticality in relation to what the player is asked to perform through playable engagement. For example, the player usually assumes the role of primary character, who is often heroic and whose aims are assumed to be just or good. A strong identification between player and character is presumed to aid in effective, immersive and therefore sustained gameplay.

Figure 2.10 The disturbed Walker. *Spec Ops: The Line* (2012) developed by Yager Development and published by 2K Games. Screen shot by author.

Typically, the use of weaponry is hyper-masculinized, highly spectacularized and cool. So-called 'militainment' games often contain jingoistic elements and present a totalizing vision that advocates for the necessity of military solutions, as opposed to diplomacy. *The Line* begins to chip away at these presumptions, and as the character's morality and sanity erode, the player's doubts, internal questions and emotional response to the carnage build-up (see Figure 2.10). As one critic observed, 'as the game goes forward, it becomes weirder and weirder that he's killing so many people.'[82] Insofar as the game intervenes in the military shooter genre, the subversion of the core mechanic into a site of critique and internal self-reflection constitutes the game's primary intervention.

Williams also articulated how part of the narrative was inspired by films like Adrian Lyne's *Jacob's Ladder* (1990), which spoke less directly to the horror of war, and more specifically to the psychological and emotional traumas experienced in its wake.[83] This sense of trauma is generated in the game by demanding a high degree of complicity, through acts that the player would likely find questionable according to typical shooter expectations. The player is slowly led from confrontations with nonspecific Arab hostiles who may simply be desperate people left behind from the mass evacuations, to outright war with US troops who become inexplicably coded as the enemy, despite their humanitarian aims. For example, in a now-iconic Chapter Eight of the game, called 'The Gate', Captain Walker's team is faced with an enemy too overwhelming to defeat in direct combat. Walker decides that in order to gain the tactical advantage, he will employ a form of chemical warfare using white phosphorous. This is a particularly brutal form of attack, which chemically burns flesh to the bone upon contact. In a cut-scene, Walker's team protests its use; however, it is impossible to continue the game without engaging in this excessive cruelty. One may attempt to evade it, by shooting at the enemy from high ground, or rappelling down and facing them directly or attempting to use stealth to evade them altogether. However, there is no viable alternative but to play through Walker's choice.

A very sophisticated use of in-game visual signifiers is mobilized, and it is one that is extremely bound up in a particular expression of whiteness, deathliness and trauma. The controls for the deployment of white phosphorous mortars comes into view: a hard-case device with toggles, buttons and a screen. A camera device is first launched that provides a hovering bird's eye view on the killing grounds below. It resembles the grainy, black-and-white utilitarian look of 'smart-bomb' vision that entered into the popular imaginary through news reportage during the first Gulf War in the early 1990s, and streamed images of remote warfare, sometimes likened to video game warfare. In view are small, moving shapes that resemble troops and military vehicles as seen from above. Toggling the on-screen crosshairs to line up with targets, one mashes a button and a mortar is released, resulting in a delayed image of white clouds spreading across the screen, followed by the sounds of human suffering. Superimposed upon this is the image of Walker himself, which appears as a colour reflection on the weapon's monitor. In this playable sequence, what one sees is the in-game 'self' of the player (i.e., Walker's visage) in a ghostly layer over the remote bomb vision of a chemical warfare attack. Further, one subsequently learns, upon surveying the damage and casualties afterwards, that the burned and dying soldiers who are writhing in agony on the ground were protecting non-combatant refugees, whom 'you' as Walker have also murdered.

This is a catastrophic mistake, and an unconscionable loss wrought by the excessive and unethical use of force by the 'hero' playable character. Internal fighting within the team flares again when one member (Lugo) reacts to the horror, claiming that they have gone too far this time. The question of who exactly has gone too far seems to refer to three things at once: to Walker and his team; to the game designers, who painfully recall the recent use of white phosphorous in Iraq by both Saddam Hussein and the United States; and the United States military itself, which has argued that it is not in violation of chemical warfare prohibitions on account of the technical classification of white phosphorous as 'incendiary'. The cut-scene envisioning burned women and children, and particularly the charred and macabre 'mother-and-child' imagery that traumatizes Walker and his team, are among the most iconic of the game (see Figure 2.11). However, the most striking and brazen image of this scenario actually reveals itself in the playable targeting of the enemy, using the tools of remote warfare that bring death from above, while reflecting the face of normative militarized masculinity back to the player. Whiteness, deathliness and trauma reach their crescendo in this image. Interesting as well is the experience of playing this section of the game while occupying a very different subject position

Figure 2.11 Victims of white phosphorous. *Spec Ops: The Line* (2012) developed by Yager Development and published by 2K Games. Screen shot by author.

from Walker. As someone of another race and gender, I was unable to readily map myself onto the reflection of Walker, resulting in a jarring interruption of immersive play. Its sudden appearance provided a stark reminder of whom the 'I' in the game is. The rare first-person view utilized during this mostly third-person game momentarily confuses player self-recognition: the mirror reflects back a strange, white male face, which insists that the player must consider themselves, both in their association or disassociation from the primary playable character, as military shooter hero.

This image of whiteness, deathliness and trauma is also key in the game's blurring of the boundary between super-soldier and homicidal maniac. *The Line* indicts the supposed civilizing mission or 'white man's burden' of protecting the world from degenerating into disorder, darkness and barbarism. In this, 'the line' that is crossed may also refer to the dissolution of stable white masculinity as it is put into crisis through a racialized encounter with the other in the Arab world. In a strong departure from the typical military shooter, in which the playable character has righteousness on his side, this game generates friction.[84] The 'full spectrum dominance' demonstrated in the excessive use of force, poorly rationalized missions and mounting insanity interrupts the core values of such games. And, as I have argued, as cultural forms of signification, the visual politics of these images betray an affective quality of deep ambivalence, fear and a perception of larger ambient anxieties surrounding eroded white dominance in US culture.

Does the strategy undertaken by Williams and his team ultimately provide an effective intervention? In his detailed analysis of *The Line* as an example of militarized entertainment critiquing itself, scholar Matthew Thomas Payne suggests that the game may be the industry's first 'anti-war military shooter'.[85] He asserts that the 'discordant feeling' generated in the player gives rise to a productive critique of the genre, and, more generally, the 'banal pleasures of militainment'.[86] Marcus Schulzke argues that the core mechanics of the game effectively prevent the player from preserving themselves from the ethical difficulties of the situations *The Line* presents:

> The game shows the potential problems of soldiers entering a
> war they barely understand and hoping that good intentions

alone will allow them to produce a good outcome. This dystopia is therefore one that calls attention to the many evils of unrestrained violence and military intervention, especially in regions that are poorly understood. The game mechanics present these messages forcefully by constraining players in such a way that they must use violence to complete the game only to find that victory can be hollow and far too costly.[87]

Indeed, the cavalier manner in which Walker and his two 'skilled' operators enter into the theatre of their purported search-and-rescue mission, their persistent demonstrated inability to communicate with the people they find there, and their patently violent mishandling of the scenarios they encounter within the narrative, in retrospect, indicates their unpreparedness for this space. What they have to their advantage is the ability to kill very, very effectively – and that is all the game mechanics permit a player to do. However, in terms of a broader and more ethical continuum of possibilities, the narrative conveys a kind of impotence, an inability to actually fix anything or save anyone. As Holger Pötzsch similarly asserts, '*Spec Ops: The Line* ultimately subverts the myth of the male, white soldier as glorious hero and saviour so central to the American and increasingly also European military imaginary.'[88] Pötzsch has connected *The Last of Us* and *The Line* in an essay that considers how the relations between design features and narrative strategies can create a constructive friction between genres and their underlying ideological bases.[89] However, he ultimately questions the effectiveness of any critique because the highly artificial construct of an apocalypse detracts from real and ongoing systemic problems in the lived world:

> The fact that the game [*The Last of Us*] uses a worn generic trope – a catastrophic event that over-night destroys all established institutions and unravels received power relations – and thus establishes a postapocalyptic context 'ex machina' significantly reduces the critical import of *The Last of Us*. By taking recourse to a sudden breakdown of order that is unequivocally connected to a clear external cause, the game loses its ability to meaningfully comment upon key tendencies in contemporary society and politics such as rapid ecological detriment,

economic downturns, growing inequalities, or resurgent practices of warfare at a global scale.[90]

The same argument could be used to critique the potency of *The Line*, in
terms of its potential to make any meaningful commentary about the lived
world. Williams himself has side-stepped the notion that the game makes
large socio-political statements, suggesting that instead it is a story about
character and, in a larger sense, a curated emotional journey of a player
who is presumed to be uncritically engaging with military shooters:

> [With *Spec Ops*], we were really trying to shine a light on the
> darkness in us as gamers and the types of games we choose to
> enjoy for entertainment. WHY we go into those games. We
> wanted people to be thinking about the inherent darkness of
> sitting down and playing a game where you kill thousands of
> people. What does it say?[91]

However, while many debated the developer's socio-political intentions,
and the relative effectiveness of its genre interventions, it is more useful to consider the politics at work in its play, and the ways in which the
game reflects back or seems to galvanize popular attitudes – or manipulate them in some way. For example, it is seldom asked why the location
of an identified 'heart of darkness', recast to tell the story of the descent
of an emotionally compromised Western figure, would be modern-
day Dubai. While the game certainly makes an effective critique against
blindly accepting the testosterone-fuelled, excessively violent scenarios
that populate the military shooter genre, in terms of a larger consideration of whiteness, masculinity and trauma, it is impossible not to notice
the specific site of Walker's unravelling. Further, one must consider the
function of the playable game spaces in relation to lived world conditions,
which mark those spaces as sites of trauma for the West. For it is certainly
not incidental that an Arab mega-city that thrives in the lived world – in
the present day – would be so summarily represented within the game
space as an apocalyptic space.

The game space of Dubai is a ruin of a global metropolis. Sandstorms
have decimated most of the city, and its remains teem with peril and dread.
Little water exists, and only a few refugees survive in the most desperate

conditions. Nature reclaims highly modern consumerist spaces that were once lavish and ambitious in their construction and now decimated by warfare. A strong sense of verticality prevails: one may enter an area that seems like a flat wasteland and suddenly realize that the sand has covered whole blocks worth of skyscrapers, which a player can only access through extreme drops into their depths. Gigantic windows that have inexplicably survived the city's destruction may suddenly crack, sending a tidal wave of orange sand in your team's direction. Roofs of buildings may seem like floors until one falls through them, up might suddenly become down. Objects of extreme indulgence like fancy cars, jet-skis, planes and yachts litter the landscape like discarded toys. One often enters into interior spaces associated with leisure and consumerism, but which have been repurposed as sites of conflict. Decorative lights may still twinkle, hearkening to a bet-ter time, while one engages in full-blown carnage and chunks of burnt flesh litter the space. The effect is of a phantasmagoric nightmare.

While, as a matter of creative license, we may see the destroyed Dubai as a manifestation of Walker's crumbling mental interiority, a politics of identity clearly influenced the decision to set Walker against a 'heart of darkness' located in the Arab world. Why this particular space? The opu-lent metropolis defines a stark figure/ground relation, through which the white, Western heteronormative male character is defined against an oppo-site or foil.[92] The Line does enact the psychological and ethical ruin of a Western soldier-ideal, whose prescribed role as a white protector against an Arab heart of darkness is revealed as defunct. Within the game world, it does launch an inspired and necessary genre critique of the military shooter. But the melancholic irony of The Line issues from the gulf between the moral address of the shooter and the ethically problematic space of the game's own politics of representation. This is a vision that ultimately shores up ideological positions around a dichotomy between whiteness and oth-erness rather than disrupting them. Therefore, the game's lauded self-criticality should not be confused with its making any statement against the predominating American view of the Arab world.

The expression of a white heteronormative hero who is not all-knowing, not all-powerful and whose lack of understanding proves to be a liability appears in both The Line and in The Last of Us. And, as I will discuss below, it resurfaces in *Tomb Raider* in the transformation of the unflappable action hero Lara Croft from an adventurer into a much more vulnerable and human survivor.

Tomb Raider, Whiteness and the Female Heroine in Peril

It is worth considering *womanhood* in particular in relation to the ideological category of whiteness. The revamping of the representation of Lara Croft provides a paradigmatic example from the same cultural moment that can be used to problematize constructions of whiteness in relation to race and gender. *Tomb Raider* (2013), developed by Crystal Dynamics and published by Square Enix, is an origin story in which the player meets a youthful Croft on her first expedition. Unlike the Lara Croft of previous games, the hyper-sexualization of her body is notably toned down: while still clad in her iconic tank top, she now wears long pants and her breasts seem (finally) more proportional to the rest of her body. She is inexperienced, though she already possesses the obsession with ancient cultures and is adventurous in the pursuit of this knowledge. Croft displays much more vulnerability and falters in her confidence. This is conveyed through body language, dialogue and the learning curve the character faces in the playable aspects of the game (see Figure 2.12). It is telling that one of the most iconic characters in all of video game history underwent such a radical reinvention in this particular cultural moment.

Scholars and critics tend to consider the Lara Croft character exclusively from the perspective of gender. Indeed, despite her popularity with players, her highly contested formulation has become somewhat of an icon for virtually everything that is wrong with the representation of female characters in games. Likewise, the conventional use of a generic white male protagonist has also come under scrutiny, resulting in interventions in character development that seem to embody but then break with type, such as the aforementioned examples of *The Line* and *The Last of Us*. Anne-Marie Schleiner contests the feminist critique of Croft, declaring her 'a product of the mechanization of bodies; her fetishized synthetic beauty resides in her slick and glistening 3D polygons, evolved from clunky robotic forms into

Figure 2.12 Lara Croft under duress. *Tomb Raider* (2013) ©2013–16 Square Enix, Ltd. Developed by Crystal Dynamics, Inc. and published by Square Enix. Image courtesy Square Enix, Ltd.

attire more appropriate for the information society.[93] Presenting a broad array of possible readings, Schleiner advocates for the subversion of gender categories by appropriating and hacking the iconic Lara.

In describing female hypersexualization in relation to *Tomb Raider* and other games, Jon Dovey and Helen Kennedy assess that, 'the visual imagery in many mainstream games seems to be entirely ignorant of the critiques that have been made of these stereotypes in other visual media and appear to import some of the worst examples in an entirely unreflexive and uncritical way.'[94] Justine Cassell and Henry Jenkins outline the problematics of Croft as a character purported to be liberated and capable, while pandering to chauvinistic teen male interests ('tits and ass', as they put it).[95] They ponder the potentialities of transgender identification made possible through the male player's engagement with a female avatar.

Helen Kennedy, in her definitive 2002 essay, 'Lara Croft: Feminist Icon or Cyberbimbo?', considers the diverging interpretations of this iconic character, in terms of what she calls 'gendered pleasures' that occur as a result of play. She surveys the broad array of feminist responses to the polarizing figure of Lara Croft, and importantly attends to the possible transgender readings of relations between player and character. Additionally, she underlines the avatar's uncanny vacillation between her objecthood as a heteronormative sexual fantasy figure, and her complete lack of a defined sexual identity. 'In the end,' she concludes, 'it is impossible to securely locate Lara within existing feminist frameworks, nor is it entirely possible to just dismiss her significance entirely.'[96] For her, feminist theory must turn its attention to games, while keeping in mind the computer-mediated particularity of their forms.

There is also an array of responses that interrupt the notion that Croft should be read through gender representation. Most notably, Espen Aarseth's comments on the figure of Lara Croft contradict the dominant feminist critiques that occurred early on. Invoking that 'invisibility' deconstructed by Dyer, he suggests that playability changes the terms of engagement and that, relative to game mechanics, the avatar is best thought of as transparent: 'the dimensions of Lara Croft's body, already analyzed to death by film theorists, are irrelevant to me as a player, because a different-looking body would not make me play differently [...] When I play, I don't even see her body, but see through it and past it.'[97] The game studies and electronic literature scholar attempts to wrest video games from narrative-based interpretation, identifying them as self-contained forms – a 'new material technology' – as opposed to a continuation of story (with its attendant representations) in interactive form.[98] In more recent research, Esther MacCallum-Stewart has returned to the subject, surveying the history of responses to the iconic character, while taking into account Croft's reinvention by a female writer in the 2013 reboot. In this essay, the author does mention the heroine's race briefly, identifying her formulation by lead graphic artist Toby Gard as the 'Hispanic Lara Cruz', before she became the British aristocrat Lara Croft.[99] But ultimately, MacCallum-Stewart focuses on the lack of nuanced discussions beyond gender, and the general scholarly neglect of fans, players and game culture producers who help shape her possible meanings. While there is no shortage of debate around Lara Croft, her whiteness remains greatly under-theorized.

Whiteness and femininity are both at play in *Tomb Raider* (2013). Particularly during the first portion of the game, many of the missions focus on Lara as unprepared, overwhelmed and in serious jeopardy. Dyer discusses the notion of the heroine in peril in relation to visual pleasure, which although related to exhausted tropes of female passivity in cinema, directly relates to the reinvention of Lara Croft as a woman who is resourceful, yet out of her depth, ambitious but inexperienced and imperilled.[100] Writing on the cinematic desperate heroine, Dyer observes:

> Heroes in jeopardy do something about it; heroines don't. And the pleasure we are supposed to get from seeing these sequences is that of a woman in peril. We're supposed to get off on her vulnerability, her hysteria, her terror. In the way such sequences are put together, we are encouraged to take up a traditional male role in relation to the woman, one that asserts our superiority and at the same time encourages us to feel the desire to rape and conquer. We are superior because we either know more than her (we know that psychopath is there but she hasn't spotted him yet), or because we can see what any sensible person would do but she, foolishly and pathetically, doesn't.[101]

This is an extension of his discussion around the fundamental inactivity of the white woman, particularly under the conditions of images of imperial expansion, such as was discussed in relation to *The Jewel in the Crown*. Dyer proceeds to make plain the ways in which the viewer of the sort of rote imagery he describes is presumptively encoded as heterosexual male, and that this constructed male gaze oscillates between that which is tantamount to a rapist (who sees the unsuspecting heroine's unprotected flesh from a privileged and predatory vantage point) and a saviour (embodied in the rescuer who comes to her aid).[102] Characterizing this 'tendency' in cinema to be organized around what is thought to exemplify heteronormative male sexuality, Dyer sees this impetus as putting women in their place, 'as objects of a "natural" male sexual drive that may at times be ridiculous but is also insistent, inescapable and inevitable. Such representations help to preserve the existing power relations of men over women by translating them into sexual relations, rendered both as biologically given and a source of masculine pleasure.'[103] Lara Croft's whiteness accords her a kind of purity. Her adventurer status aligns her with the colonial vision of the white explorer in an exotic land, while her white femininity paints her somewhat as a victim, but simultaneously as the critic of – or even the cause of – the downfall of empire. Within the third-person perspective of the game, the player is then cast not truly as Lara, but as an omniscient invisible entity who must protect the endangered Lara from an assortment of possible deaths.

In *Tomb Raider*, Lara's deaths are illustrated in various startlingly gruesome forms including impalement, butchering, being crushed by boulders, gunned down, stabbed, torn apart by wolves, shot with arrows, hacked at, strangled and burned.[104] In addition to their gory detail, they notably depart from earlier iterations of the Lara Croft franchise, which paint the heroine as much less fragile, and have a much stronger focus on puzzle-solving. Still, this revamped Lara received critical acclaim, and contained many of the same elements of adventure and discovery the franchise is known for.[105]

Simon Parkin of the *Guardian* pointed out the darker, more desperate tenor of the reboot:

> Incrementally, she [Lara] stops cringing in the bushes and steps into her role of a heroine modelled on the aristocratic British explorers of the early 20th Century: pioneering, fearless, cultured and somewhat standoffish. We watch as she loses innocence at the hands of experience.
>
> In contrast to the previous titles then, *Tomb Raider* is a game about loss as much as it is about discovery – even if that loss is generally only expressed in the storyline, not the systems. It's also a game about survival, in a way the previous games were not.[106]

Survivalism and loss, as well as the identified theft of innocence, thematically figure into *Tomb Raider* in a way that feels very much like *The Last of Us*. In this case, the female form of whiteness is cast against the backdrop of a mysterious Pacific island called Yamatai, filled with hostile inhabitants who are cult followers bent on female sacrifice to their Solarii Sun Queen. Separated from her shipwrecked crew, Lara must learn to navigate the terrain alone and, increasingly, defend herself against both the elements and the obsessed, deranged islanders. As opposed to an unflappable heroine, she is the underdog, initially the victim, and must quickly learn to handle herself in the unrelenting environment. She is no daredevil, as she unsteadily negotiates the perils around her. Scavenging, again, plays a strong role in the playable elements of the game. Players must search for tools and parts that allow Lara to find and upgrade weaponry, and otherwise provide the means for survival. Like *The Last of Us*, the urgency around finding what one needs, if even in small amounts, feels dire. In addition, the discovery of clues, artefacts and documents that unveil additional knowledge of her location and her attackers provide narrative complexity. Like Walker in *The Line* and Joel in *The Last of Us*, the scenario presents another traumatized form of whiteness, although in this case, one that interestingly vacillates between the visual representation of a vulnerable female figure and the urgent drive to protect that playable figure from harm.[107] The plentiful desperate grunts and cries that Lara emits as she navigates the dangerous terrain expresses this to great effect. It also resonates in small, animated touches such as the way she grasps an injured arm while her character awaits your next move.

In a brief playable cut-scene that received much media attention, a male scavenger abducts Lara, physically intimidating her by suggestively rubbing a hand against her thigh. A representative of Crystal Dynamics initially described this scenario as an attempt to abduct and rape Lara, but the language around this was quickly amended to indicate that there was no sexual assault represented. However, the scene is decidedly gendered, and the so-called 'pathological situation' that was intended to indicate physical intimidation and fear conveys a strong affective sense of impending sexualized domination (see Figure 2.13).[108] Thus, the dynamics of simultaneous predator/protector that Dyer notes in relation to the embattled heroine is embodied in the player's interaction with Lara as a vulnerable woman to be looked at, and also a victim to be saved. Certainly, she is not passive to the degree that Dyer describes in relation to earlier cinematic representation. She finds her agency and transforms into the figure that we recognize, the indomitable Lara Croft. But she too is an embattled figure, set against the backdrop of an uncivilized place, and cast in the role of the victimized other while mobilizing a visual politics of whiteness that largely goes unacknowledged in analysis.

Figure 2.13 Lara accosted. *Tomb Raider* (2013) ©2013–16 Square Enix, Ltd. Developed by Crystal Dynamics, Inc. and published by Square Enix. Image courtesy Square Enix, Ltd.

Conclusion: A Trauma Narrative of Whiteness

The overwhelming absence of a discussion of whiteness as core to each of the aforementioned games points to a larger, understudied area in playable media. Namely, whiteness operates in duplicitous ways as both a universal expression of humanity – which has ideological consequences – and as a specific form of identity politics that goes unrecognized as such. 'The combination of extreme whiteness with plain, unwhite whiteness,' Dyer explains, 'means that white people can both lay claim to the spirit that aspires to the heights of humanity and yet supposedly speak and act disinterestedly as humanity's most average and unremarkable representatives.'[109]

This undertaking is not about simply deconstructing these specific representations and naming a bias that exists as a form of intellectual catharsis. Rather, it seeks to understand the power at play in these pervasive images. These three games, though inclusive of many themes and dimensions, simultaneously reveal a set of concerns related to a social grouping of heteronormative whiteness, particularly in relation to navigating a scenario of losing power and dominance. These are the 'aesthetics of ambivalence' of which I speak, affective qualities that trade on notions of the white male normative hero, but which in fact betray a larger form of whiteness that is deeply in crisis, desperate and which strategically mobilizes itself as a form of otherness. It is a whiteness that appropriates the moral high ground of victimhood through its embattled status as a form of alterity, even while it trades on itself as normative.

If we suspend the idea of these games as representing the normative and consider how they are in fact the expression of a particular group, and if we can make the whiteness of these games 'strange', it becomes possible to see several things. In the first case, it reveals a trauma narrative of ideological whiteness that repeats itself unendingly in the innumerable fear-based narratives of contagion, besiegement, apocalypse and the crumbling of civilization (see Figure 2.14). Second, it becomes clear that, rather than merely a strategy for representing a universal form of humanity, these games in fact fixate on whiteness, even while proclaiming themselves as nonparticular. How can both of these function simultaneously? How can whiteness possess the ordinariness of universalism, while also assuming a traumatic narrative of alterity and disenfranchisement? This double-signification

Figure 2.14 Joel battles a hunter. *The Last of Us* (2013) image provided by Sony Interactive Entertainment America LLC. ©Sony Interactive Entertainment America LLC. Created and developed by Naughty Dog LLC.

connects to the effort to preserve whiteness from denaturing it to the point that it becomes specified (and therefore non-dominant) rather than universal. This is mobilized, at least in part, by a representational logic ordered around the normativity of whiteness, and a phobic response to difference. Expressions of whiteness appear again and again in games as both normative and under duress, unremarkable and exalted, deserving of, and denied that which was deserved. That is to say, these games must be understood *as* the visual politics of dominant culture and, therefore, at the time in which they were made, an expression of the totalizing logics of whiteness.

3

The Landscapes of Games as Ideology

Landscape might be seen more profitably as something like the 'dreamwork' of imperialism, unfolding its own movement in time and space from a central point of origin and folding back on itself to disclose both utopian fantasies of the perfected imperial prospect and fractured images of unresolved ambivalence and unsuppressed resistance.[1]

W.J.T. Mitchell, *Landscape and Power*

[C]ompleting the game means penetrating its space, defeating obstacles, coming to the end of the story. The designer of game environments employs the visual tricks of the garden designer to create an active space, where narrative and spatial progress merge. The visitor to the digital gamescape is no mere spectator, however, but an actor.[2]

Eugénie Shinkle, 'Gameworlds and Digital Gardens'

Introduction

In his informative look back at *Prince of Persia: Sands of Time*, a game developed by Ubisoft Montreal and published by Ubisoft in 2010, creator

141

and designer Jordan Mechner mentions the following maxim: 'Build a Playground for Your Hero.'[3] Rather than focusing on the 'hero', this chapter concerns itself with the 'playground': the game space built as a complex site where the player/hero enacts their journey. Game spaces are central to player experience. This has long been understood from a production standpoint, and has even been explored in relation to the transformation of the lived world through gamification.[4] Yet the fundamental role and cultural meanings of in-game landscape have received little critical investigation.[5] Particularly in regard to a politics of representation, it makes sense that most of the focus would fall to the figures imaged, rather than the spaces within which they move. But navigating and engaging with game space in a sustained way is highly complex, and indicative of larger cultural value systems. The world-making of games has become a paradigmatic form of contemporary visual culture that models relations between player and space in significant ways. Within the study of video games, the construction of space has largely been theorized from a formal perspective. However, turning a visual studies lens to gamescapes in order to understand these landscapes as ideology, we can begin to see how these spaces naturalize a certain set of relations through a highly curated framing of the playable environment. This chapter asks: how can the combined knowledges of formal game studies and visual studies provide new insights to game space and the potent cultural 'dreamwork' it undertakes?

Although there are many AAA titles that present extremely compelling environments, I have chosen the culturally loaded *Metal Gear Solid V: The Phantom Pain*. The chapter will place particular emphasis on its spatial features, as well as the game's constructed and highly ideologically weighted landscapes. *The Phantom Pain*, a Japanese title, was developed by Kojima Productions and published by Konami Digital Entertainment in late 2015. I specifically chose this mainstream stealth-themed game for several reasons, including its status as an iconic title that resonates with mass audiences and its legendary director Hideo Kojima. Moreover, *The Phantom Pain* belongs to a legacy brand (*Metal Gear*) that dates back to 1987, which is undeniably one of the most successful franchises in console game history.

Figure 3.1 Snake on D-Horse in Afghanistan. *Metal Gear Solid V: The Phantom Pain* (2015) developed by Kojima Productions and published by Konami. Image courtesy of ©Konami Digital Entertainment.

The Phantom Pain additionally utilizes the Fox Engine, a proprietary game engine developed by Kojima Productions and notable for its advanced photorealism, rendering power, possibilities for 'realistic atmosphere' and enhanced sandbox capabilities.[6] After its release, *The Phantom Pain* was especially lauded for the freedom of engagement possible within its massive spaces, and critics identified it as a major technological benchmark for its detail and open-world potentials (see Figure 3.1).[7] In this, it epitomizes the best mainstream games have to offer in terms of the sought-after objective of a highly convincing 'world', and it generally conforms to the typical use of a game landscape as a theatre for asserting dominion over space through the player's mastery of gameplay.

While the game is an iconic tactical stealth action adventure with elements of speculative fiction, it is the space itself (rather than the hero or the action) that concerns me here. Through its invoked themes, its loaded geographical manifestations and its symbolic embodiment of neoliberal ideals, the constructed landscape models a visual culture of global capitalism. But I am also interested in W.J.T. Mitchell's query in relation to ideological constructions of land, from his now-canonical *Landscape and Power*, which 'ask[s] not just what landscape "is" or "means" but what it *does*, how it works as a cultural practice'.[8] He explains:

> Landscape as a cultural medium thus has a double role with respect to something like ideology: it naturalizes a cultural and social construction, representing an artificial world as if it were simply given and inevitable, and it also makes that representation operational by interpellating its beholder in some more or less determinate relation to its givenness as sight and site. Thus, landscape (whether urban or rural, artificial or natural) always greets us as space, as environment, as that within which 'we' (figured as 'the figures' in the landscape) find – or lose –ourselves.[9]

Mitchell's description regarding still imagery, in which landscape is constructed *as* cultural medium – as opposed to merely rendering the thing-in-itself – takes on heightened significance when considering game space. As a *playable* space, it lends itself even more to the 'dreamwork of imperialism' to which the art historian refers. Particular kinds of fantasies are enacted within a fully realized simulation that purports itself as given and inevitable, although it is not. And, in relation to third-person perspective games, the configuration of a playable character in the frame repeats the paradigmatic situation of figure within the pictorial landscape, albeit a dynamic one, in which we, too, lose and find ourselves. As I discuss in this chapter, with games like *The Phantom Pain*, the contextualization of landscape becomes vital for what it *does*, in terms of understanding how setting (just as much as spectacular action) may drive meaning. Additionally, the 'givenness' of the game's site as constructed landscape shapes relations to space that echo a set of ethical relations to the lived world.

I have stressed that game representations in general are thoroughly intentional (see Chapter 2). Henry Jenkins and Kurt Squire have, already in the early beginnings of game studies, made a similar assertion regarding in-game environments:

> Game worlds are totally constructed environments. Everything there was put on the screen for some purpose – shaping the game play or contributing to the mood and atmosphere or encouraging performance, playfulness, competition, or collaboration.

> If games tell stories, they do so by organizing spatial features.
> If games stage combat, then players learn to scan their envi-
> ronments for competitive advantages. Game designers cre-
> ate immersive worlds with embedded rules and relationships
> among objects that enable dynamic experiences.[10]

The awareness of games as utterly purposeful in their design, and intended
for particular rule-based engagements with the space (which may also be
innovatively repurposed by the player), points to a central concern for
much of game design: world-building. While effective strategies around
game space development are key for immersive gameplay, I am also particularly interested in the ways open-world games speak to the complexities
of power in light of current social and cultural anxieties. The constructions
of game landscapes are revelatory in this regard, because they model systems of engagement that betray values, priorities and biases.

In their highly influential *Game Cultures*, Jon Dovey and Helen
Kennedy remark on the centrality of cultural context for an understanding
of how space functions in games: 'Although games and play take place in
their own time and space, this "location" is intimately related to the wider
cultural landscape [...] it can be argued that we can only understand the
game space through its relation to the non-game space.'[11] The importance
of understanding this situatedness of meaning within a culturally inflected
time and space cannot be overstated. Games – though different from novels, films, songs, television shows and plays – similarly possess meanings
that shift in relation to cultural context, as well as the myriad subjectivities brought to their interpretation by user experience. Dovey and Kennedy
also point to the earlier work of Lev Manovich, which underscored how
movement through game space partly constitutes its enjoyment, since time
and narrative become mapped onto spatial movement.[12] The co-authors
make reference to 'cultural landscapes', which implies literal game space,
but more importantly, connective relations to the lived world. Jenkins and
Squire seem to refer more directly to the literal construction of game space,
which has subsequently been conceived as world-building (in the sense that
Mechner wrote of when he mentioned building a playground for a hero).

This chapter invites the reader to ponder the multiplicity of the term
'landscape' in relation to the world-building that is manifested in games,

larger cultural landscapes and the connectedness between these possible spaces. As a part of a larger project of modelling how to generatively apply cultural analysis of the image to game studies, I read *The Phantom Pain's* first site, Afghanistan, for meanings conveyed through its playable landscapes.[13] Bringing together studies of game space from medium-specific theorizations from game studies and the theorization of landscape from the history of art and visual culture, this chapter proposes a critical framework for the world-building at play in dominant games. As the seminal work of W.J.T. Mitchell and Leo Marx will help me explain, video games *as visual culture* always make a set of claims about land, space and place.[14]

Metal Gear Solid V: The Phantom Pain

Metal Gear Solid V: The Phantom Pain begins in 1984 in a remote hospital in Cyprus. The story finds the once-great hero, Snake (aka 'Big Boss'/'Boss'), in a compromised position: recently awoken from a nine-year coma, disoriented, one-eyed and highly traumatized. The legendary character is clearly past his prime and in a weakened condition. With a body riddled with shrapnel and scars, not to mention an amputated left hand, Snake is far from battle-ready. At first, he can only use his elbows to drag his sluggish, atrophied body.

What unfolds is a vendetta narrative that explores themes of the psychological toll of war and the atrocities of military conflict. In an opening interlude, the player controls Snake, who wears only a pair of scrubs. Without a weapon or even shoes, he must navigate a besieged hospital with the help of a mysterious guide. Once he negotiates the corridor-based engagement with enemies and the destructive supernatural entities that pursue him, the land opens up before him into a grand expanse of steep hills and valleys. Snake is rescued, outfitted with a bionic prosthetic hand, patched together and reintegrated into private mercenary work in Afghanistan (see Figure 3.2). The player divines after some time that this is a vendetta narrative, and a series of missions will be executed in order to build and grow the mercenary group, the Diamond Dogs, and their stronghold that was destroyed in a previous game. The narrative and gameplay that follow contain elements of horror and fantasy, in addition to more conventional attributes of the

Figure 3.2 Snake the mercenary. *Metal Gear Solid V: The Phantom Pain* (2015) developed by Kojima Productions and published by Konami. Image courtesy of ©Konami Digital Entertainment.

military genre such as the use of missions, strategy, stealth, increasingly spectacular weapons, combat, scavenging and navigation.

The cinematics and naturalistic physics of space in *The Phantom Pain* are impressive technological feats, allowing for free traversal of the terrain and offering myriad opportunities for large and small missions in a highly articulated, photorealistic environment. One's initial companion or 'buddy' – a white steed, code-named 'D-Horse' – accompanies the character and helps to cover the ground faster than Snake can on foot. Players eventually unlock other buddies including the useful canine 'D-Dog', the mechanical bi-pedal transport device called 'D-Walker' and the bikini-clad, mute female assassin, Quiet. Given the time of the game's release, it bears mentioning that the much-criticized Quiet reads as both a blatant stereotype, and a dig against the mounting critique against retrograde female imagery in games (see Introduction).[15] Initially experimenting within the space, one can duck and cover, run, charge, dive, climb and use an array of weaponry, as well as engage in hand-to-hand combat. While an instructive voice-over suggests that it is up to the player to decide whether to handle missions with stealth or aggression, a combination of both will likely produce the best results. A player must take into account various natural and built elements, including identifying good places to hide or stash downed enemies, to observe the passage of time in terms of the most opportune moments to launch a mission, and to use the harsh weather – namely, sandstorms – as cover from the enemy. Snake's first mission is to recon intelligence ('intel') and then use it to rescue an old ally from Soviet-controlled Afghanistan. The mountainous landscape is craggy and harsh, with ruins dotting the landscape and brushy valley regions. One engages with the space from the third person with occasional first-person perspective when necessary for gameplay. The action is seen from a floating camera-eye perspective, mostly above and behind the player-character's figure. Particles of dust, droplets of water and Snake's blood when he is injured all gather on that window, providing the sense of being in an action *film* (a mediated experience) as opposed to being immersed in the action-adventure itself.[16] The aural components of the game confirm this, as one can hear a rustling noise that imitates wind resistance against a microphone, when running or on horseback, suggesting *mediated* sound. Each 'Episode' or mission has its own title sequence, another reference to cinema. The figure-ground relations are such that the playable character is usually fairly small and dead-centre in the image, which in filmic terms might convey a sense of entrapment or diminutive relation to the land. However, the practical function of this is that the player may see the character being controlled, as well as roughly 180 degrees of the surrounding space.

In Episode Three, entitled 'A Hero's Way', Snake's mission is to capture or eliminate a Soviet Spetsnaz Commander known for his brutal scorched-earth campaigns against guerrillas in the region, particularly the mujahideen. Once deployed, Snake must cover a great deal of ground in order to reach the zone in which his target may be found. The durational nature of traversing the space and the changing light across the environment provides indexical reference to the passing of time and a sense of distance. The land is immediately striking for its specific type of terrain: arid, brush-covered and severe. Using the advantages of the ruins dotting the area, the high ground for remote visual identification of foes, as well as the cover of night, this game configures the land strongly in terms of its use-value for the completion of objectives (see Figure 3.3). The space is, however, startlingly devoid of local people, eliminating the possibility of friendly fire or collateral

Figure 3.3 Snake surveils. *Metal Gear Solid V: The Phantom Pain* (2015) developed by Kojima Productions and published by Konami. Image courtesy of ©Konami Digital Entertainment.

damage. The land yields resources like medicinal plants and raw diamonds, but is just as easily a site of unexpected danger, such as animal attacks or passing Soviet trucks filled with enemy soldiers. Interior spaces similarly contain details that lend a certain texture and authenticity to a notion of militarized Afghanistan as represented in lived-world news media.

Scavenging leads to the discovery of useful intel, objects that can help reconstruct and fund home base, or 'Mother Base', a repurposed oilrig in the Seychelles (see Figure 3.4). This remote site, accessible by helicopter, presents a starkly different environment. A rig juts from an azure, oceanic horizon seemingly at a remove from any shore. It is as sun-drenched as Afghanistan in the day, but with a completely separate visual texture and spatial quality: it is Technicolor instead of beige, definitively industrial. The mega-construction (whose colour is initially orange, but ultimately customizable) is a stark contrast to the desert and, though militarized and severe, offers a welcome reprieve filled with comrades (the Diamond Dogs) who venerate Snake (as 'Big Boss'). Exploration of its spaces reveals all manner of useful supplies, as well as providing remote support and upgrades while in the field. The detail is painstaking, enlivened and offers great variety of possible interactions.

Figure 3.4 Mother Base. *Metal Gear Solid V: The Phantom Pain* (2015) developed by Kojima Productions and published by Konami. Image courtesy of ©Konami Digital Entertainment.

The various simulated landscapes of *The Phantom Pain* give the appearance of a more immersive or 'real' experience.[17] In relation to his discussion of another military-themed game, *Spec Ops: The Line*, Matthew Thomas Payne has indicated that this idea of the 'real' in games is a slippery proposition at best, because naturalistic imaging is falsely confused with authenticity and realism:

> Realism – understood as a set of claims about the world – is not necessarily synonymous with verisimilitude, or a media technology's ability to re-present worldly sights and sounds. And yet, the entertainment industry purposefully conflates the war game's ability to render photorealistic graphics and surround sound with broader notions of experiential realism.[18]

In this critique of militainment, Payne contends that the photorealism of the imagery and immersive aural elements of these games provide a formal fidelity, while often eliding larger and much more problematic realities of war that tend to be far less cinematic. *The Phantom Pain* lapses into moments of fantasy and horror so exaggerated as to be impossible to conflate with the 'real'. It evokes certain spaces, but does not replicate them. Its affective qualities of space, place and mood invoke an impersonal mechanical vision, even while it elaborately stages the irrational and psychological. While the game itself approaches photorealistic detail, it is important to differentiate its lack of fidelity to actual spaces as well as its hyperreality. Used by Jean Baudrillard, this term describes a sense in which the real itself is inaccessible, and can only be understood within a system of signs that reduplicate the real again and again until the object of the representation becomes lost and unattainable. What remains is simulation that staves off its own 'crisis of representation' by hysterically repeating itself.[19]

The experience of moving through *The Phantom Pain*'s Afghanistan is not faithful to the actual Afghanistan. But what concerns me here is how the highly mediated space of the game simulates particular ideas about a lived place, even while it traffics in ideology – and does so as an extension of power. For example, throughout the game, spaces are visually treated as uninhabited, except by occupying Soviet soldiers. That is to say, in the clusters of buildings and rundown maze-like villages, through which one engages in semi-urban warfare, the inference made by the nature of the space is that they no longer contain Afghanis engaged in their everyday lives. These sites have been taken over by the Soviets and are now outposts for the 'enemy'. This manoeuvre eliminates ugly complications that may arise from the presence of non-combatants, and displaces the sense that such military engagements routinely injure and kill civilians as a by-product. Although it is highly culturally loaded, the space is treated as politically non-particular. The excessive repetition of the game's episodes (mostly: creep into enemy territory, abduct a human asset, return to base) takes place in a site that has strong current US political and cultural resonance with national traumatic dimensions. The hysterical (i.e., panic-stricken and irrepressible) impulse toward re-enactment is not without critical significance, and is tied specifically to the landscape in which it occurs.

That *The Phantom Pain* is a Japanese product does not lessen the reality of its sophisticated address of American anxieties, and in fact it is interesting to consider the forms of critique taking place. What potential criticisms of US dominion over space may be built into a simulated scenario of Snake in his initial setting of 1980s Afghanistan? Snake is a normative white male rugged hero, an American-born private military contractor who operates beyond nation-states. He is set against a backdrop in which Soviets are constructed as adversaries and, as will become clear, his role would generally conform to a US-aligned position. *Metal Gear Solid* creator/director Kojima's self-described obsession with American movies is apparent in his video games, and is featured in his public facing profile on social media, such as his official Twitter page. During an interview at the Tribeca Games Festival in 2017, the director even described how Snake's iconic bandana is a reference to the one worn by Michael (played by Robert De Niro) in *The Deer Hunter* (dir. Michael Cimino, 1978). Other games like the *Grand Theft Auto* franchise (1997–), particularly beginning with *GTA III*, are known for the impressive open-world possibility and myriad ways in which to engage with space via land, sea or air. Though much of the popular outrage about *GTA* focuses on its representations of criminal activity, the actual game experience is largely one of sheer exploration and discovery. Not only does it impart an impactful sense of place, but the gameplay also demands that one learns the space well in order to progress through missions. But is important to remember that *GTA*'s jaded renderings of 'fictive' cities based upon actual ones (those stereotyped versions of places like Los Angeles, Miami and New York) are bitingly satirical interpretations, engineered by non-nationals. In the case of *GTA*, brothers Sam and Dan Houser who co-founded Rockstar Games are English with a core team originating in Scotland, and highly influenced by filmic representations of American crime stories.[20] Their numerous Rockstar Games offices are global. Many mainstream games like the *GTA* and *Metal Gear Solid* series overtly appeal to the representational logics of an American audience, likely due to the global popularity and cultural cache of American film. As a result, things like representations of a normative American male protagonist, situated in a fraught global site of political intensity for the US, then told from the perspective of a Japanese force in the global game industry, becomes extremely complicated.

Game Spaces and World-Building: Formalism

This is not to say that games are the same as films. Given the specificity of playable media, it is vital to account for characteristics of form, and how this may provide insight into games as highly constructed landscapes. Scholars of digital media in general, and game studies in particular, have engaged with notions of space from the moment the technology permitted even the most rudimentary spatial representations. Much of the early writing has been organized around defining what makes games formally distinctive from other media. Janet Murray, in her seminal *Hamlet on the Holodeck,* foregrounds the ability to render navigable space as a key asset of digital media.[21] New media scholar Lev Manovich has identified eminently traversable space as a 'key form' of new media.[22] In the same year as Manovich, games scholar Espen Aarseth declared: 'The defining element in computer games is spatiality. Computer games are essentially concerned with spatial representation and negotiation, and therefore a classification of computer games can be based on how they represent – or, perhaps, *implement* – space.'[23] Focusing on the three axes of action, time and space, Aarseth argues that the landscapes of games are highly unrealistic in the sense of how they conform to the lived world. Even the most 'open' of these generated landscapes are designed with play in mind, skewed in order to design a curated gameplay experience. Though nuanced readings of their works reveal differences in their approaches, it is certain that game space and its navigation constitute one of the elements that differentiate games from previous media forms.

Henry Jenkins has argued for 'an understanding of game designers less as storytellers and more as narrative architects'.[24] In his 'Game Design as Narrative Architecture', Jenkins describes game consoles as 'machines for generating compelling spaces'. In earlier writings he has even gone so far as to suggest that these simulated spaces compensate for disappearing lived-world territories of play.[25] Jenkins, in relation to the potential of games, points not to their ability to reproduce literature in playable form, but their evocation of pre-existing literary familiarity and visual literacy, as places where the mise-en-scène may be built up, and as sites for engaging with emergent narratives.[26] These spatial stories, Jenkins argues early on, 'are pushed forward by the character's movement across the map' and telling these stories well becomes about 'designing the geography of imaginary worlds, so that obstacles thwart and affordances facilitate the protagonist's forward movement towards resolution'.[27] The challenge, for him, is to create a balance between openness and structure so that the potentials of playable media are maximized, while retaining narrative coherence in the episodic presentation.

Several spatial formations must intersect within a video game in order for world-building to be successful. Michael Nitsche, in his book-length analysis, identifies five distinct 'planes' for approaching the subject of game space. These include the 'rule-based space' that sets the mathematically delimited parameters for what is possible in the space; the aural and visual presentation or 'mediated space' that is seen onscreen; the 'fictional space' or imagined comprehension of what is experienced; the 'play space' or interplay between the human and hardware; and finally the 'social space' which includes other players and observers in their direct or indirect engagement with the game.[28] As Nitsche argues, these in-game and extra-game elements work in concert to provide a whole experience, and a sense of presence in the immersive space.[29] While surveying a history of approaches to various dimensions of game spaces such as player reception, the notion of a 'magic circle' (which separates play from other everyday activity), and design of level architecture, Nitsche suggests that the confluence of these elements engenders an experience of game space:

> The better this world operates, the less the players have to understand the code logic underneath, which was so crucial for the knobs-and-dials system. A game world does not ask interactors to understand the internal computer processes and the mathematical logic of the code. Players do not have to translate the metaphors and the 3D game spaces back into their technical generation, but instead are asked to connect them to a consistent fictional world.[30]

The structure of the game's virtual space, Nitsche argues, affects how the player may engage with a space, and it also may inform the experience of their missions, and general interactions within it. One of the key identifications made regards the simulation of a camera, where there is in fact none. Arguing that the virtual camera mediates engagement with game space and therefore the building of the world depends upon it,[31] Nitsche writes:

> In order to shape this camera work, virtual cameras can mimic all of the mentioned real-camera behaviors in their presentation of a

video game space without any physical restraints. Paradoxically, this freedom of digital cameras can initially result in a shrinking of applied artistic practice. A virtual camera lacks the functional parts of a real camera apparatus that codefine [sic] cinematic language. There are no lenses, filters, shutters, no iris, or film stock in a virtual camera; the camera does not weigh anything and does not make any noise – yet all these elements are responsible for a range of cinematic effects and the development of cinema's form. Without these defining features, virtual cameras lack an important incentive for artistic development: the creative encounter with the limitations of the technology.[32]

This also applies to gamic landscapes, since the mimicking of 'camera work' always 'frames' and mediates the game, which suggests a meaningful affective experience. If we revisit the kinds of mediated 'seeing' that are possible in *The Phantom Pain*, for example, this directly relates to how the virtual camera images a particular moment in the visual representation of the game, which in turn connects to the presumption of a pre-existing visual literacy of film and television in the player/viewer. Specific camera angles may evoke particular known filmic and televisual genres, or

Figure 3.5 Observing from a distance. Snake in the foreground is blurred, while the focal point at a distance is sharp, emulating a conventional lens. *Metal Gear Solid V: The Phantom Pain* (2015) developed by Kojima Productions and published by Konami. Image courtesy of ©Konami Digital Entertainment.

Figure 3.6 Snake conducts an extraction. Notice the lens 'flare' aesthetic. *Metal Gear Solid V: The Phantom Pain* (2015) developed by Kojima Productions and published by Konami. Image courtesy of ©Konami Digital Entertainment.

expressive cues. For example, the simulation of lens-like depth-of-field renders objects within a focal point sharply, while other objects in the foreground or background are blurry (see Figure 3.5). Or, depending upon which direction Snake faces, and what time of day, bright light from the sun may enter the 'camera' and scatter, creating a simulated lens 'flare' – something that is not native to the form, but added for dramatic effect (see Figure 3.6). Additionally, elements such as directional sound and a sophisticated aural environment contribute to the rendering of a convincing sense of spatial experience. Non-diegetic sound like music may alert the player to pending danger, indicate that a combatant is near, or simply provide atmosphere or emotional affect. In other words, these elements in combination help to relate a sense of 'being there' or sustained presence within the environment.

The notion that the virtual 'camera' does not provide the context for a 'creative encounter with the limitations of the technology' is well taken, but with a caveat. The virtual camera sets the terms by which the visual access to the game is made possible, and it surely does not inherently possess the same aesthetic markers ('limitations' of film stock, lenses, filters, shutters, etc.) that a conventional camera apparatus does, and which does lend specificity to the visual image. However, digital media present their own limitations and aesthetic languages. These are defined by, for example, rendering capacities and numbers of polygons.

In an example like *The Phantom Pain*, which refers so directly to film, the virtual camera of the video game functions as an apparatus that organizes relations between the player/audience, the playable character, and the space. Theorization around the nature of these relations has some precedent in modern social theory. Particularly with respect to the technological image and its reproductions, philosopher Walter Benjamin has famously articulated the relations between actor, camera and audience in a recorded performance, such as in a film. 'The audience's identification with the actor,' Benjamin writes, 'is really an identification with the camera. Consequently the audience takes the position of the camera; its approach is that of testing.'[33] This notion of 'testing' is significant and refers to a correlation Benjamin makes between the actor and mechanical equipment like the film camera. In this relation, the film actor is increasingly tested in terms of their ability to translate their expressivity into a form legible to the camera, and transmissible through its organizing systems. He relates this to the increase in the testable in relation to the individual under extended economic conditions of capitalism. In this system, 'vocational aptitude tests' increasingly delimit the measure of the individual. 'The film shot and the vocational aptitude test are taken before a committee of experts. The camera director in the studio occupies a place identical with that of the examiner during aptitude tests.'[34] A game 'camera' or cinematics reconfigure this relation again so that the identification that the player/viewer may have with the playable character, is actually an identification with the computational. This is about calculation, processing and problem-solving, and encourages a framing of the landscape through this rationalizing lens.

In Episode Eight, 'Occupation Forces', one is asked to locate and eliminate a Colonel, then stop the deployment of his tank unit. Loaded with gear, Snake must stealthily move through a compound, gathering intel and incapacitating enemies. The land is steep and craggy, with the compound built into it. One's purpose is always the collection of resources in the form of intel, manpower and raw materials for use at Mother Base. In the process of completing missions like this, one accesses the heads-up display on the player's screen that allows for the marking of enemies and locations, commands, alternative screens that image relevant maps on the iDroid, menus of available weapons for selection, active weapon status, cross hairs for particular weapons, measures of relative distance and mission updates. This is just some of the information overlaid onto the in-game visual space. As with many military-style action stealth games, *The Phantom Pain* offers a tremendous amount of information that a player must constantly absorb and negotiate in order to succeed. In addition, players must continue to consider the development of the Mother Base and persistent management of its resources during their missions. Effective management results in additional resources in the field, such as the ability to conduct remote strikes on a marked target.

On the iDroid, layers of menus and sub-menus drive the management of one's resources. For example, in the management of Mother Base, one sees under that tab on the iDroid screen options: customize, development, resources, staff management, base facilities (for construction and expansion of the base) and a database. Choosing 'Base Facilities', a sub-menu appears with different aspects of the Mother Base Command Platform, which provides information for your combat units, R&D teams, the base development unit, support unit, intel team, medical team, waiting room, sickbay and a brig. Many of these can in turn be managed. In separate tabs, one can look at a map of the immediate gameplay territory or select from unlocked missions. The highly individuated levels of selection suggest extreme personalization and asset micromanagement to the point of absurdity.

The persistent aptitude tests configure a relation in which the player identifies with the computational. This becomes the 'culture' that engagement with the game imparts. Nitsche does discuss the function of games as culture, suggesting that, '[g]ames have become widespread cultural artifacts. As a result video game spaces increasingly become places of cultural practice and cultural significance.'[35] When he discusses this, he refers to how people engage with each other within the context of virtual communities. For him, games become places where culture is *enacted*: social spaces. This presents a more sociological or anthropological notion of 'culture' – one consistent with the study of 'game culture' as 'player culture' or the study of 'game communities'.[36] Within this framing, it would be likely that the most optimum object of study would be games that largely create scenarios and sites for sustained communal online engagement, such as multiplayer online games.

Nitsche's assertion is valid, but 'culture' has slippery meanings and in his case aligns more with the sociological than with visual culture studies (see Introduction). This chapter suggests that the complex representational practices, and underlying ideologies that may be revealed through the close consideration of games as visual culture, speak to the contexts in which they were made. As such, I am less interested in games as a place where people engage with each other in a mediated sphere for social interaction or community, than games as concentrated forms in which a given society finds its cultural expression through a politics of representation. But if we agree with Nitsche that games spaces are sites of cultural practice and cultural significance, it is necessary to take into account just how player experiences are enframed by those spaces.

Mark J.P. Wolf, who has written extensively on game worlds and how effective world-building occurs across many forms, contends that playable spaces themselves demand critical attention. Wolf's *Building Imaginary Worlds* connects the spaces of games to the development of other kinds of world-building, such as those that can be found in literature, table-top games, dollhouse play, building sets, role-playing games and the like, as well as text-based adventures and graphical adventure games.[37] He groups these disparate but, according to him, connected phenomena under what he calls the 'imaginary world tradition', suggesting that what players of games experience in the simulated spaces of playable media finds its precedence in thousands of years of human storytelling and play:

> The notion that 'things could have been otherwise than what they are' is the idea behind the philosophy of possible worlds, a branch of philosophy designed for problem-solving in formal semantics and, that considers possibilities, imaginary objects, their ontological status, and the relationship between fictional worlds and the actual world. Possible worlds theory places the 'actual world' at the center of the hierarchy of worlds, and 'possible worlds' around it, that are said to be 'accessible' to the actual world. These worlds are then used to formulate statements regarding possibility and necessity.[38]

our dominance over it. Once you've mastered a particular space, moved past its goalpost, you can reassume play at that point no matter the outcome of a particular round. These mechanisms help us to map our growing mastery over the game world, our conquest of its virtual real estate. Even in the absence of such a mechanism, increased understanding of the geography, biology, and physics of the different worlds makes it easy to return quickly to the same spot and move further into the frontier.[46]

The two scholars also discuss what they call 'warp zones' or secret ways to move from one portion of the game to another as a means of pushing out the territory of the game, of maps and tours that share various dimensions of the activated site for players, and the central importance of narratives in the legitimation of their claims to particular lands. This is consistent with many games today, though these observations were made in 1995. For example, in *The Phantom Pain*, one has several possible means of moving from one site to another via warp transport or 'fast travel', initially symbolized by a helicopter pick-up. Eventually, in a more creative and cheeky use of resources, one may use a large cardboard box to ship Snake between transport sites, allowing for fast travel between locations. Games scholar James Newman argues that for Fuller and Jenkins 'at least part of the pleasure of videogame play is derived from the transformation of the place to space, the eradication of the unknown and the bringing of uncertain geographies under the control and influence of the player.'[47] As Newman describes the connection between game space and travel narratives, the 'heart of these narratives [is] the transformation and mastery of geography – the colonization of space.'[48] Newman himself characterizes the progress through a particular game as quite often contiguous with progress through its world, and suggests that 'gameplay may not be seen as bounded in space, but also as a journey through it.'[49]

William Huber similarly connects the speed with which one moves through game space to a sense of domain over it:

> Velocity compresses the experience of place and creates the passing landscape, or spaces of transition. There can be affective shifts associated with moving through a space quickly through which one once moved slowly – even without conflict, a kind of mastery is produced, and the satisfaction of this telescoping

mobility is a significant element in the aesthetics of the play of these games.[50]

This connection between velocity and mastery also describes a historical precedent of the imperial drive toward expansion, embodied in the domestication of the frontier and the colonial impulse. The persistent notion of a predatory eye, the gathering of resources and global expansion resonates strongly with the procedural rhetorics of *The Phantom Pain*. As Fuller and Jenkins suggest, 'Cultures endlessly repeat narratives of their founding as a way of justifying their occupation of space.'[51] In relation to the troublesome site of Afghanistan for the United States, it serves as a logical site for enacting foundational stories of establishing the nation, within the logic of the game as a site without indigenous people, and as a space that is ideologically constructed to demand its own domestication. This is manifested in the very form of the game space which provides a site for repeating and perfecting precision engagements that unlock enhanced possibilities for play and access to expanded territories.

Comparatively few scholars address game space in relation to the cultures that inform them. In her writing on game space, Bernadette Flynn has discussed game experience as cultural practice and underscored the importance of looking at the aesthetics of navigation as constitutive of that cultural practice.[52] She questions the kinds of representational contexts that are created, what choices designers make, and how they choose to situate players within those spaces. She advances the notion of a particular kind of engagement with the space – picking up clues, strolling through the space, witnessing the built world – as consistent with a kind of flânerie, something she sees as more possible in games of discovery and puzzle-solving than those of high action. Flynn's writing highlights the significance of the space itself as constitutive of the experience of gameplay early on in game studies, as opposed to the foregrounded actions and plot points. In her writings, she challenges Jenkins particularly around his early focus on narrative as experienced through navigation of the game world, arguing instead that the spatiality of the game is distinctive from earlier forms, and contributes to an experience of 'play action' that outstrips earlier conventions around play, story or plot.

Arguably one of the most important documents to model a framework for studying games and culture is *Tomb Raiders and Space Invaders: Videogame Forms and Contexts*. In it, co-authors Geoff King and Tanya Krzywinska describe the functional use of varying degrees of utility, accessibility and comparative freedom of game worlds, depending upon technological limitations – but also what various types of gameplay necessitate. The scholars maintain that, 'the world of the game is often as much a protagonist, or even antagonist, as its inhabitants.'[53] They do not discuss the spaces of games in relation to the history and scholarship around 'landscape' as a highly constructed and mediated form of looking at a site. However, they do – like Fuller and Jenkins – connect the exploration of gamescapes with that of European colonial exploration, and its more contemporary connections to global capitalism. Among other things, King and Krzywinska argue that '[i]f the appeal of spatial exploration in games is closely connected with a continual search for avenues of fresh stimulation, this might also be strongly resonant with broader processes within capitalist/consumerist culture, which relies on the constant creation of new "desires" to be satisfied.'[54] It is very difficult not to see a similar engine for the stimulation of new desires in *The Phantom Pain*, in its core mechanic of persistent collection, which ranges from a kind of desperate scavenging to a plundering of any available raw and refined resources. While they connect what they call 'management' or 'strategy' games that utilize such elements in gameplay to titles like *Civilization* or *Sim City*, which simulate a god's-eye perspective and objective distance over a system, these characteristics are also found in aspects of games like *The Phantom Pain*. Indeed, a significant dimension of the game consists of the collection of human, animal, plant, mineral and other collateral resources that the player then allocates toward various objectives that mostly expand and enhance Mother Base (see Figure 3.6).

Framed in the third-person perspective, *The Phantom Pain* affords a specific viewpoint that encourages a particular set of relations to the land. King and Krzywinska deconstruct the mobilization of linear perspective and its connectedness to the player-character, in terms of the action of the game and the 'impression of a world that is centred on, and revolves around, the position of the player and/or the player-character.'[55] *The Phantom Pain* largely conforms to this perspective. The virtual camera generally floats behind and slightly above the player-character, and the space imaged is most frequently that which would be in front of the character. With Snake placed in the middle of a space organized around a Cartesian logic, the player that controls him operates within a highly curated manipulation of perspective. In a presentation on the relationship between the language of the garden and the space of nature in video games, scholar Eugénie Shinkle identifies how world-building in games is shaped to communicate and guide:

> Familiar and easily navigable, with a wide field of vision and a distinct foreground, middleground, and background, Cartesian space enhances the player's sense of presence by enabling them to situate themselves in space and understand the orientation of visual objects. Positive and negative space is used to create areas of depth and areas of blockage; players will tend to move straight ahead into areas of depth without too much prompting, with massed objects and paths directing their progress when necessary.[56]

This importantly identifies the design of the space respective to the tendencies of the player to respond to it in particular kinds of ways. But these cues, which are initially formal elements, give rise to more complex cultural logics. As Shinkle argues in the epigraph above, these are communicated through a discourse of landscape, in which the player becomes an actor.

> Like the perspectival foundation on which it is constructed, landscape representation is a paradigmatic form; a means of inscribing deeply-held cultural attitudes into an apparently neutral space of representation. Viewing a landscape is, of course, not a natural way of seeing, but a visual habit that transforms experience. And landscapes, in turn, are not simply representations of particular states of nature, but created contexts within which politics and ideology take shape. The discourse of landscape – its definition, its conventions, its history – authorizes a specific cultural vision of nature, and its political potency is, in part, a function of its ability to naturalize this vision, to conceal deeply rooted cultural sensibilities behind a screen of benign realism.[57]

She applies this logic to the landscapes of games, which in turn become spaces that borrow from the pre-existing discourse of landscape. Within these highly ideologically concentrated sites, which are often deceptively taken to be 'realistic' representations, players enact relations to the world. However, this 'screen of benign realism' that Shinkle identifies constricts the potential range of activities and engagements with space to relations like domination, penetration, goal-orientation and control.

As King and Krzywinska have pointed out, it is only possible to understand a game world in relation to the context of its non-game space.[58] Pre-video game theorists of play such as Johan Huizinga initially argued for the sanctity of play as occupying a 'magic circle' that separated the special activity from the normal world, its concerns and rules. However, this has been long contested.[59] In her essay 'There is No Magic Circle', Mia Consalvo challenged the usefulness of this formal approach for video games, illustrating the tremendous amount of seepage along the boundaries between territories of play and the lived world. In addition to her primary discussion of cheating in games as a paradigmatic example of how in-game players' behaviours might relate to their extra-game lives, Consalvo valorises the 'real lives, real commitments, expectations, hopes, and desires' of the real people who play games.[60] The work of King and Krzywinska, as well as Consalvo, constitutes a distinct intervention in games scholarship that gestures toward a critical cultural approach to games. Although their work unlocks potentials for games scholarship, this avenue of inquiry nonetheless deserves greater expansion to meet the increasing complexity of game representations and technological capacities.

Calling games a form of 'landscape representation that communicates ideas about how the world is and how it should be', geography scholar Michael W. Longan argues that simulated terrains mirror aspects of the lived world.[61] His represents one of few analyses of the relationship between landscape and game space and seeks to understand games as tools for learning about the lived world. He states that games potentially reveal the 'often hidden social processes behind the production of real world landscapes' – calling attention to the scholarship around landscape from a visual studies perspective that already understands landscape as ideological.[62] Longan argues that games contain deeply moral considerations embedded in the very instantiation of their landscapes and gestures towards the need to develop more sophisticated understandings of those representations.[63] Likewise, Miguel Sicart points out that computer games 'create game worlds with values at play'.[64] Players, he says, engage with these spaces, understanding that while they may cheat or test the system, they are mostly subject to its rules. These rules, he argues, generate a world suited to the goals of play.[65] There are ethics involved in rule-making, and of course the spaces that are generated would be, as Sicart characterizes them, 'ethically relevant' to analyze.[66]

While questions of form regarding building a better game space or convincingly rendering a game world are key to successful game development, games are also visual culture. Although separate from other media forms, they do call upon pre-existing literacies and traffic in more than the spectacularly technological. Development of some of the most sophisticated games in both the mainstream and alternative or 'indie' contexts display a nuanced relationship between the environment created and the affective relations to the player, between 'actual' world concerns and the 'in-game' space. Like King and Krzywinska, Consalvo, Longan and Sicart argue, this research underscores the entangled relations between the lived world and the game world. Truly, the rule-based worlds of games are landscapes that model value systems and ethical considerations, *not only on the level of action within the place, but within the place itself.* As a means to better understand landscape as a cultural construction rather than objective vision, and the embedding of value systems and rhetorical elements within manifestations of space in image-making practices, the next section explores landscape representation and cultural power from a visual studies perspective.

Theorizing Game Space as Ideological Landscape

In his essay on imperial landscape, W.J.T. Mitchell describes how representations of the land in Western imaging practices, as they emerged in the seventeenth century, were specifically connected to social engineering[67] around imperialist expansion into the West.[68] Calling upon a history of scholarship on the development of landscape painting and its penchant for particular kinds of representations, he asserts these images are always already 'secondary representations'.[69] That is, nature itself is mediated by cultural constructions around its meaning, before then undergoing a secondary transformation under the process of representation. Utilizing a history of scholarship around landscape representation, including the work of Jay Appleton, Ann Bermingham and Kenneth Clark, among others,[70] Mitchell asserts that landscapes are central to the construction of particular ideologies about the land, nation and social identities that shore up how cultural power functions.[71] Key to Mitchell's analysis is his understanding of 'place', 'space' and 'landscape', which he defines as a 'specific location', a 'practiced place', and a 'site encountered as an image or "sight"', respectively.[72] He attributes these definitions largely to the influence of Henri Lefebvre's concept of triangulation as a strategy against binary thinking about space and place, and sense of how landscape is constituted through mediation. And, he additionally appropriates concepts from Michel de Certeau, particularly his theorization of space as activated through various registers of engagement.[73] Like Mitchell, this chapter presumes the notion that these three concepts operate in tandem; as Mitchell puts it, they 'dictate a process of thinking space/place/landscape as a unified problem and a dialectical process'.[74]

Although Mitchell never specifically identifies games as a medium of expression, this notion of 'secondary representations' – as necessarily formulated cultural constructions by virtue of having re-mediated already mediated natural occurrences – applies particularly well to playable media. This is because of the nature of games as utterly constructed, both on the level that they literally 'simulate' a sense of space and place, and because they are the secondary manifestation of code, which is technical but also necessarily cultural.[75] I similarly assert that in relation to games, 'landscape is better understood as a medium of cultural expression', and that representations of that landscape (in this case, within games) reveal 'ways of seeing the landscape, *but as a representation of something that is already a representation in its own right* (emphasis added)'.[76] This is significant because, like Stuart Hall identified in his canonical essay, 'Encoding, Decoding', the messages within media have a 'complex structure in dominance' that reflect power relations at each stage in the production and consumption of the text.[77] Importantly, these messages may have an apparent sense of realism, but as Hall argues, this '[n]aturalism and "realism" – the apparent fidelity of the representation to the thing or concept represented – is the result, the effect, of a certain specific articulation of language on the "real." It is the result of a discursive practice.'[78] These codes, in other words, may be so universally accepted as to appear natural, but it is extremely important to understand that this is the by-product of the code having reproduced a largely unquestioned perception in the viewer (or in this case, player). In an absence of understanding how these many layers of meaning-making take place, through representation and secondary orders of representation (which drifts in orders of degree away from the thing in itself), the highly ideological images of games may become taken for granted as realism. Actually, they have already been mediated through multiple layers of cultural intervention at several points in their process of production. The visual power of so-called photographic realism in games may obscure this, and their technical frameworks may naturally invite formal approaches. However, it is vital to consider games as *at least* second order representational formulations.[79] This is one of the ways in which games are quite literally culture – that is to say, as I have argued elsewhere in this book, they are *necessarily formulated cultural constructions*. This is evidenced in their landscapes, and so it is possible to look to in-game landscapes themselves, for insight into the cultures in which they originate.

Of note as well is the 'practised' dimension of the place; that is to say, actions within virtually all playable media are repeated until perfected enough to proceed.[80] Most importantly, Mitchell ties the gaze upon the land, via Appleton, to 'the eye of a predator who scans the landscape as a strategic field, a network of prospects, refuges and hazards' – a mode of looking that is eerily concomitant with the opportunistic eye of the shrewd player.[81] These definitions and concepts provide useful means of thinking through a paradigmatic example of an immersive game space that presents itself as aesthetic, but that must be carefully observed and understood affectively in terms of what Mitchell calls the 'violence and evil written on the land, projected there by the gazing eye'.[82] Within *The Phantom Pain* itself, there are specific and elaborate ways of looking at the landscape; this activity is in fact exceedingly bureaucratic in its character. One can observe the enemy from a distance via in-game binoculars. Seeing them through this technologized vision (which is a doubling again of a view on a simulated space through the 'enhancement' of simulated binocular vision) permits the identification of enemy soldiers and then the marking of combatants with a red triangle. Once classified as enemies, soldiers with markers can always be seen and their distance from the player is noted numerically in metres. In short, they no longer possess the element of surprise, a key advantage for the player during engagement. Significant objects of interest are noted as well, and observation of the space often reveals additional intel through remote communications that will prompt a player about their mission and best strategy.

Within this scenario, observation carries with it a kind of dominion; it is opportunistic. Seeing, while no guarantor of success, maps territory, hostiles and key targets. Scavenging for intel may become as (or even more) important than the hunt for objects, and it begins to take on bureaucratic dimensions when elaborate schemas of collection of information and resources (like raw diamonds, processed materials, fuel, medicinal plants, specialists in bionics and translation) directly allows for Mother Base to be expanded and the main character's abilities to be enhanced. Gameplay even allows for micromanagement of Mother Base's resources and redistribution of individual recruits, per their special abilities. Under categorical types of engagement with Mother Base – such as development, resources, staff management, base facilities and database – a player enhances their functionality in the field through the strategic use of resources. Eventually, one's income to the base is enhanced through various indirect means, such as the establishment of a 'Merc Deployment Unit Function', which allows the player to dispatch mercenaries to other conflict zones for profit. Managing and allocating all these hoarded resources can begin to feel like work. This complex demand to multitask and simultaneously understand the game through various visual references (on the ground during active play; through the 'iDroid' screen that presents a map and multiple tabs and pull-down menus for the activation and administration of various resources; and the binocular view) presents a quintessential twenty-first-century multiplex management strategy. In their overview of how values are communicated through games, Mary Flanagan and Helen Nissenbaum effectively argue that even these seemingly neutral diagrams contain beliefs, moral positions and politics.[83] In relation to the simulated Afghan landscape, a map becomes a complex representation of potential objectives and notions of progress.

Looking is also done within the framework of a space/place/landscape that has overdetermined signification for the present-day US audience. *The Phantom Pain* is set in 1984, during the historical moment now known as the Soviet Union's 'Vietnam War' – named so because of the Red Army's unsuccessful ten-year attempted invasion of Afghanistan and the sense that this conflict contributed directly to the erosion of the Soviet Union's power.[84] During this clash, the Soviet Union engaged in a war against the mujahideen, guerrilla Afghan freedom fighters, sending upwards of roughly 118,000 Russian troops by the time in which the game takes place.[85] The United States, Saudi Arabia and Pakistan collaborated in the funding and training of the mujahideen, who were successful in forcing a Soviet retreat by 1989. Although there are some instances of chronological inconsistency within the game, it nonetheless contains specific references to key US interventions. For example, in one episode, Snake must recover a weapon called a 'Honey Bee' from hostile forces: a tactical ground-to-air missile launcher. The shape and size of the fictive weapon meaningfully resembles the actual hand held 'Stinger' anti-aircraft missile, which the United States is known to have provided to the mujahideen, and which were decisively effective against Soviet planes and helicopters.[86] In the wake of the actual conflict, the political and religious Taliban movement arose from within the mujahideen. While the audience for this game may know little of the specifics of the Soviet-Afghan War of 1979–89, the more recent 2001–14 US-led war in Afghanistan ('Operation Enduring Freedom – Afghanistan'), which came as a result of the World Trade Center attack on 11 September 2001, was an unprecedented mediatized event and remains a raw national trauma.[87] The choice of this particular historically laden 'playground' for the hero of this game certainly instils a potent affective quality that ties into a cultural imagination and national feeling about a particular place.

Mitchell conceives of the viewer of the land as a kind of predator. Setting aside the form of strategic looking that scans the landscape with binoculars in order to 'mark' enemies, there is a larger sense in which games encourage the address of the game space and all that is within it from the viewpoint of its prospective use-value for the player. It is an opportunistic and exploitative form of observation. This predatory viewing is not limited to military tactical shooters, since many forms of games demand strategies around the effective use of space. Mitchell, in relation to the history of Western landscape painting, connects this active predatory looking to imperial expansion. He describes a set of binary hierarchal relations between Western and non-Western aesthetics of landscapes. Among these is the notion that the non-Western native of the land does not see the land for its abundance and promising economic value. They are constructed as failing to 'exploit, develop, and "improve" the landscape' in such a manner that normalizes its rapacious appropriation by the West.[88] The genius of this position is that the construction of the land as underused (by the predatory, desiring eye) provides its own verification by virtue of what it sees. 'Landscape,' Mitchell concludes, 'thus serves as an aesthetic alibi for conquest, a way of naturalizing imperial expansion and even making it look disinterested in a Kantian sense.'[89] This sets up an interesting paradox, in fact, that runs the gamut between desiring or opportunistic looking and the naturalization of expansion as originating from a disinterested place.

In *The Phantom Pain*, the landscape as an already mediated site of the game further undergoes a second mediation of playable engagement, which allows the experience to come into being. The experience is activated in particular ways, and encourages seeing the landscape from a particular perspective. For example, during gameplay, one's relation to the game space is largely tied to the impulse toward collection. This is evidenced in a core game mechanic that uses a 'Fulton Recovery Device' – that is, a balloon apparatus to which one may harness collected assets like animals, objects and tranquilized enemies. Once attached, it quickly inflates and then spirits the 'package' back to Mother Base. One cannot set aside the cheekiness of seeing a befuddled, partially tranquilized enemy or wild animal dangling from the harness and then yelping with confusion as they are harmlessly yanked straight up into the sky and out of the frame. This has a startling visual effect, and with repetition, it conveys an offhand technological and physical mastery over a lesser prey. It makes light of Snake's dominion over anything he can collect (see Figure 3.7).

Figure 3.7 Snake activates Fulton Recovery Device. *Metal Gear Solid V: The Phantom Pain* (2015) developed by Kojima Productions and published by Konami. Image courtesy of ©Konami Digital Entertainment.

As a character, 'Snake' introduces a highly technologized and militaristic intervention onto the landscape of Afghanistan (and later, the Angola–Zaire border area): one that normalizes engagement with a space in a seemingly distanced or disinterested way.[90] That is, while there may be a desire for objectives to be completed, the onscreen emissary of the player possesses a certain nonchalance, a coolness, a dispassionate relation to the undertaking. Like many military games, the primary character is often relatively inexpressive, verbally or physically. With his back mostly turned to the player, facial expressions do not come into play; iconic masculine stoicism that typifies such representation compounds this. And, of course, as I have mentioned, the territory of the game is often mediated by in-game technologized vision enhancements of GPS mapping, binoculars or weapons scope – all of which foreground mechanized and, by implication, rationalized looking.

In addition to a view of the landscape that configures the looking as opportunistic, yet rationalized and disinterested, there is the matter of how landscapes are mobilized in the service of empire. Scholar of American studies Leo Marx famously explicates the power of the pastoral ideal during the discovery and colonization periods, and how it serves an

173

American theory of society.[91] Searching out the 'more elusive, intangible effects of change – its impact on the moral and aesthetic, emotional and sensory, aspects of experience', he turns to what may be found in the poetry and fiction of the time.[92] In his canonical work, *The Machine in the Garden: Technology and the Pastoral Ideal in America*, originally published in 1964, Marx exploits the ideology of the wilderness, specifically the desert, as an access point to foundational American constructions of landscape. He describes the curious dual image, which oscillates between an Edenic vision and hostile wilderness:

> To depict America as a garden is to express aspirations still considered utopian–aspirations toward abundance, leisure, freedom, and a greater harmony of existence.
>
> To describe America as a hideous wilderness, however, is to envisage it as another field for the exercise of power. This violent image expresses a need to mobilize energy, postpone immediate pleasures, and rehearse the perils and purposes of the community. Life in a garden is relaxed, quiet and sweet [...] but survival in a howling desert demands action, the unceasing manipulation and mastery of the forces of nature, including, of course, human nature. Colonies established in the desert require aggressive, intellectual, controlled and well-disciplined people.[93]

In the above, he refers to an Elizabethan-era (early 1600s) imagination of the New World, and its ideological condition of being in an uncivilized state. The notions of this space varied, as Marx well describes, from the garden to the wilderness. What is key here is that the land, as formulated into *landscape*, was in both cases envisioned as a progression toward a 'benign and ordered nature'.[94] That is, Marx shows how there was a cultural captivation with the New World as a land that would *become* the pastoral space of English ideals and utopian notions. However, he importantly notes that the pastoral and the primitive were often interchangeable in terms of how poets of the period envisioned the new continent.[95] In the cases where travellers encountered nature's rough treatment upon reaching the New World, they spun literary tales of a dangerous wilderness, filled with treachery and severity. Notions of America circulated between these two poles: the garden and the howling desert. This, Marx argued, marked two positions in relation to the land that one could more rightly describe as imagined worlds that were extensions of ideologies driving imperialist expansion. On the one hand was the notion of the Arcadian vision of plenty, an Edenic nature, which came along with the sense that humans' experience within it would be one of 'abundance, leisure, freedom, and a greater harmony of existence'.[96] On the other was the notion that Marx described above, of a space that demanded intellectualism, discipline, mastery, manipulation, aggression and self-sacrifice. To some degree, the embedded cultural imagination around severe landscapes, particularly in relation to the desert, is associated with these qualities of the West. But these were also political landscapes, designed to stimulate the collective imagination in such a manner as to encourage a particular cultural, political and economic push toward expansion.

As Marx himself readily admits, turning to fiction and poetry does not produce empirical results in terms of historical record – but it does tap into a certain *zeitgeist* and illuminate how its ideological needs and its cultural formations intersect.[97] Similarly, one might debate the intrinsic cultural value of mainstream video games, and conclude that even the better exemplars hold little, if any. Yet, in the affective experience of these games as cultural expressions, we may find similarly eloquent and telling expressions of nebulous drives and anxieties, and the formulation of a similar national push toward political, social, cultural and economic aims.

In this, *The Phantom Pain* provides a paradigmatic example of a natural environment-turned landscape. Figure/ground relations in this imagined space – in the first part of the game, specifically Northern Kabul, Afghanistan – surely differ from the conventional images of earlier expressive forms like poetry, fiction and painting of an imagined pastoral American land. In this procedural game world, the view and engagement is shifting, commanding a particular set of relations to the space. It is discursive, rather than fixed, but fundamentally structural in the sense that the 'image' still operates within the bounds of a constructed rule-based system (a game made of software) that is delimited, culturally contextual and necessarily ideological. Its playability as a media form renders it distinct from earlier forms of landscape. However, the landscape of *The Phantom Pain* similarly configures the space as overarchingly devoid of 'natives', and

Figure 3.8 Snake on D-Horse. *Metal Gear Solid V: The Phantom Pain* (2015) developed by Kojima Productions and published by Konami. Image courtesy of ©Konami Digital Entertainment.

instead illegitimately occupied by an invading Soviet force. And, it presents the Afghan landscape as a new wilderness space to be dominated and domesticated through aggressive, intellectual, controlled and well-disciplined manipulation (see Figure 3.8).

There is No Such Place: Afghanistan in *The Phantom Pain*

This comes to the matter of the persistent affective quality of the game (the moral and aesthetic, emotional and sensory dimensions of experience, of which Marx wrote) and its connection to the agitation of a particular kind of feeling about the place it purportedly represents. In respect to the portion of the game presented in the Northern Kabul region, the landscape is consistent with popular news imagery and films, which present a certain bracketed vision of the place as bombed out, arid and asynchronous with modernity. For example, the limited US news reportage from the conflict at the time suggested that without modern weaponry, Afghan freedom fighters are 'eighteenth-century [men] fighting a twentieth-century war.'[98] In another example, documentarians Hilda Bryant and Richard

176

Pauli describe the landscape of Afghanistan as 'mud holes of an ancient people pulverized by heavy Russian artillery'.[99] For the sake of agitating for anti-Communist intervention in the region, 'many reports showed the Afghans to be a mountain-dwelling, medieval, and tribal people facing a faceless military machine' in the form of the Soviet Union, with its superior technological force.[100] The formal aesthetic sensibility of the game, as has been described, mirrors the Afghan landscape of the American cultural imaginary: rocky, arid, brushy, unforgiving, sun-beaten and brutal from a sensorial perspective.

But for the sake of this discussion, most importantly, Afghanistan is configured *as in need of intervention*. Neda Atanasoski has discussed the strange transfiguration of Afghanistan in the American popular imagination in her research on humanitarian militarism, and its connection to postsocialist imperialism.[101] Particularly, the construction of 1980s Afghanistan as a site in need of humanitarian intervention has morphed from a sense that communism and inhumanity must be fought, into a post-9/11 ideology of rescuing innocents (especially women) from repressive fundamentalist Islam. In her essay on US media representations of the Soviet–Afghan War, Atanasoski writes:

> The contradiction between the messianic overtones of President Ronald Reagan's foreign policy promising a postsocialist future and the place of Islam and Muslims in that future came to a violent head after 9/11. Currently, the memory of U.S. military and humanitarian aid to the mujahideen has become an alibi for the perpetual military occupation of Afghanistan. The implication that humanitarian investments unaccompanied by U.S. military oversight fail to properly 'discipline' Islam frames the necessity for U. S. imperialism in the Middle East [...] Throughout the Reagan presidency, the Afghan freedom fighters were enfolded into a U.S. narrative of secular progress, which would bring about a free world, as well as into a messianic narrative of deliverance from Communist oppression [...] Yet because of the objectification of the mujahideen for the purposes of a U.S. global vision, after the fall of the Berlin Wall they themselves came to embody the totalitarian and oppressive evil once associated with Communist ideology.[102]

Atanasoski discusses how, despite an enforced Soviet media blackout that rendered the conflict largely a 'hidden war' from most of the press, those images and news reports that did enter into the US largely framed the American role as one of necessary moral intervention into a progressing communist imperialist expansion. And the blackout suggested a new 'heart of darkness' for a colonial imperialist power (the Soviets), a moral darkness that the United States might battle, in order to cover up its own stench of past imperial violence in Vietnam. Through humanitarian intervention against the Soviet Union's presence in Afghanistan, the US could publicly redeem itself by fighting against totalitarianism – even though, as Atanasoski well argues, the connectedness between US actions in Vietnam and the USSR's actions in Afghanistan were similarly imperialist. However, with the defeat of the Soviet Union in the region, the US ceased its militarized humanitarian aid, leaving a crippled war-torn country in turmoil. The rise of the Taliban occurred in the vacuum of this 'hollow ideal' of American humanitarianism.[103] In an impressive form of ideological acrobatics, the US transforms the guerrilla freedom fighters they once covertly backed into the enemies of freedom and democracy in the world.[104] Atanasoski ultimately contends that, paradoxically, the 'buried memory of the Soviet-Afghan War reaffirms US morality in the Middle East in the present.'[105]

Set upon this fraught theatre of war, the moral, aesthetic, emotional and sensory dimensions of gameplay in *The Phantom Pain* are overdetermined by this morass of complex relations. Whether or not an individual player is aware of the historical details, these affective elements nevertheless circulate in the cultural imaginary, manifesting themselves in popular films and other media imagery.[106] These contribute to a 'feeling' that connects both to the visual trigger of the imaged place and the traumatic weight of the September 11 attacks, which were attributed to Osama bin Laden and al-Qaeda. For it was Afghanistan toward which the US first directed its military arsenal, with the aim of invading in order to root out the Taliban, who was believed to have harboured al-Qaeda. The game's setting, then, is a landscape. It is a simulated and controlled version of something that is in itself mediated within the Western dominant image-making machine in order to signify in particular ways. Those significations, as I have described them, includes a complex fear/fascination with Afghanistan that has existed for 40 years, and which forms a flashpoint for affective engagement. This simulated landscape also constitutes a way of seeking to conceptually frame the space as a part of bracketing the historical and domesticating it into a particular understanding. On this subject, in relation to visual culture, Richard Dyer has written:

> The idea of a landscape, framed and perspectively [sic] organized, suggests a position from which to view the world, one that is distant and separate. Moreover, the very grasping and ordering of the land on canvas or in a photograph suggests a knowledge of it, bringing it under human control. Even the wildest, most dwarfing landscapes may also suggest Western man's heroic facing up to the elements or at any rate, in his apprehension of their sublimity, making him aware of his special perception of the divine.[107]

The contradiction is that this game simultaneously immerses a player by creating a durational, haptic experience of a landscape, even while the extreme framing and perspectival organization has a distancing effect from what one might call the thing-in-itself. It is a fantasy. Despite its apparent photorealism and historical contextualization, there is no such country, there are no such people.[108] This recalls the theorizing of Jean Baudrillard as well, who declared, to the ire of many, that 'the gulf war did not take place'.[109] With this statement, Baudrillard challenged the notion that the televisual representation of the first Gulf War, as a media event, in any way addressed the lived experience of the war. In its mediation into images, at the virtual speed of real-time reportage, the war became inaccessible, viewable only through the lens of 'mass-manipulative rhetoric'. Likewise, the landscape of *The Phantom Pain* with its experiential force might be thought of as a manifestation of the dreamlife of a culture, or as Mitchell indicated in the above epigraph, the '"dreamwork" of imperialism', which reveals at once the utopian vision of a 'perfected imperial prospect', while also trafficking in 'fractured images of unresolved ambivalence and unsuppressed resistance'.[110] From a visual studies perspective, the game's representation of Northern Kabul operates as an incredibly experiential, affective display of a particular world(view). It is real in the sense that innumerable hours can be spent there, in the space/place/landscape; nevertheless, it does not take place.

Conclusion: A Particular View of a Particular World

Video games that render land make claims about space, place and landscape. As the many forms of landscape that came before them, games are tools of power, and particularly in relation to lived spaces, may be thought of as connected to imperialist expansion. As 'practiced' forms of place, the spaces of games in which players move often tend toward a predatory vision of landscape, in the sense that the space is observed from a privileged position, and often assessed in an ongoing, activated manner for its use-value or exploitability for success within the rule-based system of play. In the case of the specific possible world of *The Phantom Pain*, the wilderness (the howling desert) of the game recalls in many ways literary and poetic precursors, which constructed North America in terms of a primitive space in need of domestication through aggressive and highly disciplinary means. This domestication process is repeated incessantly in the theatre of war, represented in episodic form. And in the case of the game's specific site of Afghanistan, the landscape is configured as in need of intervention. This is the extension of a historical rupture initiated by the US intervention in Afghanistan in the 1980s, and complicated by a fraught web of unintended consequences, including but not limited to 9/11. The game's representations are not a given, nor are they natural, but a complex calibration of rich significations within which it becomes possible to enact an array of relations to that history and its ambient effects.

This chapter is primarily concerned with landscape as a highly politically and culturally mobilized form of visual representation, and the ways it bears upon how we think about game spaces. These critical tools are extremely useful and draw attention to the primary role of culture in shaping the formal dimensions of landscape. The politics of identity of the dominant group (with the greatest power to represent their subjectivities) addresses its concerns through the medium of video games to its audience. Game worlds encourage ways of thinking about particular spaces, and while they do not entirely dictate our understandings, they can be persuasive, particularly when they aspire to 'realism'. Game spaces, like landscapes, are highly formulated cultural constructions. They are practiced through action, which is necessary for movement through and engagement with games. Film theorist Dudley Andrew once said that,

> Worlds are comprehensive systems which comprise all elements that fit together within the same horizon, including elements that are before our eyes in the foreground of experience, and those which sit vaguely on the horizon forming a background. These elements consist of objects, feelings, associations, and ideas in a grand mix so rich that only the term 'world' seems large enough to encompass it.[111]

As in film, the world-building of video games consists of a framing that constitutes itself as representing that which can be seen within it, *in relation to what is presumed to persistently exist beyond it*. There is a sense that what cannot be seen nevertheless exists, and lives in a totality beyond the frame of the playable image.

In the case of *The Phantom Pain* as one of many potential examples, the complex engagement with a troubling, fraught history of the US with Afghanistan forms the affective and literal 'ground' upon which the game is built and enacted. The space is configured as bureaucratic, and seen through the violent predatory gaze, which reconfigures the land as something to be exploited and disciplined by Snake and his well-oiled Diamond Dogs (see Figure 3.9). Notions of progress toward goals in the game are linked to seeing, mapping, claiming and managing. It is impossible to fully understand the game decontextualized from its moment of coming into being. Given that landscape has been shown to legitimize conquest, the predatory gaze directed toward a game world for the purposes of better exploiting its puzzle-solving potentials comes as no surprise. Ideological needs and cultural formations intersect in mainstream games, which seem to convey much more about our desires, than their lived-world counterparts. In the end, whether players are specifically aware of cultural references made, the

Figure 3.9 Snake aka Big Boss and the Diamond Dogs. *Metal Gear Solid V: The Phantom Pain* (2015) developed by Kojima Productions and published by Konami. Image courtesy of ©Konami Digital Entertainment.

game world still works on players in terms of their affective engagement with the space. It behoves game designers to fully understand the nuanced cultural references they invoke, as well as the reality that space is more than an immersive setting. It is also constitutive of the value systems set forth, and delimits possible worlds. Likewise, critically activated game players will likely demand more of game worlds than the incessant repetition of narratives of conquest, and logics of bureaucracy.

4

The World is a Ghetto: Imaging the Global Metropolis in Playable Representation

I have increasingly come to believe that our understanding of the city cannot be viewed independently of the cinematic experience. [Jean] Baudrillard's much-quoted notion of starting from the screen and moving to the city accepts a duality between the real city and the reel city that no longer exists. I propose instead that to understand this relationship better, we should start not from one and move to the other, but engage with both simultaneously. In what Baudrillard calls the 'collapse of metaphor...the obscenity of obviousness...our chasms of affectation,' culture keeps imitating and duplicating itself in a delirious self-referentiality. In a pervasive game of mirrors reflecting each other, art imitates life, life imitates art, art imitates art, life imitates life.[1]

Nezar AlSayyad, *Cinematic Urbanism*

Introduction: Speculative Futures, Genre and the Global Metropolis

In his *Cinematic Urbanism: A History of the Modern from Reel to Real*, urban historian Nezar AlSayyad describes a challenge he set forth to his students: 'Imagine if there was no real New York or real Los Angeles or no trace left of them and the only thing we have are films that depict them or use them as a backdrop for their cinematic story. What kind of history would we write?'[2] This chapter continues a close consideration of game space, focusing on visual representations of the megacity as a global node, with its extreme economic inequities and playable dystopian environments. Like AlSayyad, I ask: if all we had were gamic representations of the global city, how would those cities be described, and what would those simulated places tell us?

This chapter compares two games, chosen for their melancholic fixation with memory and forgetting within a larger narrative of urban dystopia. *Max Payne 3* (2012) is a mainstream blockbuster from Rockstar Games, a multinational game developer and publisher most known for titles such as *Grand Theft Auto*, *Midnight Club*, *Red Dead*, *Manhunt* and *L.A. Noire*. *Max Payne 3* transplants a quintessentially American hardboiled police detective from grimy, rainy New York City to the sunny international locale of São Paolo, Brazil. Released almost nine years after *Max Payne 2*, the game continues the saga of the titular protagonist and his perpetual attempts to forget the tormented memories of his dark past. *Remember Me* (2013) is a sci-fi action-adventure game in the third person by DONTNOD Entertainment, a French video game developer, and published by Capcom. In a futuristic 'Neo-Paris,' the primary playable character, Nilin, is an elite memory hunter who possesses the power to access and strategically manipulate the memories of others. After her own memory is brutally erased, the racially mixed, cyberpunk heroine navigates a dystopic scenario in which the commodification of memory has led to inequity and dehumanization. Over the course of gameplay she recovers her own past and rare skill set. In a smart-technology future in which encoded, commoditized and exchanged memories are big business, Nilin must navigate a hostile and carceral world in which the new 'memory economy' has given rise to an extreme surveillance society.[3] Unlike *Max Payne 3*, *Remember Me* is notably not part of a franchise, although it would still solidly be characterized as a mainstream video game in terms of its budget, large production team and distribution.

Both games are highly cinematic and draw upon pre-existing visual literacies from Hollywood genre films. In the case of *Max Payne 3*, the game presents a playable hardboiled detective narrative. *Remember Me* offers a futuristic, cyberpunk sci-fi scenario. These games also provide iconic representations of the global condition, through two visualizations whose poetics specifically address the megacity, violence and memory from differing approaches. Since the two titles rely so much on filmic tropes, the unique intervention of cinematic urbanism – theorization of the urban condition as imaged in film – is key. Imaging of the global metropolis, within the context of larger socio-cultural anxieties around urban sprawl, overpopulation, placelessness and the rise of non-Western nodes in the global network, looms heavily in these games. The scholarship of film theorists Nezar AlSayyad, David B. Clarke and others ground this analysis in the visual and critical studies approach modelled throughout this book. To fully understand the powerful stories told about global cities, these critical tools provide fresh insight into the mirror-like interplay between playable urban representations and increasingly globalized life.

Each of these games is a formulated cultural construction, intended to appear 'realistic' in its representations in terms of pictorial naturalism. *Remember Me* is overtly a form of speculative fiction; one could argue that *Max Payne 3* represents a kind of science fiction as well. After all, the core mechanic of 'Bullet Time', by which a player can slow action and trace a bullet along its path through time and space, constitutes a kind of superpower. Through these two games, this chapter suggests that these simulated and controlled versions of already highly mediated forms of Western image-making betray particular kinds of relations, most notably in regard to a postmodern subject under the duress of globalization. Finally, this chapter considers the respective 'heroes' or primary playable protagonists within each game. In the case of *Remember Me*, I look at the ethnically ambiguous figure as a cypher for the global entity – specifically the female, technologically augmented and ethnically mixed Nilin, whose memory has been wiped. Nilin, who desperately seeks to recuperate her memory, is contrasted against Max Payne, the titular character who suffers profound alienation and decontextualization. This is marked by his perpetual attempts to blot out his traumatic memories using alcohol, pills and violence-induced adrenaline. In a larger sense, this chapter addresses the dual-edged anxiety of the non-Western world configured as mega-ghetto and the disorientating effects of global capitalist flows, which manifest themselves through the mobilization of metaphors around amnesia or forgetting.

A note about game genre is in order. In her essay on the relationship between geopolitics and games, Rachel Hughes considers the interrelations between the two, and importantly, the 'historical intimacy between commercial and state interests in the computation and simulation of conflict', as well as the mobilization of particular geopolitical viewpoints within particular genres.[4] 'Consciously or otherwise,' Hughes writes, 'genre is as integral to the meaning-making of political strategists and military generals as it is to game designers and players of digital games.'[5] Hughes describes the 'looking-moving-feeling' of the military genre of action games as engendering ' "anticipatory looking" (and rapid response) [which] arguably matters more than the player's game strategy, experience-level and dexterity in manoeuvring their avatar through the gameworld.'[6] This 'generic resonance between geopolitics and gaming' or 'game world geopolitics', as she terms it, is significant because her research pointedly draws into consideration the importance of genre in relation to geopolitical representational practices within simulations, and how they may impact lived world attitudes.[7] And, more significantly, this reframes the discussion of games and their impacts away from the moral panics around their influences as, for example, murder simulators, and more productively toward how, 'rather than understanding games as ideologically driven attempts to mirror the world, gaming ought to be understood as a type of practice that participates in the world.'[8] Considering genre as a form of typified affect, actions and givens, Hughes says genre is 'future-orientated' in that it initiates a certain sense of expectations around certain games that conform to them, and it also impacts the experience of gameplay itself.[9] Hughes writes:

> Generic games are thus doubly anticipatory: while genre itself allows for anticipation, the game as simulation […] is not a reflective experience but an anticipatory one, demanding extensive temporal immersion and experimentation. Contemporary geopolitics, in its intensified engagement with simulation, also participates in this doubly anticipatory field. As in games, generic 'effects of reality and truth' in the writing and practice

of global space come with expectations about forms of conduct, character sets and affective experiences. Such expectations are critical to the legitimacy and futures of particular global actions and administrations.[10]

Despite the superficial divergence in the use of terms around mirroring set forth by AlSayyad and the above suggestion made by Hughes that games do not merely 'mirror the world', both of these positions suggest that their respective media in question do more than illustrate, but are in dynamic relation with, or in other words participate with the lived world.

Both of the games in question conform to genre expectations: *Remember Me* models a dystopic science fiction scenario and *Max Payne 3* adopts the neo-noir detective narrative. Their respective genre conventions participate in a future-orientated form of world-building through their use of stylistic devices that signal a certain set of truths, norms and affective capacities. This is tied to the sense of space associated with each respective genre. As I have mentioned, a large part of this analysis contains a consideration of backdrop, in the case of *Max Payne 3* the city spaces of a present-day São Paolo, and for *Remember Me* a near-future Paris, rebuilt after a devastating twenty-first-century European war. In both cases, particular game mechanics and scenarios are tied to their respective character's memory and forgetting. These are also inflected by site-specificity, such that a genre-informed sense of place and narrative combine with fearful depictions of potential global futures in telling and generative ways.

Like the 'game of mirrors' between the reel city and real city described by AlSayyad, the imaging of the metropolis within video games can be thought of as not merely fixed representations that illustrate a particular ideological bent, but something much more dynamic and engaged with the actual world. These imagined cities, while surely not singularly responsible for the world as it is, or as it will be, provide insight into lived world fears by modelling a microcosm of anticipated conditions – affective fictions that are critical to our capacities to imagine potential geopolitical futures.

AlSayyad's work adopts an intersectional approach, radically bringing together the study of urban space and cinema studies. Although his research does not specifically focus on video games, his theories of cinematic urbanism are methodologically useful in the consideration of the construction of playable urban space, especially when it appropriates cinematic aesthetics. Particularly germane is his assertion that the 'distinction between what is real in the everyday, and how we imagine the everyday' is becoming porous.[11] If we think of this in relation to the procedural rhetoric of the city as imaged in games, a complex and telling picture emerges. Likewise, Barbara Mennel similarly notes how the cinematic city has been key to understanding the tectonic shifts from modernity to postmodernity, as well as national to globalized contexts.[12] 'Global cities,' she writes, 'provide settings for narratives about migration, but the cinematic representation of global cities also offers new global versions of older tropes associated with the city, such as alienation, now reflected in the representation of tourists, business travelers, and the displacement of migrants within global networks.'[13] As such, playable representations provide an equally insightful look into core concerns around the global city. The dystopias generated in *Max Payne 3* and *Remember Me*, as it will become clear, channel socio-political anxieties around globalization, placelesness, memory and the postmodern megacity.

Max Payne 3: Noir Figure, Exotic Ground

The original *Max Payne* was released for consoles and PC in 2001, with its sequel *Max Payne 2: The Fall of Max Payne* released in 2003, both developed by the Finnish company Remedy Entertainment. With their brooding score and noir-inspired voiceover, the series features a hardboiled anti-hero with rage issues, a shattered sense of idealism and little left to lose. Max, complete with black trench coat and inner demons, has suffered both tragedy and professional dishonour, most notably through the murders of his wife and infant daughter, for which he was initially framed. The first two games make strong aesthetic reference to graphic novels. They often feature still or minimally animated cutscenes that contain elements like still images, framed panels and text. A classic crime noir narrative voiceover accompanies these interludes. Its dismal iteration of a violent New York, with its seemingly perpetual gloom and rain, dingy tenements and drug nests, make for a highly atmospheric sense of place (see Figure 4.1). The overall game aesthetics clearly evoke both print-based and cinematic references intended to be legible to a player as operating

Figure 4.1 Max in his noir element. *Max Payne 3* (2012) developed by Rockstar Studios and published by Rockstar Games. Image by Rockstar Games and ©Take-Two Interactive Software, Inc.

within a visual culture of films. Like David Fincher's neo-noir detective thriller *Seven* (1995) and Michael Mann's *Manhunter* (1986), *Max Payne 3* images a battle-weary and emotionally compromised figure struggling against formidable malevolence. The original *Max Payne* also introduces a key core mechanic of 'Bullet Time', which effectively allows the playable character to observe the movement of bullets in slow-motion, in a kind of intense focus that enables enhanced targeting and the spectacular imaging of the in-game camera as it follows the bullet's path from its chamber to its bloody kill-shot. In addition, the game allows for a 'Shoot Dodge' movement through which players can – like true action heroes – acrobatically hurl their characters through the environment to evade gunfire. At the moment of its release, this particular feature of the original game would have been readily associated with several prominent cinematic references, most notably the films of John Woo, such as *A Better Tomorrow* (1986) and *Hard Boiled* (1992), and the Wachowski siblings' iconic *The Matrix* (1999).

In *Max Payne 3*, an infinitely more jaded and traumatized Max greets the player. No longer a member of the police force, he now finds himself in São Paolo, hired as security detail to a wealthy Brazilian family headed by the real-estate mogul Rodrigo Branco. Max is markedly older. In his rumpled suit, thicker and more fatigued by the world than in previous games, he is no less a magnet for violence. When Branco's trophy-wife (Fabiana) is abducted, Max quickly finds himself out of his element, and up against favela gangs, covert police forces and crime scenarios beyond even this hardened ex-cop's comprehension. The killing is designed to be grim, cinematically spectacular and frequent. As one character tells Max, 'You're in the jungle now'.[14] This is suggestive of a kind of 'heart of darkness' or an otherwise wild territory beyond the civilized, where one encounters the savage and hostile. Max appropriately undergoes drastic changes in keeping with his new scenario. By the time the action heats up, he's shaved his head – perhaps a nod to Marlon Brando's depraved 'Kurtz' figure from *Apocalypse Now* – and he's clad in a garish Hawaiian-shirt disguise that is incongruously cheerful, considering that he is slaughtering his way through the favela.

The Bullet Time and Shoot Dodge effects are enhanced, making for what one reviewer described as an exhausting experience of 'brutal and unapologetic' violence.[15] Capturing the action-packed spectacle of its mechanics, critic Evan Narcisse writes of the game's cinematic allure:

> The kills you can pull off in MP3 [*Max Payne 3*] feel beautifully choreographed, especially when you pause the game mid-game and spin the camera around to take everything in. There's an odd tension at the core of *Max Payne 3*'s gameplay. It holds a cover mechanic nested inside a system that dares – hell, encourages – you to be reckless. If you gamble poorly and are at death's door, you can use your last bit of energy in a Last Man Standing slo-mo sequence to take out an enemy and limp away to keep on fighting. None of this creates any kind of dissonance. Instead, it feels in line with the character. 'Throw caution to the wind and then, in those moments, that's where you find your reward,' it whispers to you.[16]

At the time of the game's release, the Bullet Time and Shoot Dodge effects were highly lauded by critics for their refinement, elegance and visual impressiveness, although they were not new to the franchise.[17] The almost balletic action sequences are surely gratifying. The game is not designed to be truly open-world, so there is very little roaming encouraged; still, the spaces are highly detailed, with disturbable objects and environments that contribute to an overall convincing sense of world-making. Here, the aesthetics of the graphic novel have given way to more modern-looking scan lines, glossiness, saturated colour and intermittent double-vision. It recalls director Tony Scott's *Man on Fire* (2004), which tells the story of an alcoholic ex-CIA mercenary hired to protect a privileged young girl in Mexico City, and several titles popularizing favela drama and action, such as Brazilian crime films including Fernando Meirelles and Kátia Lund's *City of God* (2002), and José Padilha's *Elite Squad* (2007). In fact, the latter example is highlighted on the official game website and cited as a direct influence.[18]

Critically, the unlikely noir setting of São Paolo was generally well received at the time of the game's release. One notable critic called *Max Payne 3*, 'one of the finest executions of *game noir* to date'.[19] Another dubbed it 'a masterpiece of underworld carnality, depravity and violence'.[20] These loaded descriptors contain a distinct racial dimension that points to the ways that the West ideologically constructs Brazil – and particularly *favelas* within key cities like Rio de Janeiro and São Paolo. There are several dimensions to the 'carnality' and 'depravity' presented within the game that become significant, which are prominently foregrounded through key elements such as the playable character's qualities, story elements and the game space itself.

According to Dan Houser, the co-founder, vice president and head writer for Rockstar Games, the theme of addiction drove aesthetic decisions, including the notable departure from the graphic novel, as well as Max's extreme disorientation within a foreign setting. Houser told *Polygon*:

> From a narrative standpoint, (addiction) is entirely central to the game – the story depends on it, and it is built into the story, and the entire flow of the game is built around it [...] From a visual design perspective, we wanted the visual effects to give the impression of a blurred somewhat hazy look that would give a sense of someone stoned on booze and heavy painkillers.[21]

Certainly, the bright and colourful iteration of São Paolo the game initially presents is as dislocating for the fan of the conventional *Max Payne* series as it is for the titular character himself. This is due both to Max's drastic physical transformation from a lean, young detective to a paunchy, hardened middle-aged burnout, and the jettisoning of the classic noir cityscape that so defines the genre. While previous games represented Max as dulling his physical and psychological aches with pills, the older character presented here is bloated and highly addicted to both painkillers and alcohol. He is, in short, a functional alcoholic while on-duty, and falling-down drunk while off. As Houser explicated further, Max's addiction included a pursuit of adrenaline kicks and violence, something that would be conveyed through the spectacular cinematic thrill of stylized action:

> We wanted Max's hazy drunken perspective to also feel vaguely similar to when he is in Bullet Time, as if Bullet Time, which is when he is at his best and almost super human, is also something of an addiction to him – like the moment when he feels most himself […] is playing the game (and the previous games) that has, to some extent put him in this state.[22]

Critic Keith Stuart of the *Guardian*, contesting this as a character inconsistency, outlined a ludonarrative dissonance within the game, caused by the friction of a seemingly self-revulsive and self-destructive Max, who despises himself for his violent past, but who springs wholeheartedly into killing sprees: 'Max is filled with doubt and self-loathing and yet his in-game actions – at least as far as the flow of the story is concerned – are resolute and deadly.'[23] This friction is surely noted; yet it seems possible to rationalize the character's actions through that thematic through-line of addiction. With his compulsion for the rush of violence, Max pursues it as ardently as his next bottle of pills. It focuses him and forces him into the moment – and away from the tormenting thoughts of the past. In keeping with his traumas around his inability to ultimately protect his wife and child, perhaps Max is forever stuck in a pattern of trying to save them, again and again, hopelessly, through his melancholic repetition of the defence of others.

More compelling is the connectedness between the playable character's addiction, and his inability to forget. Max seeks a relief from these pains, which he attains temporarily through his blackout drunkenness and pill-popping, as well as throwing himself into the fray when presented the opportunity. Intermittent representations of the protagonist at home alone foreground this immediately: binge drinking, downing painkillers, stumbling about, and out of control. Perhaps suicidal, or merely self-flagellating, Max is surely at his bottom, which stems from his inability to assimilate the past into something he can manage. In short, he is a tragic figure because he is so completely trapped in the past that he is unable to thrive in the present. The scenario presented is also one of extreme alienation from place. This troubled figure moves in a mode so disconnected from the space around him that it produces the effect of a playable São Paolo as utterly fictive, and estranged from the actual place in itself, though it may bear aesthetic or affective resemblance in the game. The mazelike, perilous iteration of the favelas only heightens this sense of dislocation. His melancholic self-destructiveness reads as particularly heightened and ideologically fraught in relation to the specific and elaborate urban and racialized scenario in which Max has been inserted. Given Rockstar's reputation for iconoclastic, satirical and critique-oriented scenarios in other titles such as the *Grand Theft Auto* series and *Red Dead Redemption*, one can only assume that the decision to uproot Max from New York is a calculated risk, given the success of the original *Max Payne* and its sequel.

The question naturally arises: Why dislocate Max? What does it mean to contextualize this classic character type within a new site? Whatever the developer's intentions around reimagining the franchise, this move effectively takes the noir detective figure, which is a construction fundamentally borne of anxiety around modernity and the city, and places him in a new condition that invokes postmodernity and the global through the megacity with its circulation of bodies in a transnational flow, stark ethnic and class-based fragmentation, militarized protection of privileged districts, large numbers of dispossessed, compression of time and vertical architectural hierarchy of classes (see Figure 4.2). This is potently illustrated in the beginning of the game, in a cut-scene in which Max is on-duty at a swanky event for his employers. The high-rise penthouse overlooks a seemingly endless, dingy favela, blanketed in a layer of pollution. Max makes a snide remark to his partner (Passos) about how there's 'nothing like the view of extreme poverty to make a penthouse cocktail party really swing', highlighting

193

Figure 4.2 Max decontextualized in Brazil. *Max Payne 3* (2012) developed by Rockstar Studios and published by Rockstar Games ©Take-Two Interactive Software, Inc. Screen shot by author.

the backdrop of social and economic disparity (see Figure 4.3).[24] No less ironic, the party is a benefit – 'something for the kids' it is explained – but apparently an excuse for the elite to network and debauch. In his decontextualization, and his obviousness as a Caucasian American ex-cop out of his element in a South American metropolis, Max immediately assumes the racialized positioning of a whiteness that is imperilled, ambivalent and compromised.[25] The dislocation of his own noir context recasts Max as minority and outsider.

In one telling scenario, Max disguises himself as a tourist by shaving his head and donning a Hawaiian shirt and sunglasses, with the reckless plan to enter the 'Nova Esperança Favela'[26] alone in pursuit of the abducted woman (Fabiana) for whom he was responsible.[27] Brazilian drums beat as players are allowed to explore the favela from within for the first time. Max is quickly greeted by the phantasmal images of poverty, narrow dilapidated alleyways and bombed-out looking cement-block neighbourhoods, skittish locals, children playing soccer, Brazilian rap music, half-naked women gyrating at a street party, and gang-members with automatic weapons – then he's mugged at gunpoint. As he wanders the favela, contemplating

Figure 4.3 Max overlooks the favela from a penthouse party. *Max Payne 3* (2012) developed by Rockstar Studios and published by Rockstar Games ©Take-Two Interactive Software, Inc. Screen shot by author.

his poor decision-making skills and his 'latest midlife crisis', he finds more trouble with the gangs and must shoot his way to the top of the hill, where Fabiana is being held. The ongoing internal monologue Max engages in, which players hear through voiceover, narrates his self-loathing and the various reasons that those around him would legitimately show him hostility as an American, 'tourist' and mercenary bodyguard to the rich people who ignore their plight. He describes their economic dispossession, with statements about how kicking a ball (professional soccer) is one of their only ways out of the favela. In typical Rockstar fashion, the visual representation of 'ghettourism' suggests one set of stereotypes about the 'jungle' into which Max has entered, while the superimposed voiceover provides a contradictory framing message that suggests satirical self-critique within the game.[28]

Before long, Max is up to his old tricks, executing hordes of attacking gang members in a frenzy of urban warfare. There is no possibility of negotiation or evasion, just efficient, and thrillingly cinematic killing. But as you clear building after building, and the bodies pile up, you begin to wonder whether it's a fair trade: Fabiana's life for so many anonymous dead. The fact that Max kills so many people is never truly rhetorically questioned within the scope of the game itself. The core mechanics of Bullet Time and Shoot Dodge tend to discourage stealth and diplomacy and encourage, wherever possible, magnificently shooting your foe in the face.

One critic responded to the potential minefield of placing a white male action archetype within this unlikely setting for the franchise by suggesting that the moral quandaries were mitigated by a lack of civilian casualties:

> Somehow, and this is quite a trick, *Max Payne 3* doesn't feel like it's exploiting the setting. There's a respect, a reverence there, or at least that's the sense I got. Maybe it's because amidst all of the spectacular carnage, the Schwarzenegger-meets-Michael Mann gun battles raging through the favelas and night clubs and abandoned pleasure palaces of Rockstar's enormous São Paolo, civilians are never your target, even by accident. As dirty as *Max Payne 3* gets, there's no glorified murder of innocent bystanders allowed.[29]

Another critic, Daniel Krupa of *IGN*, writes of the tension between the graphic violence depicted within the game, and the milieu in which it unfolds:

> it focuses on some of its most visceral manifestations – ragged bullet wounds, charred flesh, dismembered limbs – but it also peers into the unseen causes that lie behind such acts of violence. It touches on the disparity between rich and poor, and how resentment and desperation can fester in the slums and the penthouses alike. This isn't only tackled in the main story, but also in nice scraps of incidental narrative recovered in clues dotted about the meticulously-crafted environments.[30]

True, there is some gesture toward the issue of race in the game's narrative as it intersects with violence and inequity; however, within the game mechanics it is mostly sidestepped. Commentary such as the two above mostly feel like rationalizations. The highly problematic optics of guiding Max through a hellish vision of the favela, and through corrupted urban spaces, are immediately clear. During gameplay, the narrative complexity is often reduced to the slow-motion kill shots of extremely impressively rendered, but ultimately anonymous, non-white men. This dynamic between a white male protagonist and attacking gangs of mostly black and brown men is so stark as to appear odd and anachronistic – particularly in terms of the way it is unproblematized within the game – a move that is uncharacteristic for the Rockstar brand.[31]

While the game trades on the cultural cache of *City of God* and *Elite Squad*, which are Brazilian films about the favelas that crossed over into mainstream US markets, the game differs greatly in tone and nuance from the original filmic references.[32] The appropriation of their settings, without the humanizing narratives of struggle and overcoming, reduce the place to a dangerous and exotic locale – a backdrop for a white male protagonist to reconnect to a sense of purpose through extreme and cathartic violence against black and brown people.[33] That is to say, the figures Max executes comprise part of an exotic background that he instrumentalizes to his own purpose. As a result, the game possesses all the harshness of *City of God* or *Elite Squad*, but without their affective qualities or meaningful socio-political interventions.

Remember Me and Urban Amnesia

Like *Max Payne 3*, *Remember Me* is also connected to noir, in this case blending a neo-noir urban setting with a post-apocalyptic futuristic space. *Remember Me* takes place in a speculative, post-apocalyptic megacity, called Neo-Paris, in the year 2084. Neo-Paris is a flooded wreckage of the original, upon which a new metropolis is built, with a vertical hierarchy of the few most privileged living at the top, and the scavenger, zombie-like, memory-corroded denizens subsisting in the multi-level ghettoes below. In this possible future, personal memories can be recorded, traded, manipulated and erased. DONTNOD describes their game concept as one in which the 'last remnants of privacy and intimacy have been swept away in what appears to be a logical progression of the explosive growth of social networks at the beginning of the 21st century'.[34] Smart technologies have restructured all aspects of society, organizing life into a memory economy that affords power to a few, while creating a surveillance society for most.

Figure 4.4 Nilin and the Sensen implant. *Remember Me* (2013) developed by DONTNOD Entertainment and published by Capcom. Image courtesy of ©CAPCOM U.S.A., INC.

The form and content of the game contain an implicit critique of both social networks and advanced technologies, which have enabled the powerful conversion of lived memory into encapsulated and eventually commoditized form. Within the narrative, the 'Sensation Engine' or 'Sensen' is an implant at the base of the neck, with a ring of light emanating from it (see Figure 4.4). It allows for the digitization of memories and their preservation, but also their commodification, theft, alteration and deletion. Players are introduced to the Sensen technology through an infomercial with talking heads who give testimonial of the profound positive and reaffirming impact of Sensen technology on their own lives: the deceased husband who may now live on in secured memory, the young lovers who can evidence their true affection by sharing their innermost feelings in an emotional mind meld and the war survivor whose traumatic memories are enshrined for posterity.

Memorize, the corporation that has introduced (and which ultimately controls) this technology, has concentrated its power to the point of dominating an advanced surveillance society. The corrupting effects of its technologies are felt in the extreme verticality of Neo-Paris, where a small minority of the privileged may live in luxury, while the vast majority are subjugated or exist as 'Leapers': derelict, cast-aside scavengers whose addiction to Memorize's Sensen technology has rendered them sub-human, disfigured and aggressive. Like all inventions of a sci-fi dystopia, the Sensen technology was purportedly developed to benefit humanity by relieving people of their miseries, enshrining positive memories and offloading traumatic ones. But the visionary innovation was eventually monetized, monopolized – and hacked – with pernicious consequences. In a future in which memory can be traded, bought, sold, erased and remixed, the protagonist Nilin finds herself at the centre of a dystopia borne as much out of a lucrative and addictive product as an unprecedented form of social engineering.

The highly capable and agile Nilin is described as an 'elite memory hunter', a hacker who can enter into people's memories, and even possesses the rare ability to recombine them, to powerfully manipulate subjects from within their deepest motivations. Episode 0, effectively an interactive title sequence, is entitled 'Rebirth/Reboot' and introduces us to the compromised figure of Nilin within a prison facility of the future called La Bastille Fortress. It is described as the most notorious penitentiary in Europe, where prisoners' memories are 'confiscated' upon their arrival, leaving them docile because they no longer understand there is anything outside the Bastille's walls to which they might escape. Their memories are kept in a Memory Confinement Center, within a highly protected panoptic tower. Nilin's retained knowledge is stripped from her and uploaded to the prison servers in an acutely painful process as Nilin – despite her toughness – curls up on the prison floor. It is to this hopeless place that Nilin will eventually return in an effort to liberate her comrades and regain her stolen memories. But first, she'll need to remember who she is, and what her role is within the dystopic system. Edge, her elusive friend, leader of the anti-Memorize resistance group 'Errorists' and the voice in her ear that remotely guides her, seems to know her from before, though his aims are opaque. Nilin's persisting amnesia, combined with larger themes around memory manipulation, have an overall destabilizing effect for the player. Even the protagonist herself is sometimes unsure of her benefactor, Edge, and his aims. This is registered through the dialogue, in which her sense of autonomy impinges upon her directives: 'Another errand?' Nilin protests during one mission, 'I'm not some obedient valet,

Edge...' By extension, the player naturally begins to wonder whether Nilin is being led astray.

Overall conceptual inspirations for the game noted by Moris, include the anime classic *Ghost in the Shell* (dir. Mamoru Oshii, 1995), *Memento* (dir. Christopher Nolan, 2000), *Strange Days* (dir. Kathryn Bigelow, 1995), the writings of Philip K. Dick and attendant contemporary cinematic manifestations such as in *Blade Runner* (dir. Ridley Scott, 1982), *Total Recall* (dir. Paul Verhoeven, 1990), *Minority Report* (dir. Steven Spielberg, 2002) and *A Scanner Darkly* (dir. Richard Linklater, 2006).[35] The French sci-fi film *The Fifth Element* (dir. Luc Besson, 1997) is a clear influence, particularly in relation to the cyberpunk female action character, as well as stories featuring data smuggling and memory commoditization like Robert Longo's cyberpunk cult classic *Johnny Mnemonic* (1995). Of course, there is also the spectral presence of William Gibson, whose neo-noir sci-fi *Neuromancer* (1984) and other writings are thought by many to have inaugurated the cyberpunk genre.

Received by critics with middling reviews, *Remember Me* was nevertheless lauded for its compelling world and original score. The game was eclipsed by *The Last of Us*, a magnum opus of a game released the following week (see Chapter 2).[36] The Paris-based developers, DONTNOD, also reported that they experienced difficulty in securing a publisher, due to the perception that a female protagonist would not be as well-received by audiences.[37] Responding to this, creative director Jean-Maxime Moris said of their chosen character: 'You have to avoid the pitfalls of making her [Nilin] just a damsel in distress or a sex bomb, because this is what you think would appeal most to the hordes of men that constitute your fan base.' He continued, 'But if you respect your public, then you refuse to dumb your work down, and eventually it pays back because what you do is different. But I'm not saying we're the only ones. I'm quite happy to see that more and more games feature female protagonists.'[38]

The key commodity within Neo-Paris is memory, and it is mobilized in the game on both a narrative and playable level to critique present-day social networking sites and the trend toward excessive sharing, as well as referencing iconic cinematic and literary precursors like *Blade Runner* (see Figure 4.5). One critic, Evan Narcisse, points directly to the connection

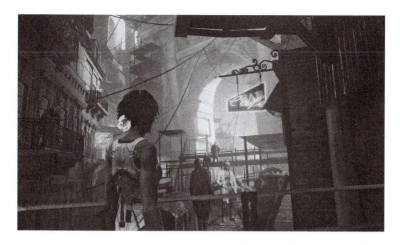

Figure 4.5 Nilin in Neo-Paris. *Remember Me* (2013) developed by DONTNOD Entertainment and published by Capcom. Image courtesy of ©CAPCOM U.S.A., INC.

between the speculative nature of the scenario presented and today's social media models of personal sharing and remote data storage:

> Would you let a significant other download your memories to their brain? Would you excise all those awful adolescent moments if you could? *Remember Me* plays like a thought experiment set in a world where millions of people have answered those questions – and the many others that extrapolate from its imaginary science. Play it so you can prepare for a future where your personal history lives in a digital cloud, even more than it does now.[39]

Another critic pointed to an interview with the creative director of *Remember Me*, who described the direct connection between social media and the fictive memory economy produced for the game:

> Today, we share our histories and the events in our lives via social networks like Facebook, Tumblr, and Twitter. [Jean-Maxime] Moris said that was fascinating to him, and so the world of *Remember Me* takes the concept one step further, allowing individuals within its universe to completely digitize and re-live past experiences.[40]

The character of Nilin can be read against that of Rick Deckard, the protagonist from *Blade Runner* – based on a Philip K. Dick story – who navigates various levels of the dystopian postmodern city, while becoming increasingly conflicted about his own position as truths are revealed. Deckard, who is tasked with the elimination of humanoids built for labour, begins to wonder whether they may indeed have personhood. In *Remember Me*, Nilin learns through the slow recuperation of her own memories that her origins spring from the Memorize Corporation, and she is literally birthed from the sufferings of her parents – one black and one white. As an ethnically ambiguous figure, and a kind of cypher for a global identity, her experience speaks to recollection as malleable. The identities that we build our foundational memories (and traumas) upon are far less stable than we think. Nilin's ally Edge tells her, 'A society whose only goal is to forget its mistakes will not survive...'[41] As Nilin navigates Neo-Paris, literally punching and kicking her way toward her own identity and the truth of the Sensen technology, one cannot help but consider the mobilization of memory as a way of exploring the melancholic dimensions of a mode of being in which there is a perpetual anxiety about what is being lost, and constant fortification against what might be taken. Indeed, this perpetual anxiety largely informs today's memory economy, with its cloud-based backup and secured data centres.[42] The notions of memory and forgetting, as well as the commerce in memory foregrounded in *Remember Me*, recall themes long-explored in the speculative fictions of Philip K. Dick, which are cited by Moris as inspirations for the game. Relating the cold-war themes of Dick's stories to memory and identity, Lance Rubin points to their persisting relevance in the contemporary context of a 'War on Terror':

> Dick's protagonists stand as powerful allegories for the confusion, paranoia, and phenomenological uncertainty about memory and identity in post-9/11 America. Rather than externalizing threats in the Manichean mantra of 'with us or against us,' *Minority Report, Imposter, Paycheck* and *A Scanner Darkly* suggest that the menaces to freedom are much closer. They articulate an internalization of the 'War on Terror,' the willful forfeiture of our humanity to those who would manipulate our

memories and identities for political ideals that disregard the
lives of individuals in the name of a professed greater good.[43]

These manipulations of memories and identities for political ideals refer, in
Rubin's description, to the strategic erasure and re-mix of national memory
as it regards the Bush, Jr. administration's post-9/11 insistence on the presence of weapons of mass destruction in Iraq, then its subsequent imperative to bring democracy and 'save' Iraqis through invasion, even after such
weapons were not found. In this, Rubin unveils an erasure of historical
memory at work in the United States: justifying military intervention;
rationalizing the outcomes of that intervention; forgetting about the circumstances which may have led to the ensuing conflict; and then wilfully
ignoring national culpability for reprehensible global economic behaviour
in order to remain comfortable.[44] *Remember Me* does not fall far from these
themes, as the cost of Nilin's recuperation from amnesia is often her painful
reliving of traumatic memories, and her tampering with the memories of
others, all for the sake of the professed greater good.

Play in the Fourth World City

Globalization and its cultural effects are at the root of these playable representations, particularly in terms of the anxieties they communicate.
Primary to these are fears of extreme economic disparity and exclusion
that result from informational global capitalism. Many scholars have captured the uniqueness of globalization as a cultural phenomenon, such as
sociologist Manuel Castells, who describes a new 'space of flows' of capital, bodies, information, labour, products and 'a specific form of social
organization in which information generation, processing, and trans-
mission become the fundamental sources of productivity and power'.[45] In
an increasingly connected world, electronically mediated exchange, the
presence of mega-cities as nodes of exchange and a solid network of managerial elite contribute to a fluid space of capital. In this 'space of flows',
one holds relevance and centrality in terms of one's connectedness to the
network society, as opposed to geographical location.[46] Max Payne is one
such figure, displayed to a new global node in the space of flows, employed

by managerial elite, and disoriented by his new identity in the network. Castells also identifies the coming of a 'Fourth World' – a new formation comprised of those left out of the utopian vision of globalization:

> a new world, the Fourth World, has emerged, made up of multiple black holes of social exclusion throughout the planet. The Fourth World comprises large areas of the globe, such as much of Sub-Saharan Africa, and the impoverished rural areas of Latin America and Asia. But it is also present in literally every country, and every city, in this new geography of social exclusion. It is formed of American inner-city ghettos, Spanish enclaves of mass youth unemployment, French *banlieues* warehousing North Africans, Japanese Yoseba quarters, and Asian mega-cities' shanty towns. And it is populated by millions of homeless, incarcerated, prostituted, criminalized, brutalized, stigmatized, sick, and illiterate persons. They are the majority in some areas, the minority in others, and a tiny minority in a few privileged contexts. But, everywhere, they are growing in number, and increasing in visibility, as the selective triage of informational capitalism, and the political breakdown of the welfare state, intensify social exclusion. In the current historical context, the rise of the Fourth World is inseparable from the rise of informational global capitalism.[47]

Castells' Fourth World is easily recognizable in the São Paolo favelas of *Max Payne 3*, as well as in the slum dwellings of Neo-Paris in *Remember Me* (see Figure 4.6). Clearly, actual cities have long informed the cultural imagination embedded within their speculative filmic counterparts. And in the case of the global city – or city under the duress of globalization – violence, exclusion, inequity and uncertainty have been at the centre of this ongoing conversation. This chapter shows how these themes extend to gamic representations as well.[48]

That said, very little scholarship exists on representations of the city in games. Early on in game studies, Celia Pearce coins the term 'narrative architecture' in her *The Interactive Book*, reading the architecture-like constructions of virtual space as environments that players engage with and enliven in order to activate the narratives within them.[49] Rowland Atkinson and Paul Willis write that such spaces need to be considered as

Figure 4.6 Neo-Paris. *Remember Me* (2013) developed by DONTNOD Entertainment and published by Capcom. Image courtesy of ©CAPCOM U.S.A., INC.

a central influence on how an increasing number of people who grow up with games understand contemporary urban life.[50] Contending that the worlds created in games are not mere abstractions or pure fiction, they instead argue that these playable representations of the city are 'powerful competing and structuring imaginaries of urban space that are suffused with connections to real-world places and urban cultures' that contribute to a reformulation of how their 'real' counterparts are understood.[51] They show that the pervasiveness of video games has given rise to a phantasmal interplay between game worlds as more than merely imaginary representations, and the lived worlds they purport to image. Alberto Vanolo similarly describes the increasingly 'blurry categories of the "real" and the "virtual"'.[52] Building upon the scholarship of Atkinson and Willis, he concludes that 'a highly visual and aestheticized experience, it involves the development of a relevant political and technological unconscious, a sort of thirdspace in which to hybridize the porous boundaries between fantasy and reality, the real and the imagined, the self and the other.'[53]

While it is important to understand the two gamic spaces in question as playable representations of cities, notably, they are also specifically dystopias. Marcus Schulzke considers the critical import of dystopias, particularly in relation to video games, identifying them as crucial sites of social critique.[54] Creating the conditions by which 'players may become active participants in creating or perpetuating the problems that make game worlds dystopian,' these complex worlds provide a meaningful critical perspective through which to reflect upon lived-world problems.[55]

It should be noted that neither of the two sites, Neo-Paris and São Paolo, should be confused with accurate re-creations of their lived world counterparts. While they may convey the affect or substantively reference known and iconic cities, they are not the same, and the prospect of traversing them is masterminded to induce certain gamic outcomes. Oscar Moralde, who writes excellently on the video game 'city-as-theme-park' notes the ways in which the haptic space of a game 'becomes a space for virtual bodily enactment; where the player consumes attractions and experiences' and in which the objective is consistent immersion within an elaborate facade. These digital cities should not be confused with real ones, he asserts, because their spaces depart from their originals to provide a kind of experience for the player, and they are often only partially articulated shells.[56] These are liminal spaces, admittedly stagey in their distillation of iconic city elements into a simulated model, yet 'real' because these spaces are experienced in a durational and sometimes quite haptic way.[57] Indeed, the traversable models of these two game spaces intersect with the navigation of collective memory, and enact a powerful social imaginary around globalization in relation to the visual culture of global cities.

The space of *Remember Me* has close ties to pre-existing literary and cinematic forms, and builds the game mechanics connected to memory into both its narrative and playable manifestation of the dystopic future city. The time period for the game, 2084, was inspired by George Orwell's *1984*. Moris explains:

> The book depicts a very vertical authoritarian society, the kind of society which is now pretty much non-existent in Western Europe and North America. But we believe a new insidious, horizontal form of control has emerged. Since the revolution of instant content sharing, people have been uploading more and more of their personal data onto social networks. What is being done with all that data, most people don't care to know, because

the 'cool' benefits outweigh the perceived threat to individual freedom.

In *Remember Me*, the last barriers of intimacy have been brought down, and people are now uploading their raw memories directly onto the network. As people exchange memories and dilute their very selves, we ask fundamental questions about identity and in that way, we are also exploring the favorite themes of another great writer: Philip K. Dick.[58]

Dick's *Do Android's Dream of Electric Sheep?*, first published in 1968, was adapted into Ridley Scott's *Blade Runner*, a clear cinematic inspiration for the dilapidated Neo-Paris cityscape imaged in *Remember Me*.[59] *Blade Runner* takes place in a future Los Angeles of 2019. Scott's masterful world-building of the film, imagines an anxious vision of the worst possible outcome of the city's imagined trajectory – as projected from the 1980s. Writing on *Blade Runner*, Marcus A. Doel and David B. Clarke described its future city in terms of:

its fractal geography; the interruption of temporality; the triumph of flexible accumulation within the hollow husks of global corporations; the fusion of the mechanisms of capital accumulation and governance, the absorption of referentiality and representation through a proliferation of simulacra and simulations; the lack of authenticity and the indeterminacy of identity; the short-circuiting of memory, genealogy, and history; the omnipresence of the Fourth World; the slow motion catastrophe of space-time decomposition; and the banality and fatality of living on in the hereafter.[60]

Doel and Clarke could just as easily have been describing the gamescape of Neo-Paris. Like the dark, polluted Los Angeles of *Blade Runner*, Neo-Paris is similarly overbuilt. Long-abandoned layers of development have so thoroughly buried parts of the city's landscape that the sun barely reaches it. Once surely advanced, clean and prosperous, the city is now decrepit, heaped with the detritus of better days, and ecologically past the point of no return. A first look at the city after escaping the Bastille offers a flooded ghetto, with shanties and modular dwellings nestled between the existing buildings. It clearly lacks sufficient infrastructure. Out of necessity,

Figure 4.7 Leapers. *Remember Me* (2013) developed by DONTNOD Entertainment and published by Capcom. Image courtesy of ©CAPCOM U.S.A., INC.

makeshift bridges and catwalks connect buildings so as to make flooded areas traversable. Haphazard power lines crosscut the slum dwelling, covered in layer upon layer of graffiti and large digital billboards that perpetually chatter out their ideologies to the denizens below. Overhead, patches of blue sky can be seen, but on the ground there are rats, garbage, homeless memory addicts and barricades that divide the slum from the more preserved and protected spaces of the favoured. Deranged 'Leapers' – an array of variously blighted citizens whose advanced addiction to the memories of others has left them damaged – scurry about in slums (see Figure 4.7). Those few who are less advanced into their decay, or the well-heeled, live above in small enclaves of privilege that resemble a futuristic version of a charming Paris neighbourhood, tended to by demure-looking, brightly coloured androids. Increasingly identifiable as robotic slaves, these humanoids are encountered throughout the game in the capacities of service: food vendors, housecleaners, servants, repair staff to larger machines and even sex workers.

The controlled jumble of construction echoes a more internal disorder of the mind, brought about by the Sensen technology. There is a clear allusion made to memory as the architecture of who a person is, and the malleability of memory as a threat to the stability of self, identity and any sense of internal cohesion. Claustrophobic, maze-like spaces predominate throughout the game – many of them in disrepair with evidence of scavenging. The brilliantly rendered combination of darkness, rain and buzzing neon drenches the game space with atmosphere, and iconic Parisian elements of architecture like the Sacré-Coeur Basilica, Notre Dame Cathedral and Eiffel Tower lend an authentic sense of place. Overlaid onto this is a severe, more modern complex of urban planning. Its reductive metal, concrete and glass minimalism contrasts starkly with the Paris of old. Much is broken, repurposed and unstable. Drones hover between all of these elements. Some undertake construction and repair, while others provide surveillance and enforcement. It is a vision of a future city that is recognizable but refreshed through its new locale, and – unlike cinema – navigable. The overall effect produced is of a megacity in disrepair, and in a larger sense, technological society past its prime. *Remember Me* depicts the aftermath of the broken promise of progress, and it is apparent that the utopian advances of the game world's 'past' have left its 'present' condition moribund. The tawny, blue-eyed Nilin moves about this space with a feline confidence, scaling ladders and negotiating leaps with nimble ease. Her path is optimized by indication of an orange, double-chevron symbol that charts out her direction, which strongly suggests to the player a goal-oriented rather than exploratory engagement with the space.

Several critics vocalized complaints about the difficulty of interacting with the game world in a meaningful way.[61] The linear nature of the adventure, and the character's overly scripted engagement with the space, was a cause of some consternation. However, reviewers clearly appreciated the 'brilliant new cyberpunk adventure' and convincing world-making of the game in terms of the story itself.[62] The creative director explained that the highly curated narrative was intended to control affective dimensions of the game:

> While we do encourage the player to deviate from the path to a certain extent to uncover pick-ups, it is true to say that *Remember Me* is a linear experience. This was a choice we made at the beginning of the project so we could tell the story of Nilin and ensure the player is immersed in the narrative, which does mean controlling the action, and therefore the emotion.[63]

Despite the limitations of a linear narrative, which somewhat contradicted the sublimity of cityscapes that beckoned the player to explore, the game offered much in the way of mechanics that reinforced the key theme of memory. Like the Bullet Time of *Max Payne*, *Remember Me* contains several innovative game mechanics, including memory-remixing, a novel combo-system for constructing optimal melee attacks using the unique 'Pressens' system and the use of mnemonic tools to locate assets. Sparingly presented, but likely the most interesting innovation, is the memory-remixing, which feels both incredibly compelling as a game mechanic and inordinately cruel in its manipulation. Within this mode, Nilin accesses a pivotal memory of her subject/victim and identifies key details. Within this partially constructed, hollow non-space of recollection, Nilin conducts memory playback and then tweaks key moments in order to alter their perception of a traumatic event. These moments present themselves as 'glitches', which bear an aesthetic quality akin to the malfunctioning of digital and analog technology, usually marked by digital data degradation, and made visible through digital artefacts. This glitch aesthetic has the affective impact of conveying the instability, breakdown and vulnerability of memories – even the ones that define our identities the most. Said one critic:

> Killing in games rarely feels personal, but the kind of mental damage you do in *Remember Me* stayed with me after I switched off the console [...]
>
> [...] We're used to games that show how technology can lead society astray, but Dontnod's portrayal feels sharp and relevant; keep on turning your blind eye, letting them sacrifice your liberty for security while pacifying you with new technology, it seems to say, and you won't like what happens.[64]

Compelling as well is the space of pure memory, which the game renders as modular and incomplete, a glitch-space emblazoned with terms like 'MEMORY' and 'TRAUMA'. Perpetually shifting, unstable and beautifully realized as a non-place, Nilin encounters her biggest boss-fights within it (see Figure 4.8).[65]

Figure 4.8 Glitch-space. *Remember Me* (2013) developed by DONTNOD Entertainment and published by Capcom. Image courtesy of ©CAPCOM U.S.A., INC.

Notably, there are virtually no gun-like weapons in the game, which consists mostly of hand-to-hand combat – a decision the creative director described as a by-product of the Sensen technology:

> In Neo-Paris, weapons are forbidden. People don't need guns when they are all happy thanks to the Sensen, and so it is easy to ban them. Control over people is exerted through the power that Memorize has over the memories that are exchanged over the network. They know who you are and who you like to hang out with. No need for prisons and no need to point guns at you to scare you anymore.[66]

Instead, Nilin has a wrist device that provides aid through engaging locks remotely, emitting pulses and otherwise supporting her during combat. There are some interesting plays on the notion of a replayable memory, such as the 'Remembrane'. Using this node, Nilin can review others' memories by activating them with her own Sensen. These appear as spectral, holographic recordings left behind that provide clues to the successful navigation of perilous spaces and the solution of puzzles along her journey.

Additionally, mnemonic images, encountered by players as a type of treasure map, are scattered among the proliferating heads-up displays (HUDs) throughout the space. These contain snapshots indicating landmarks that identify secret locations where assets may be found that improve Nilin's skills through upgrades, or fill in details of the game world – if remembered well by the player. *Remember Me* begins with the incarcerated and the memory-poor, the sick, the stigmatized, the human rubbish, with those most expelled from power and outside the utopian global vision. It begins with the Fourth World. Across the time and space enlivened by experiencing the game, players traverse nearer and nearer to the non-place of pure control and power at the centre of Neo-Paris' society of surveillance.

Bullet Time, Memory Remixing and Harvey's Space-Time Compression

Conceptually speaking, the most original interventions of the two games in question concern how they address shifts in notions of space and time associated with the postmodern, globalized condition. As I have previously mentioned, AlSayyad (through David Harvey) identifies among the key qualities of postmodernity and its megacities: the circulation of bodies in a transnational flow, stark ethnic and class-based fragmentation, militarized protection of elite districts, dispossessed masses, shifts in the notion of time and space (such as their compression) and a vertical architectural hierarchy of classes. Time and space become socially, culturally and economically compressed due to increasingly flexible modes of accumulation. In his *The Condition of Postmodernity*, Harvey theorizes the 'time-space compression' that emerges as a result of capitalism, which advances its aims across great distances and differing times, often with near instantaneity. Likewise, he discusses how spatial barriers are reduced through advancements in transportation and communication. The term 'time-space compression' refers to:

> processes that so revolutionize the objective qualities of space and time that we are forced to alter, sometimes in quite radical ways, how we represent the world to ourselves. I use the word 'compression' because a strong case can be made that the history

of capitalism has been characterized by speed-up in the pace of life, while so overcoming spatial barriers that the world some-times seems to collapse inward upon us [...] As space appears to shrink to a 'global village' of telecommunication and a 'space-ship earth' of economic and ecological interdependencies [...] as time horizons shorten to the point where the present is all there is (the world of the schizophrenic), so we have to learn how to cope with an overwhelming sense of *compression* of our spatial and temporal worlds.[67]

Harvey asserts that if the encoding and reproduction of social relations occur within the frameworks of space-time, it therefore follows that shifts in the way space-time experiences get represented will likely impact the coding and reproduction of social relations, too. For example, develop-ments in the concepts of space and time during the Renaissance, he argues, prefigured the coming Enlightenment rationality, and this could be evi-denced in the increasing rationality of space in mapmaking of the time. By the Enlightenment, space was highly rationalized as an almost utopian pursuit of total ordering culminating in modernism as a cultural force.

Insofar as the postmodern is concerned, increases in flexible accumula-tion, the valuing of instantaneity, and overall acceleration in time and pro-duction in Western capitalism since the 1960s, has for Harvey given rise to a kind of stress – particularly among those under the duress of constant adaptation to these new realities. The command of time-space compres-sion would, then, demark a formidable social power. Interestingly, Harvey also turns to *Blade Runner* as one effective example of the cinematic imag-ing of postmodern urban time and space as fragmented, collapsed and uncertain.[68]

If it is true that, as Harvey says, 'conceptions of time and space are nec-essarily created through material practices which serve to reproduce social life,' what kinds of material practices of time-space in the form of repre-sentations exist in these gamic examples?[69] What do they tend to say about the social relations from whence they arise? In the case of *Max Payne 3*, I have already mentioned the core game mechanic of Bullet Time, which effectively allows the playable character to manipulate time and space by observing the movement of his bullets in slow-motion as they find their targets, and enemy bullets as they approach. In gameplay, this manifests itself as time slowing for all the action in the game, except for the playable character, who then possesses the advantage of aiming with real-time speed at slow-moving targets. So activating Bullet Time, which allows for a limited 'adrenaline' rush of focus, results in a heightened capacity for precision when aiming and firing at foes. In this iteration of the game, a simple vertical adrenaline meter marks how much of it remains before the Bullet Time runs out. Similarly, the Shoot Dodge function is a slow-motion dive that is used to evade a mortal attack, although it is possible to be injured. In both cases, time and space shift in the emulation of the heightened focus that is narratively described as Max's preternatural skill for gunplay. The material practice evidenced in this game is one of a central relationship to time-space compression that expresses itself as bursts of control within a larger framework of postmodern chaos, with its fragmentation, transnational flow and constant threat of obsolescence due to the fluctuations of global capitalism.

Remember Me expresses time-space compression through three innovative core game mechanics: the use of 'S-Pressens', memory remixing and the strategic theft and digital replay of memories as 'Remembranes' or augmented reality projections. 'S-Pressens' are five special abilities or powers slowly unlocked for Nilin that allow for advantages during close combat. These are indicated in a 'Sensen Wheel' heads-up display on the lower left, when summoned using the controller. 'Sensen Fury' generates a flowing attack with numerous uninterrupted hits; Sensen DOS stuns enemies; Sensen Camo renders Nilin temporarily invisible to foes; 'Logic Bomb' turns an enemy explosive; and 'Sensen RIP' (or 'Rust In Pieces') appropriates control of an enemy robot, which in turn attacks its own and ultimately explodes. The selection wheel for the aforementioned slows the action onscreen, so that Nilin battles in slow motion. Once selected, several of the S-Pressens impact space-time relations for Nilin; for example, the Sensen Fury seems to render her faster in relation to her enemies, more lethal, and even to somewhat defy the laws of physics.

Memory remixing is perhaps the most startling and fascinating in terms of playability and narrative ingenuity. Accessing the memories of a target, Nilin can modify them to her advantage by shifting subtle details in order to manufacture useful outcomes. For example, in an early memory

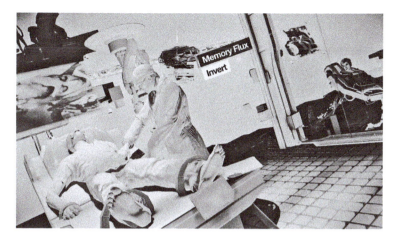

Figure 4.9 Memory Remix. *Remember Me* (2013) developed by DONTNOD Entertainment and published by Capcom. Image courtesy of ©CAPCOM U.S.A., INC.

remix, Nilin hacks the memory of Olga Sedova, a bounty hunter she needs as an ally. Through accessing Olga's memory of her husband, who is being treated for memorial degeneration, Nilin learns that Olga's primary motivation for hunting her is to fund his expensive memory transfusions (see Figure 4.9). By adjusting subtle details of the traumatic memory of her husband's hospitalization, Nilin succeeds in convincing Olga that the transfusion treatment failed, her husband died and there is no motivation to pursue the hefty bounty for Nilin's capture. This is represented within a spectral, glitchy non-place of the virtual, with some details of the memory highly rendered and others schematic. HUDs cue the player to key glitch moments in which the memory can be altered through subtle remixes of detail. In this case, a patient's loosened hand strap, the slight shifting of a utility trolley or the switching of a capsule, for example, produces varying outcomes until the desired one is achieved. In this mechanic, space-time is virtually modified in the mind of the affected character, while the memory being hacked is presented as fragmented, flowing and malleable, not stable.

Throughout the game, Nilin steals the memories of allies and enemies and then uses the resulting 'Remembranes', ghostly real-time projections that appear within the places they were recorded (see Figure 4.10).

Figure 4.10 Nilin activates a Remembrane. *Remember Me* (2013) developed by DONTNOD Entertainment and published by Capcom. Image courtesy of ©CAPCOM U.S.A., INC.

Overlaid onto the present, Remembranes collapse both past and present into one time-space. They help guide Nilin through unfamiliar, perilous and restricted spaces of the city by marking a safe path, or revealing combination codes and so on. But they also produce a kind of malleability or indeterminacy around the fixity of time; the past becomes present, while the present is suspended in order to experience the past in a temporal display. In this simultaneity, Nilin temporarily controls time-space compression, bending it to her needs, albeit briefly.

Two Playable Cities: The Favela and the Cyberpunk Metropolis

The post-apocalyptic city, such as represented by Neo-Paris, and the dystopian São Paolo of *Max Payne 3* have a strong symbolic function linked to socio-political anxieties of their day. In an essay tracing the relations between the cinematic representation of apocalypse, and the post-9/11 era, Mathias Nilges argues that such images provide a way of 'working through or at least highlighting psychological contradictions produced by moments of severe crisis'.[70] Focusing on the notion of beauty, the scholar considers the presence of the sublime, and the perceived desire for a cathartic and destructive 'antidote to a world that produces the fears we wish to escape'.[71] Nilges foregrounds the ways in which destruction is actually presented as having engendered a new pastoral condition, such as in *I Am Legend* (dir. Francis Lawrence, 2007) and *The Day After Tomorrow* (dir. Roland Emmerich, 2004), in which the United States returns to a simpler existence after total devastation. Further, Nilges argues that these disasters as imaged are often 'mobilized to restore future possibilities that appear to be lacking in the present'.[72] The solution presented in many of these apocalyptic narratives is one of a nostalgic return to the past, Nilges asserts. It is a regressive return that requires an order and a patriarchal structure – and, in the absence of its restoration, produces all manner of instabilities such as dread and anxiety:

> In a global socioeconomic situation that is founded on decidedly anti-paternalistic structures (diversity, difference, deregulation, the abolition of restricting forms of bureaucracy, production, and national protectionism that stands in conflict with the nature of global trade and production, in short, freemarket anarchism), paternalism becomes part of those structures that paradoxically begin to be perceived positively. Whereas progressive movements of the 60s and 70s fought paternalism (in its various manifestations as hegemonic production, gender norms, nationalism, moral and identity structures that resulted in exclusion and domination), the loss of paternalistic structures in the present, especially after 9/11, is increasingly understood not as liberating but as frightening.[73]

How does this translate into the two differing iterations presented? In the case of *Max Payne 3*, it seems an iconic example of what Nilges describes: Max represents a shoot-first-ask-questions-later paternalistic order that stands in for a certain form of domination that is defunct, or at least feels anachronistic. Transplanted to the sunny, hellish favelas, the hypermasculine noir detective wanders in confusion of his role there – and about solutions that never seem to come. Instead, there are only cathartic acts of destruction (as imaged through his Bullet Time-enhanced killing sprees) and intense efforts to forget (his binges on booze and painkillers). Like so many iconic defunct white male action heroes who, as Nilges describes, stand in for 'protection in the present world', Max himself becomes a cypher for all that has been destabilized, through both 9/11 as exemplar of the inability to fend off terrorist attack, and unprecedented socio-economic globalization.[74] It is no wonder that the game possesses an odd feel, despite its effective formal elements and well-liked anti-hero. *Remember Me* similarly contains overt anxieties about having gone too far with technology, and in doing so having eliminated most of the population. It makes for an effectively glitchy, disorienting experience of the game space as indeterminate and profoundly mediated.

When considering these two very dissimilar worlds in relation to each other, angst around economic and cultural globalization emerge as a consistent theme. Both *Blade Runner*'s 2019 Los Angeles and the gamic 2084 Neo-Paris are post-industrial; that is to say, they are by-products of economic globalization with its radical new forms of neo-colonization and transnational inhumanity in the name of the free movement of goods, services, capital technologies and information across traditional regional borders. In his explication of the cinematic urban vision of Los Angeles demonstrated in films like *Blade Runner* and *Falling Down*, Nezar AlSayyad identifies how each renders 'the ultimate postmodern city, where utopian aspirations have turned into a dystopic hell'.[75] Drawing upon Ridley Scott's visualizing of the 'spatially and politically fragmented' city, the scholar describes how 'tremendous power corporations can hire entire ethnic communities to manufacture parts of a larger system of whose overall purpose is never revealed to them'.[76] Describing *Blade Runner*'s Los Angeles, AlSayyad writes:

> The city of the future is depicted as a montage of the most sordid physical aspects of the urban present. This is the city as a Third World bazaar, where the language in the streets has devolved into a strange immigrant 'city-speak'. While the masses struggle, the elite live in luxurious multi-storeyed, pyramidal structures.[77]

Building his analysis of the cinematic postmodern Los Angeles on the scholarship of Mike Davis, Edward Soja, David Harvey and Fredric

Jameson, AlSayyad illuminates the supercity as a militarized panoptic space, a machine for generating particular kinds of social relations.[78] The city is remade into a site of consumption, whose economies drive novel and fragmented organization within the city that no longer conforms to the previous mode of 'modern' industry.[79]

This image of the postmodern dystopia is echoed in playable form in *Remember Me*. The nuanced game references the ecologically damaged and starkly class-divided *Blade Runner* vision of Los Angeles in innumerable ways, but among the most pronounced is the mobilizing of parity between class standing and vertical positioning. Class separation is represented spatially and architecturally, with extreme verticality of structures that typically have the socially expelled at the bottom, and the privileged at the top. *Remember Me* features several objectives that require Nilin to snake through interior spaces of wealth that are filled with the amenities of modern life including sleek, futuristic interior design, domestic robot servants and advanced forms of automation. These spaces of rarefied air are notably more sanitary and orderly, with evidence of luxury in the form of items like pianos, modernist furniture, plants, fully stocked homes and all the comforts of life. Exploring the first district for the elite presented during gameplay, called the 'St-Michel Rotunda', the player as Nilin encounters sidewalk cafés, distinctive Parisian signage for which the 'actual' city is so recognizable, clothing and flower shops, fresh food, cleaner streets, an absence of Leapers, automated stations to transact in pleasant memories and the simulation of a commercial promenade. However, the space is also clearly protected by a highly armoured and militarized 'S.A.B.R.E. Force', who are basically the 'high-tech police death squads' described by Mike Davis within his seminal deconstruction of Los Angeles (see Figure 4.11).[80]

The world of *Remember Me* is an advanced information economy of flexible accumulation, with the primary commodity being memories. *Blade Runner* also expresses an obsession with memory, which it depicts as the building-block of stable identity. In the case of the film, it refers to the borrowed human memory as key to stabilizing the constructed personas of humanoid slaves, called 'Replicants'. The slum-dwelling Leapers of Neo-Paris are not artificial humans, but unfortunates whose excessive abuse of memory have robbed them of their humanity, deformed them and

Figure 4.11 Nilin battles S.A.B.R.E. Force. *Remember Me* (2013) developed by DONTNOD Entertainment and published by Capcom. Image courtesy of ©CAPCOM U.S.A., INC.

ultimately doomed them to the servitude of the so-called 'Reconversion Project'. Developed by Memorize, this project is championed as a way of reintegrating Leapers into constructive roles. Scylla Cartier-Wells, President of Memorize, can be heard proclaiming its success across the city's oppressive propaganda screens:

> Citizens of Neo-Paris: the Leaper threat has been addressed. Thanks to the Reconversion Project, they now serve you faithfully. From sanitation to S.A.B.R.E. Force, they have become productive servants of society. The Reconversion Project by Memorize: humane responses to barbaric perils.

This is a proposed final solution: Leapers as slaves, utterly alienated, dehumanized and subjected absolutely to the mega-corporation through the imposition of a hive consciousness. Leapers are reconfigured into 'obedient, disposable tools' according to the anti-Memorize activist leader, Edge. Within the logic of *Remember Me*, Leapers are the Third World Other, without personhood, just like *Blade Runner*'s enslaved Replicants.

The dystopian 'Reconversion Project' of *Remember Me* evokes social cleansing, which *Max Payne 3* also obliquely references in regard to the

Brazilian favelas. Within narrative voiceover, Max describes São Paolo as being 'like Baghdad with G-strings', pointing to the combination of extreme violence and indulgence, a place both dangerous and sexually or exotically enticing, and a highly dysfunctional metropolis.[81] This conforms in intriguing, insightful ways with AlSayyad's compelling observations of another cinematic example of a dystopic Los Angeles, as is imaged in Schumacher's 1993 film *Falling Down*. Marketed with the tagline, 'A Tale of Urban Reality',[82] the film images a white male unemployed defence worker named William Foster (played by Michael Douglas) whose alienation in the face of his own crumbling privilege, and the escalating diversity around him, results in psychological implosion and cathartic violence. (See also my discussion on the film and its imaging of whiteness in Chapter 2.) AlSayyad describes him aptly as 'an obsolete, universal "everyman"' who 'traverses a landscape that he constructs as fragmented, hostile, violent, unreadable – and therefore out of control'.[83] After abandoning his car in the middle of a heat wave in gridlocked L.A. traffic, Foster – whose home is fractured by divorce, who lacks the purpose of work, and whose city is in a state of social and moral decay – goes on a rampage. In a fit of rage aimed at the inhabitants of a city he no longer recognizes or feels a part of, the white male victim of postmodernity, in his short-sleeved white work shirt, black tie and slacks, unremarkable briefcase in hand, turns vigilante.

The Los Angeles of this film is not one of the future, but of the 'present day' of the 1990s. However, it is the most dystopic iteration possible of a multicultural, fragmented mega-ghetto with no internal cohesive sense of communal identity to hold it together as a city. The space itself is imaged as claustrophobic, overbuilt, overpopulated, hot, dirty, smoggy, brutal and no place for the honest ordinary white man.[84] Foster punishes various cyphers for his problems: the Korean grocer who opportunistically inflates prices at the local corner store, the beggar, the hostile city-goer, the young Latino gang members who harass him, the inept manager of a fast-food franchise, a survivalist white-power surplus store owner, the privileged golfers who enjoy ample space in a private course while others are compacted within urban space, the suburbanites who have retreated to gated communities, and ultimately himself. Carl Abbott, in his analysis underscores the fraught context into which the film was released. Namely, the terrorist bombing of the World Trade Center's north tower occurred on *Falling Down*'s release day: 26 February 1993. Two days later, the Branch Davidian compound in Waco, Texas was raided by the government, which tipped off an extended conflict lasting 51 days and resulting in the deaths of more than 80 people. The 1992 Los Angeles Uprising (or 'L.A. Riots') protesting the Rodney King trial outcome was also a fresh wound on the American psyche, particularly in terms of the way it produced a racial divide.[85]

As Abbott described it, '[r]ace, gender, and economic status certainly bring out certain aspects of *Falling Down*, but the film takes on additional character when approached in terms of both space and place.'[86] The professor of urban studies diverges in interpretation from the notion of a white masculinity in crisis, one he attributes largely to the then-new popularity of 'gender studies.'[87] That said, Abbott does characterize William Foster as a 'less a flâneur than an explorer', continuing, 'Foster has to perceive and deal with difference, and to treat L.A. itself as a frontier to be explored. There is a savage tribe to be fought, and even familiar settings like fast food franchises and golf courses seem in his manic state to be the sites of exotic, inexplicable rituals.'[88] This language of 'explorers', 'frontiers', the 'exotic' and 'savages' suggests a place outside of civilization, and signals the logic of conquest. It is slightly unclear whether this is purely projected onto Foster's frame of mind, reflective of the author's position. Regardless, its loaded nature is telling in its oppositional relations between explorer and a strange land, between Foster and his alienated city – and similarly between Max and São Paolo.

Both the futuristic Neo-Paris of *Remember Me* and the 'present-day' São Paolo of *Max Payne 3* invoke an urban metropolis, filled with eclecticism, decentralization, masses of dispossessed, hostility, fragmentation and violence. In many ways, both of these playable representations are about the disorientation and decontextualizing effects of global capitalist flows. This intersects strongly with a sense of the influential presence of otherness, often indicated in the dystopian representation of the postmodern city as a global mega-ghetto. AlSayyad has discussed the intersection of race, ethnicity and the city in his writing on cinema and urban modernity. Pointing to the often stark but under theorized mapping of race and ethnicity onto space, he identifies how 'more often than not, "blackness" has been

Figure 4.12 The playable favela. *Max Payne 3* (2012) developed by Rockstar Studios and published by Rockstar Games ©Take-Two Interactive Software, Inc. Screen shot by author.

conflated with other forms of marginality, poverty, and disenfranchisement to provide a generalized Other to "whiteness."[89] This is most obviously present in *Max Payne 3*, which places a white male anti-hero against a backdrop of blackness and exoticization that comes pre-loaded with a generous helping of stereotypes (see Figure 4.12).

This creates a kind of wicked problem for the game representation, through which the dominating extra-diegetic ideologies about Brazil in general and its metropolises more specifically, bear down upon the diegetic game world. The mega-ghettos of the favelas have been cast as a national embarrassment and public eyesore, in the face of Brazil's setting as the stage for global spectacles of international sport. In 2007, Brazil was confirmed as the host of the 2014 World Cup. In 2009, the nation also won the bid for the 31st Summer Olympic Games to be held in 2016. The cleaning up of favelas in Rio de Janeiro in preparation for the World Cup constituted what many described as a 'slum "pacification" program' through which more than a thousand police and soldiers overtook the Complexo da Maré favela, with tanks, occupying the Rio de Janeiro shantytown in an effort to control the rampant drug trafficking.[90] While this internationally reported incident occurred after the release of *Max Payne 3*, this kind of militarized enforcement was well underway since the announcement of Brazil's bid for the Olympic Games in 2008. In November 2012, roughly the time that *Max Payne 3* was released, *The Economist* reported that while the homicide rate in São Paolo had fallen between 1999 and 2011, the numbers were creeping up again to over 10 per 100,000 in 2012, largely as a result of ongoing hostilities between the police and drug gangs.[91]

The so-called 'Favela Pacification Program' initiated that year has constituted what some call a 'social cleansing' and includes the forced displacement or eviction of reportedly 19,000 families by 2013, as well as ambitious infrastructure and building projects designed to support the two global sports events.[92] According to one report in 2013 by Owen Gibson and Jonathan Watts for the *Guardian*, these actions intended to modernize the city for the coming international spectacles have been complicated by rampant gentrification, deft manipulation of building codes to the government's interests and pandering to foreign investors.[93] This is complicated by the obvious irony of displacing favela residents – many of whom reportedly do not benefit from even the most basic water, power, sanitation and sewage infrastructures – while lavish stadiums, an Olympic village and urban beautification programs are underway.[94] Photo essays illustrating the highly militarized police, and particularly the elite Special Operations Battalion or 'BOPE' (dramatized in *Elite Squad*), circulate globally in major news outlets like *BBC News*, *Vice News* and *Al Jazeera*.[95]

In addition to the aforementioned breakout favela films *Elite Squad* and *City of God*, these kinds of news reports would surely be present in the public consciousness, and would be conjured in the minds of players in relation to the 'playground' built for our reluctant anti-hero Max. In the case of *Max Payne 3*, which contains a highly detailed but ultimately fabricated iteration of an actual city, the slippage between the space of the game and the reinforcement of stereotype is a much shorter leap. With the more fictive Neo-Paris, the site occupies a space of fantasy, however this does not preclude its symbolic potency as a site of the imaginary. Castells' and others' articulations of the growing global urban sprawl, of overpopulation, placelessness and the rise of non-Western nodes as multiple sites of anxiety find their reflection in these gamic articulations. Their procedural rhetorical functions are complex, but both convey a series of myths or stories, that are told again and again, about possible futures in the face of new fearsome realities.

Conclusion: Playing Possible Futures

What are the claims about space, place and city made in these two games? How do these games shore up or in some way interrupt the functionings of power? They each in their own way point to a paradigm of expulsions, profound exclusions that come as a by-product of geopolitical and economic shifts, and a resultant Fourth World. Both in some way image those left out of the utopian dream of globalization. They also suggest, in a larger sense, that violence, exclusion and inequity form a large component of the social imaginary around games, particularly in a fraught context of larger cultural manifestations that contend with similar anxieties. Within these game spaces specific kinds of social relations take place, in simulated megacity spaces.

In the case of *Max Payne 3*, there is a larger focus on an oppositional set of relations by which the global city, imagined as violent mega-ghetto,

Figure 4.13 Max in trouble in the favela. *Max Payne 3* (2012) developed by Rockstar Studios and published by Rockstar Games ©Take-Two Interactive Software, Inc. Screen shot by author.

Figure 4.14 Max in a gun battle, with Shoot Dodge and Bullet Time functions. *Max Payne 3* (2012) developed by Rockstar Studios and published by Rockstar Games. Image ©Take-Two Interactive Software, Inc.

is navigated by a subject under its duress, who is trapped in memories of the past. Max can only engage with his present through spectacular acts of violence, and perpetually enacts a paternalistic desire to restore order to a heart-of-darkness scenario. He is an interloper, a displaced diasporic subject, in a space he does not understand (see Figure 4.13). Like *Falling Down*, the game calls upon a deeply embedded set of myths of conquest, and tropes of otherness. This is modelled through its spaces, and alluring forms of playable cinematic violence place the player within a world with little potential for transformation – except through destruction. This world quickly projects players into the mode of anticipating what will come next, their 'looking-moving-feeling' (according to Rachel Hughes) acutely attuned to what may be on the horizon of gameplay itself. It is a horizon of perpetual aggression, though gloriously rendered (see Figure 4.14). In connection with the anticipatory genres of neo-noir and science fiction, the future orientation of this game conveys anxieties about what is to come, through its dystopic rendering of one possible bleak reality.

Likewise, *Remember Me*, with its focus on memorial plasticity and its liminal protagonist, is anticipatory in a very different way. While its future orientation is similarly dystopic, it presents a post-apocalyptic vision that gestures ambivalently toward the recuperative potentials of memory and forgetting, and suggests a subject who does not exemplify the paternal order, but who is literally borne of the traumatic conditions of that dystopia. More in keeping with the cyberpunk female protagonist, Nilin is an intersectional figure, technologically augmented, within a crumbling built environment. This echoes Evan Watt's assertion (as explicated in Chapter 2) that physical structures often stand in for social constraint, and their ruin can be thought of as potentially providing a generative space for liberatory subversion.[96] Both the site and the figure embody something that more resembles the rejection of paternalistic structures, through the central presence of diversity, through intersectional identity and through the literal site of the game as technological 'progress' quickened toward its most dysfunctional outcomes (see Figure 4.15). Themes around the manipulability of memory and identity for the sake of ideals, like 'freedom', invoke larger notions of national identity that are shored up through dubious means, including the spin and remix of national memory foundational for the sake of political means or for public good.

I present these models not as examples to be judged as 'good' or 'bad' representations, but as two complex responses to massive economic, social, political and cultural shifts associated with globalization. Analysis of these

Figure 4.15 Nilin in Neo-Paris. *Remember Me* (2013) developed by DONTNOD Entertainment and published by Capcom. Image courtesy of ©CAPCOM U.S.A., INC.

two playable mega-ghettos provides a tremendous mirror through which to access and reflect upon the intricacies of an incredibly persuasive 'dream life' of a culture. As AlSayyad keenly observed in the epigraph that opens this chapter, representations of the city and life mutually constitute each other in continual interplay. This is no less true in gamic cities. They participate with the world. Like his metaphor of the 'pervasive game of mirrors reflecting each other', games also engage with the lived world, so that 'art imitates life, life imitates art, art imitates art, life imitates life'.[97] These imagined cities are surely not exclusively responsible for the lived world as it is, or as it will be. But they do provide insight into 'real-world' anxieties by modelling a microcosm of present and anticipated conditions.

Playable representations matter. They are affective fictions critical for our imaginative capacities to envision potential geopolitical eventualities. Their extremely potent anticipatory images suggest that the tools of cultural analysis are needed – more than ever – to both unveil their significations within the context of their making, and to make sense of what dreams we carry into the future.

Notes

Introduction: Is the 'Culture' in Game Culture the 'Culture' of Cultural Studies?

1. Mary Flanagan, 'Response by Mary Flanagan to Celia Pearce, "Towards a Game Theory of Game"', in Noah Wardrip-Fruin and Pat Harrigan (eds), *First Person: New Media as Story, Performance, and Game* (Cambridge: The MIT Press, 2004), p. 145.
2. Lawrence Grossberg, *Cultural Studies in the Future Tense* (Durham: Duke University Press, 2010), p. 1.
3. This phrase '"dream life" of a culture' comes from: Stuart Hall, Sut Jhally and Media Education Foundation, *The Origins of Cultural Studies: A Lecture* (Northampton: Media Education Foundation, 2006).
4. Mieke Bal, 'Visual Essentialism and the Object of Visual Culture', *Journal of Visual Culture* 2, no. 1 (1 April 2003), pp. 17–18, doi:10.1177/147041290300200101.
5. Ibid., p. 18.
6. Adrienne Shaw, 'What Is Video Game Culture? Cultural Studies and Game Studies', *Games and Culture* 5, no. 4 (1 October 2010), p. 404, doi:10.1177/1555412009360414.
7. Corey Mead, *War Play: Video Games and the Future of Armed Conflict* (Boston: Eamon Dolan/Houghton Mifflin Harcourt, 2013).
8. Anna Everett and S.C. Watkins, 'The Power of Play: The Portrayal and Performance of Race in Video Games', in *The Ecology of Games: Connecting Youth, Games and Learning* (Cambridge: The MIT Press, 2007), pp. 141–64.
9. Adrienne Shaw, *Gaming at the Edge: Sexuality and Gender at the Margins of Gamer Culture* (Minneapolis: University of Minnesota Press, 2015), pp. 3–4.
10. There are many texts available that address Stuart Hall's life, his key ideas and broad intellectual influence. Please see among others: James Procter, *Stuart Hall*, Routledge Critical Thinkers (London; New York: Routledge, 2004); Stuart Hall, David Morley and Kuan-Hsing Chen (eds), *Stuart Hall: Critical Dialogues in Cultural Studies*, Comedia (London; New York: Routledge, 1996); Chris Rojek, *Stuart Hall*, Key Contemporary Thinkers (Cambridge: Polity, 2003); Helen Davis, *Understanding Stuart Hall* (London; Thousand

Oaks: SAGE Publications, 2004). Additionally, see the following for an excellent anthology of critical projects inspired by Hall's interventions: Stuart Hall, et al. (eds), *Without Guarantees: In Honour of Stuart Hall* (London; New York: Verso, 2000).

11. Procter, *Stuart Hall*, p. 1.

12. Ian Bogost, *Persuasive Games: The Expressive Power of Videogames* (Cambridge: The MIT Press, 2010), pp. vi–viii; James Newman, *Videogames*, 2nd edition (London; New York: Routledge, 2013), pp. 5–7.

13. Leigh Alexander, '"Gamers" Don't Have to Be Your Audience. "Gamers" Are Over', *Gamasutra*, 28 August 2014, http://www.gamasutra.com/view/news/224400/Gamers_dont_have_to_be_your_audience_Gamers_are_over.php.

14. Monica Anderson, 'Views on Gaming Differ by Race, Ethnicity', *Pew Research Center*, 17 December 2015, p. 2, http://www.pewresearch.org/fact-tank/2015/12/17/views-on-gaming-differ-by-race-ethnicity/ (accessed 8 April 2017).

15. Entertainment Software Association, 'U.S. Video Game Industry Generates $23.5 Billion in Revenue for 2015', Press Release (Washington, DC: Entertainment Software Association, 16 February 2016), http://www.theesa.com/article/u-s-video-game-industry-generates-23-5-billion-in-revenue-for-2015/ (accessed 8 April 2017).

16. Nielsen Company, 'Gaming Gone Global: Keeping Tabs on Worldwide Trends', *Nielsen*, 31 May 2016, http://www.nielsen.com/us/en/insights/news/2016/gaming-gone-global-keeping-tabs-on-worldwide-trends.html (accessed 8 April 2017).

17. Entertainment Software Association, '2015 Annual Report: A Year of Innovation and Achievement', Annual Report (Entertainment Software Association, 2015), p. 16, http://www.theesa.com/article/2015-esa-annual-report/ (accessed 8 April 2017).

18. Entertainment Software Association, 'Games: Improving the Economy' (Entertainment Software Association, 4 November 2014), p. 1.

19. The Princeton Review, 'Top Graduate Schools for Video Game Design – College Rankings' (Natick, MA: IAC/InterActive Unit, 2015), http://www.princetonreview.com/college-rankings/game-design/top-graduate-schools-for-video-game-design (accessed 8 April 2017).

20. D. Fox Harrell, *Phantasmal Media: An Approach to Imagination, Computation, and Expression* (Cambridge, Massachusetts: The MIT Press, 2013); Jane McGonigal, *SuperBetter: A Revolutionary Approach to Getting Stronger, Happier, Braver, and More Resilient** (New York: Penguin Press, 2015); Mary Flanagan and Helen Nissenbaum, *Values at Play in Digital Games* (Cambridge: The MIT Press, 2014); Miguel Sicart, *The Ethics of Computer Games* (Cambridge; London: The MIT Press, 2011); Miguel Sicart, *Beyond Choices: The Design of Ethical Gameplay* (Cambridge: The MIT Press, 2013); Mary Flanagan, *Critical Play: Radical*

Game Design (Cambridge: The MIT Press, 2009); Miguel Sicart, *Play Matters*, Playful Thinking (Cambridge: The MIT Press, 2014); Noah Wardrip-Fruin, *Expressive Processing: Digital Fictions, Computer Games, and Software Studies* (Cambridge: The MIT Press, 2009); Katherine Isbister, *How Games Move Us: Emotion by Design*, Playful Thinking (Cambridge: The MIT Press, 2016).

21. http://gamestudies.org (accessed 8 April 2017).

22. http://journals.sagepub.com/home/gac/ (accessed 8 April 2017)

23. Steven E. Jones, *The Meaning of Video Games: Gaming and Textual Strategies* (New York: Routledge, 2008), p. 1.

24. Ibid., p. 3.

25. Jon Dovey and Helen W. Kennedy, *Game Cultures: Computer Games as New Media*, Issues in Cultural and Media Studies (Maidenhead, Berkshire, England; New York: Open University Press, 2006); Geoff King and Tanya Krzywinska, *Tomb Raiders and Space Invaders: Videogame Forms and Contexts* (London; New York: I.B.Tauris; Distributed in the U.S. by Palgrave Macmillan, 2006); Alexander R. Galloway, *Gaming: Essays on Algorithmic Culture*, Electronic Mediations 18 (Minneapolis: University of Minnesota Press, 2006); Jones, *The Meaning of Video Games*; Nick Dyer-Witheford and Greig de Peuter, *Games of Empire: Global Capitalism and Video Games*, Electronic Mediations 29 (Minneapolis: University of Minnesota Press, 2009); Mark J.P. Wolf and Bernard Perron (eds), *The Routledge Companion to Video Game Studies*, Routledge Companions (New York: Routledge, 2014); Brian Schrank and Jay David Bolter, *Avant-Garde Videogames: Playing with Technoculture* (Cambridge: The MIT Press, 2014); Matthew Thomas Payne, *Playing War: Military Video Games After 9/11* (New York: NYU Press, 2016); Jennifer Malkowski and TreaAndrea M. Russworm (eds), *Gaming Representation: Race, Gender, and Sexuality in Video Games* (Bloomington: Indiana University Press, 2017).

26. Dyer-Witheford and de Peuter, *Games of Empire*.

27. Michael Hardt and Antonio Negri, *Empire* (Cambridge: Harvard University Press, 2001), p. xix.

28. Bronwyn Davies and Peter Bansel, 'Neoliberalism and Education', *International Journal of Qualitative Studies in Education* 20, no. 3 (May 2007), pp. 247–59, doi:10.1080/09518390701281751. See p. 247.

29. Noam Chomsky and Robert W. McChesney, *Profit Over People: Neoliberalism & Global Order*, 1st edition (New York: Seven Stories Press, 1999); Elizabeth Martinez, Arnoldo Garcia, and National Network for Immigrant and Refugee Rights, 'CorpWatch: What Is Neoliberalism?', *CorpWatch*, January 1 1997, http://www.corpwatch.org/article.php?id=376 (accessed 8 April 2017). See also: David Harvey, *A Brief History of Neoliberalism* (Oxford: Oxford University Press, 2007).

30. Stanley Fish, 'Neoliberalism and Higher Education', *Opinionator*, http://opin-ionator.blogs.nytimes.com/2009/03/08/neoliberalism-and-higher-education/

(accessed 22 April 2015); Stanley Fish, 'Aim Low', *The Chronicle of Higher Education*, 16 May 2003, http://chronicle.com/article/Aim-Low/45210 (accessed 8 April 2017); Sophia McLennen, 'Neoliberalism and the Crisis of Intellectual Engagement', *Works and Days* 26–27 (2009, 2008), pp. 259–470; Harvey, *A Brief History of Neoliberalism*; Henry Giroux and Susan Searls Giroux, *Take Back Higher Education: Race, Youth, and the Crisis of Democracy in the Post-Civil Rights* (New York: Palgrave Macmillan, 2004); Henry Giroux, 'Academic Unfreedom in America: Rethinking the University as a Democratic Public Sphere', *WORKS AND DAYS* 51/52, 53/54, no. 26 & 27 (September 2008), pp. 45–71; Jeffrey J. Williams, 'The Pedagogy of Debt', *College Literature* 33, no. 4 (2006), pp. 155–69; Jeffrey J. Williams, 'The Post-Welfare State University', *American Literary History* 18, no. 1 (Spring) (2006), pp. 190–216; Williams, 'The Pedagogy of Debt'; Miyoshi Masao, 'Ivory Tower in Escrow', in Miyoshi Masao and H.D. Harootunian (eds), *Learning Places: The Afterlives of Area Studies* (Durham: Duke University Press, 2002), pp. 19–60.

31. Giroux, 'Academic Unfreedom in America: Rethinking the University as a Democratic Public Sphere', p. 46.

32. Ibid., p. 46.

33. Lisa Nakamura, *Digitizing Race: Visual Cultures of the Internet*, Electronic Mediations 23 (Minneapolis: University of Minnesota Press, 2008), p. 3.

34. Alexander R. Galloway, 'Does the Whatever Speak?', in Lisa Nakamura and Peter Chow-White (eds), *Race After the Internet* (New York and London: Routledge, 2012), p. 118; Alexander R. Galloway, *The Interface Effect* (Cambridge; Malden: Polity, 2012).

35. American Psychological Association, 'APA Review Confirms Link Between Playing Violent Video Games and Aggression', http://www.apa.org, 13 August 2015, http://www.apa.org/news/press/releases/2015/08/violent-video-games.aspx (accessed 8 April 2017); Taylor Wofford, 'APA Says Video Games Make You Violent, but Critics Cry Bias', *Newsweek*, 20 August 2015, http://www.newsweek.com/apa-video-games-violence-364394 (accessed 8 April 2017).

36. Slavoj Žižek, 'Tolerance as an Ideological Category', *Critical Inquiry* 34, no. 4 (2008), p. 660, doi:10.1086/592539.

37. Wendy Brown, *Regulating Aversion: Tolerance in the Age of Identity and Empire*, 3rd printing, 1st paperback printing edition (Princeton: Princeton University Press, 2008).

38. Žižek, 'Tolerance as an Ideological Category', p. 679.

39. Ibid.

40. Alex Hern, 'Battlefield 1 Halts "#justWWIthings" Campaign before Remembrance Sunday', *Guardian*, 31 October 2016, sec. Technology,

https://www.theguardian.com/technology/2016/oct/31/battlefield-1-justw-withings-campaign-remembrance-sunday (accessed 8 April 2017).

41. Dyer-Witheford and de Peuter, *Games of Empire*.

42. Ernest Adams, 'Single-Player, Multiplayer, MMOG: Design Psychologies for Different Social Contexts' (Game Developers Conference, San Francisco, March 2010), http://www.gdcvault.com/play/1012332/Single-Player-Multiplayer-MMOG-Design (accessed 8 April 2017).

43. Nina B. Huntemann, 'Militarism & Video Games: An Interview with Nina Huntemann', interview by Michelle Barron, Transcript, 2013, Media Education Foundation, http://inspire.dawsoncollege.qc.ca/wp-content/uploads/2013/06/Miloitarism-and-Video-Games1.pdf.

44. Graeme Turner, *British Cultural Studies: An Introduction*, 3rd edition (London; New York: Routledge, 2003); Houston A. Baker, Manthia Diawara, and Ruth H. Lindeborg (eds), *Black British Cultural Studies: A Reader*, Black Literature and Culture (Chicago: University of Chicago Press, 1996).

45. Stuart Hall (ed.), *Culture, Media, Language: Working Papers in Cultural Studies, 1972–79* (London: [Birmingham, West Midlands]: Hutchinson; Centre for Contemporary Cultural Studies, University of Birmingham, 1980), p. 7.

46. Stuart Hall, 'Cultural Studies and Its Theoretical Legacies', in Lawrence Grossberg, Cary Nelson, and Paula A. Treichler (eds), *Cultural Studies* (New York: Routledge, 1992), p. 278.

47. Lawrence Grossberg, Cary Nelson, and Paula A. Treichler (eds), *Cultural Studies* (New York: Routledge, 1992); Simon During, *Cultural Studies: A Critical Introduction* (London; New York: Routledge, 2005); Michael Ryan and Hanna Musiol (eds), *Cultural Studies: An Anthology* (Malden, MA; Oxford: Blackwell Pub, 2008).

48. Procter, *Stuart Hall*, p. 19.

49. Norma Schulman, 'Conditions of Their Own Making: An Intellectual History of the Centre for Contemporary Cultural Studies at the University of Birmingham', *Canadian Journal of Communication* 18, no. 1 (1 January 1993), http://www.cjc-online.ca/index.php/journal/article/view/717 (accessed 8 April 2017).

50. Hall, *Culture, Media, Language*. This text is a collection of 'Working Papers' from the CCCS during the 1970s and as such provides a great sampling of the kinds of critical undertakings made under Hall's leadership.

51. Hall, 'Cultural Studies and Its Theoretical Legacies', p. 282.

52. Ibid., p. 282. For two excellent documents on feminism and cultural studies, see: Anne Balsamo, 'Feminism and Cultural Studies', *The Journal of the Midwest Modern Language Association* 24, no. 1 (1 April 1991), pp. 50–73, doi:10.2307/1315025; University of Birmingham, *Women Take Issue: Aspects of Women's Subordination* (London: Hutchinson, 1978).

53. John Storey, *What Is Cultural Studies?: A Reader* (Bloomsbury USA, 1996); John Storey, *Cultural Studies and the Study of Popular Culture*, 3rd edition (Edinburgh: Edinburgh University Press, 2010); Lawrence Grossberg, *Bringing It All Back Home: Essays on Cultural Studies* (Duke University Press, 1997); Grossberg, *Cultural Studies in the Future Tense*; Turner, *British Cultural Studies*; Angela McRobbie, *The Uses of Cultural Studies: A Textbook* (London; Thousand Oaks: SAGE, 2005); Gilbert B. Rodman, *Why Cultural Studies?* (Hoboken: Wiley, 2014).

54. Rodman, *Why Cultural Studies?*, pp. 39–40.

55. During, *Cultural Studies*, p. 38.

56. Ibid., p. 39.

57. Griselda Pollock, 'Becoming Cultural Studies: The Daydream of the Political', in Paul Bowman (ed.), *Interrogating Cultural Studies: Theory, Politics and Practice* (London; Sterling, 2003), p. 133.

58. Stuart Hall, 'Introduction', in Stuart Hall (ed.), *Representation: Cultural Representations and Signifying Practices*, Culture, Media, and Identities (London; Thousand Oaks: Sage in association with the Open University, 1997), p. 2.

59. Ryan and Musiol, *Cultural Studies*, p. xvi.

60. Ibid., pp. xvi–xvii.

61. Ibid., p. xviii.

62. Mieke Bal, 'From Cultural Studies to Cultural Analysis: A Controlled Reflection on the Formation of Method', in Paul Bowman (ed.), *Interrogating Cultural Studies: Theory, Politics and Practice* (London; Sterling: Pluto Press, 2003), p. 30.

63. Stuart Hall, 'Notes on Deconstructing "the Popular"', in John Storey (ed.), *Cultural Theory and Popular Culture: A Reader* (New Jersey: Pearson / Prentice Hall, 1998), p. 448.

64. Ibid., p. 453.

65. Axel Honneth, *The Struggle for Recognition: The Moral Grammar of Social Conflicts*, Reprint (Cambridge: Polity Press, 2004).

66. Soraya Murray, 'High Art/Low Life: The Art of Playing Grand Theft Auto', *PAJ: A Journal of Performance and Art* 27, no. 2 (1 May 2005), pp. 91–8.

67. Espen Aarseth, 'Computer Game Studies, Year One', *Game Studies: The International Journal of Computer Game Research* 1, no. 1 (July 2001), http://gamestudies.org/0101/editorial.html.

68. Espen Aarseth, 'Computer Game Studies, Year One', *Game Studies: The International Journal of Computer Game Research* 1, no. 1 (July 2001), http://gamestudies.org/0101/editorial.html (accessed 8 April 2017).

69. Galloway, *Gaming*, p. 2.

70. Ibid., pp. 71–2.
71. Shaw, 'What Is Video Game Culture?', p. 413.
72. Ibid., p. 410.
73. Shaw, *Gaming at the Edge*, p. 6.
74. Noah Wardrip-Fruin, 'Playable Media and Textual Instruments', *Dichtung Digital*, 2005, http://www.dichtung-digital.de/2005/1/Wardrip-Fruin/index. htm (accessed 8 April 2017); Marita Sturken and Lisa Cartwright, *Practices of Looking: An Introduction to Visual Culture*, 2nd edition (New York: Oxford University Press, 2009), p. 175.
75. Flanagan, *Critical Play*.
76. Ibid., pp. 253–4.
77. Ibid., pp. 254.
78. Dyer-Witheford and de Peuter, *Games of Empire*.
79. Shaw, 'What Is Video Game Culture?', p. 405.
80. Ibid., p. 404.
81. Ibid., p. 409.
82. Ibid., p. 411.
83. Ibid., p. 416.
84. Derek Conrad Murray and Soraya Murray, 'Uneasy Bedfellows: Canonical Art Theory and the Politics of Identity', *Art Journal* 65, no. 1 (1 March 2006), pp. 22–39, doi:10.1080/00043249.2006.10791193.
85. Bal, 'Visual Essentialism and the Object of Visual Culture'.
86. Nicholas Mirzoeff, *An Introduction to Visual Culture*, 2nd edition (London; New York: Routledge, 2009), p. 12.
87. Griselda Pollock et al., 'Responses to Mieke Bal's "Visual Essentialism and the Object of Visual Culture" (2003)', *Journal of Visual Culture* 2, no. 2 (1 August 2003), doi:10.1177/14704129030022012; Mieke Bal, 'Responses to Mieke Bal's 'Visual Essentialism and the Object of Visual Culture' (2003), Mieke Bal's Reply to the Responses', *Journal of Visual Culture* 2, no. 2 (1 August 2003), pp. 260–8, doi:10.1177/14704129030022012.
88. Murray and Murray, 'Uneasy Bedfellows'.
89. Ibid., pp. 37–39.
90. Sturken and Cartwright, *Practices of Looking*, p. 23.
91. Among the many fine texts that explicate visual culture studies, see: John Berger, *Ways of Seeing*, Reprint edition (London: Penguin Books, 1990); October, 'Questionnaire on Visual Culture', *October* 77, no. Summer (1996), pp. 25–70; James Elkins, *The Object Stares Back: On the Nature of Seeing* (San Diego: Mariner Books, 1997); Stuart Hall (ed.), *Representation: Cultural Representations and Signifying Practices*, 1st edition (London; Thousand Oaks: Sage Publications & Open University, 1997); Jessica Evans and Stuart Hall (eds), *Visual Culture:*

The Reader (London; Thousand Oaks: SAGE Publications in association with the Open University, 1999); W.J.T. Mitchell, *What Do Pictures Want?: The Lives and Loves of Images* (Chicago: University of Chicago Press, 2005); Mirzoeff, *An Introduction to Visual Culture*; Amelia Jones (ed.), *The Feminism and Visual Culture Reader*, 2nd edition (London: Routledge, 2010); Gillian Rose, *Visual Methodologies: An Introduction to Researching with Visual Materials*, 3rd edition (London; Thousand Oaks: SAGE Publications Ltd, 2011); Richard Howells and Joaquim Negreiros, *Visual Culture*, 2nd edition (Cambridge: Polity, 2012); Norman Bryson, Michael Ann Holly and Keith Moxey (eds), *Visual Culture: Images and Interpretations* (Wesleyan, 2013); Nicholas Mirzoeff (ed.), *The Visual Culture Reader*, 3rd edition (London; New York: Routledge, 2013).

92. Hall, Jhally and Media Education Foundation, *The Origins of Cultural Studies: A Lecture*.

93. Ian Bogost, *Unit Operations: An Approach to Videogame Criticism*, 1st edition (Cambridge: The MIT Press, 2006).

94. Bogost, *Persuasive Games*, p. ix.

95. Ibid.

96. Ibid., p. viii.

97. Ibid., p. 339.

98. Brendan Keogh, 'Across Worlds and Bodies: Criticism in the Age of Video Games', *Journal of Games Criticism* 1, no. 1 (22 January 2014), p. 3.

99. Keogh, 'Across Worlds and Bodies'.

100. Ibid., p. 7.

101. Ibid., pp. 7–8.

102. Ian Bogost, 'Videogames Are a Mess: My DiGRA 2009 Keynote, on Videogames and Ontology', *Bogost.com*, 3 September 2009, http://bogost.com/writing/videogames_are_a_mess/ (accessed 8 April 2017).

103. Keogh, 'Across Worlds and Bodies', pp. 18–19.

104. David Sudnow, *Pilgrim in the Microworld* (New York: Warner Books, 1983). Thank you to Noah Wardrip-Fruin for introducing me to this text.

105. Clara Fernández-Vara, *Introduction to Game Analysis* (New York: Routledge, 2014), pp. 210–15.

106. Jay David Bolter and Richard Grusin, *Remediation: Understanding New Media* (Cambridge: The MIT Press, 2003).

107. Shaw, *Gaming at the Edge*, p. 231.

108. Raiford Guins, *Game After: A Cultural Study of Video Game Afterlife* (Cambridge: The MIT Press, 2014).

109. Ibid., p. 11.

110. BBC News, 'Blog Death Threats Spark Debate', *BBC*, 27 March 2007, sec. Technology, http://news.bbc.co.uk/2/hi/technology/6499095.stm (accessed

8 April 2017); Shira Chess and Adrienne Shaw, 'A Conspiracy of Fishes, Or, How We Learned to Stop Worrying About #GamerGate and Embrace Hegemonic Masculinity', *Journal of Broadcasting & Electronic Media* 59, no. 1 (2 January 2015), pp. 208–20, doi:10.1080/08838151.2014.999917.

111. Anastasia Salter and Bridget Blodgett, 'Hypermasculinity & Dickwolves: The Contentious Role of Women in the New Gaming Public', *Journal of Broadcasting & Electronic Media* 56, no. 3 (July 2012), pp. 401–16, doi:10.1080/08838151.2012.705199.

112. Ibid., p. 406.

113. Anita Sarkeesian, 'One Week of Harassment on Twitter', *Feminist Frequency*, 20 January 2015, http://femfreq.tumblr.com/post/109319269825/one-week-of-harassment-on-twitter (accessed 8 April 2017). See also: Hari Sreenivasan, '#Gamergate Leads to Death Threats against Women', *PBS NewsHour*, 16 October 2014, http://www.pbs.org/newshour/bb/gamergate-leads-death-threats-women-gaming-industry/ (accessed 8 April 2017); Leigh Alexander, 'Sexism, Lies and Video Games: The Culture War Nobody Is Winning', *Time*, 5 September 2014, http://time.com/3274247/video-game-culture-war/ (accessed 8 April 2017); Jenn Frank, 'How to Attack a Woman Who Works in Video Gaming', *Guardian*, 1 September 2014, http://www.theguardian.com/technology/2014/sep/01/how-to-attack-a-woman-who-works-in-video-games (accessed 8 April 2017); Keith Stewart, 'Gamergate: The Community Is Eating Itself but There Should Be Room for All', *Guardian*, 3 September 2014, http://www.theguardian.com/technology/2014/sep/03/gamergate-corruption-games-anita-sarkeesian-zoe-quinn (accessed 8 April 2017); Emma M. Woolley, 'Don't Believe the "conspiracy", Gaming Has Bigger Problems than "corruption"', *The Globe and Mail*, 27 August 2014, http://www.theglobeandmail.com/technology/digital-culture/dont-believe-the-conspiracy-gaming-has-bigger-problems-than-corruption/article20230850/ (accessed 8 April 2017); Tracey Lien, 'Why Are Women Leaving the Tech Industry in Droves?', *Los Angeles Times*, 22 February 2015, http://www.latimes.com/business/la-fi-women-tech-20150222-story.html#page=1 (accessed 8 April 2017); Liz Ryerson' 'On "Gamers" And Identity, «First Person Scholar', *First Person Scholar*, 10 September 2014, http://www.firstpersonscholar.com/on-gamers-and-identity/ (accessed 8 April 2017).

114. Among the others targeted are Jenn Frank, Leigh Alexander, Mattie Brice and Samantha Allen. See: Sreenivasan, '#Gamergate Leads to Death Threats against Women'.

115. Helen Lewis, 'Gamergate: A Brief History of a Computer-Age War', *Guardian*, 11 January 2015, http://www.theguardian.com/technology/2015/jan/11/gamergate-a-brief-history-of-a-computer-age-war (accessed 8 April 2017); Simon

Parkin, 'Zoe Quinn's Depression Quest', *The New Yorker*, 9 September 2014, http://www.newyorker.com/tech/elements/zoe-quinns-depression-quest (accessed 8 April 2017); Chris Plante, 'An Awful Week to Care about Video Games', *Polygon*, 29 August 2014, http://www.polygon.com/2014/8/28/6078391/video-games-awful-week (accessed 8 April 2017); Fruzsina Eördögh, 'The Anti-Feminist Internet Targets "Depression Quest" Game Creator Zoe Quinn', *Motherboard*, 19 August 2014, http://motherboard.vice.com/blog/zoe-quinn-slut-shaming-the-feminist-conspiracy-and-depression-quest (no longer available); Sam Biddle, 'The Psychopaths of GamerGate Are All That's Left, and They're Terrifying', *Gawker*, 2 February 2015, http://internet.gawker.com/the-psychopaths-of-gamergate-are-all-thats-left-and-th-1683271908 (accessed 8 April 2017).

116. Katherine Cross puts forward a useful definition of 'Social Justice Warriors' as the following: 'The phrase "social justice warrior" was originally coined on Tumblr to describe a dangerous tendency among some leftist activists to aggressively and angrily pursue political goals according to strict ideological codes, often to the detriment of others, with no clear collective gain, but significant personal aggrandizement'. See: Katherine Cross, ' "We Will Force Gaming to Be Free": On GamerGate & the Licence to Inflict Suffering', 8 October 2014, http://www.firstpersonscholar.com/we-will-force-gaming-to-be-free/ (accessed 8 April 2017).

117. Chess and Shaw, 'A Conspiracy of Fishes, Or, How We Learned to Stop Worrying About #GamerGate and Embrace Hegemonic Masculinity', p. 210.

118. There were also many sympathetic male participants who presented their own experiences with sexism while observing the treatment of women around them, such as wives and colleagues.

119. Bridget Blodgett and Anastasia Salter, '#1ReasonWhy: Game Communities and the Invisible Woman', in *Proceedings of the 9th International Conference on the Foundations of Digital Games* (Foundations of Digital Games 2014, Society for the Advancement of the Science of Digital Games, 2014), http://www.fdg2014.org/proceedings.html (accessed 1 May 2017).

120. Griffin McElroy, 'IGDA Draws Backlash, Member Resignations over Female Dancers at GDC Party (Update: IGDA Responds)', *Polygon*, 28 March 2013, http://www.polygon.com/2013/3/28/4157266/igda-gdc-party-brenda-romero-resignation (accessed 8 April 2017). See also: Brenda Romero and Leigh Alexander, 'GDC Vault – #1ReasonToBe', *GDC Vault*, 2014, http://www.gdcvault.com/play/1020593/ (accessed 8 April 2017).

121. Brianna Wu, 'Rape and Death Threats Are Terrorizing Female Gamers. Why Haven't Men in Tech Spoken Out?', *The Washington Post*, 20 October 2014,

http://www.washingtonpost.com/posteverything/wp/2014/10/20/rape-and-death-threats-are-terrorizing-female-gamers-why-havent-men-in-tech-spoken-out/ (accessed 8 April 2017).

122. Hiawatha Bray, 'Brianna Wu Appears at PAX East Videogame Convention', *BostonGlobe.com*, 8 March 2015, https://www.bostonglobe.com/metro/2015/03/08/brianna-appears-pax-east-videogame-convention/hEzlyb5ggIf03vKy-cUa2aL/story.html (accessed 8 April 2017).

123. Lisa Nakamura, 'Racism, Sexism, and Gaming's Cruel Optimism', in Jennifer Malkowski and TreaAndrea M. Russworm (eds), *Gaming Representation: Race, Gender, and Sexuality in Video Game Studies* (Bloomington: Indiana University Press, 2017), pp. 245–50.

124. Alexander, 'Sexism, Lies and Video Games: The Culture War Nobody Is Winning'.

125. Anna Everett, Alex Champlin and John Vanderhoef, 'Race, Space, and Digital Games: An Interview with Anna Everett', *Media Fields Journal* 8 (2014), p. 2.

126. Ibid., p. 5.

127. Donna St. George, 'Study Links Violent Video Games, Hostility', *The Washington Post*, 3 November 2008, sec. Technology, http://www.washingtonpost.com/wp-dyn/content/article/2008/11/02/AR2008110202392.html (accessed 8 April 2017); Roni Caryn Rabin, 'Video Games and the Depressed Teenager', *The New York Times*, 18 January 2011, http://well.blogs.nytimes.com/2011/01/18/video-games-and-the-depressed-teenager/ (accessed 8 April 2017); Nathan Grayson, 'Why Aren't We Discussing Videogame Violence?', *Rock, Paper, Shotgun*, 28 December 2012, http://www.rockpapershotgun.com/2012/12/28/why-arent-we-discussing-videogame-violence/ (accessed 8 April 2017); St. George, 'Study Links Violent Video Games, Hostility'; Leo Kelion, 'EA Boss Denies Video Games Encourage Violent Attacks', *BBC News*, 21 January 2013, http://www.bbc.com/news/technology-21274482 (accessed 8 April 2017); Sean Coughlan, 'Violent Video Games Leave Teens "Morally Immature"', *BBC News*, 6 February 2014, http://www.bbc.com/news/education-26049333 (accessed 8 April 2017); Patrick Stafford, 'How to End Video Games' Bullying Problem: Change the Games', *The Atlantic*, 22 May 2014, http://www.theatlantic.com/entertainment/archive/2014/05/how-to-fix-video-games-bullying-problem/371344/ (accessed 8 April 2017).

128. Dennis Scimeca, 'BioWare Developer Manveer Heir Challenges Colleagues to Combat Prejudice with Video Games', *VentureBeat*, 20 March 2014, http://venturebeat.com/2014/03/20/bioware-developer-manveer-heir-challenges-colleagues-to-combat-prejudice-with-video-games/ (accessed 8 April 2017).

129. Sabrina Tavernise, 'Numbers of Children of Whites Falling Fast', *The New York Times*, 6 April 2011, http://www.nytimes.com/2011/04/06/us/06census.html (accessed 8 April 2017). See also: William H Frey, *Diversity Explosion: How New Racial Demographics Are Remaking America* (Washington, DC: Brookings Institution Press, 2015).

130. Nakamura, 'Racism, Sexism, and Gaming's Cruel Optimism'.

131. Carolyn Petit, 'Why Political Engagement Is Critical to Games Journalism', *A Game of Me*, 23 August 2014, http://agameofme.tumblr.com/post/95611752882/why-political-engagement-is-critical-to-games (accessed 8 April 2017).

132. Anna Anthropy, *Rise of the Videogame Zinesters: How Freaks, Normals, Amateurs, Artists, Dreamers, Dropouts, Queers, Housewives, and People like You Are Taking Back an Art Form*, Seven Stories Press, 1st edition (New York: Seven Stories Press, 2012).

133. Ian Bogost, *How to Talk about Videogames* (Minneapolis: University of Minnesota Press, 2015), p. 181.

134. Nakamura, *Digitizing Race*.

135. Richard Dyer, *White: Essays on Race and Culture* (London; New York: Routledge, 1997), p. 4.

136. Manuel Castells, *End of Millennium: The Information Age: Economy, Society, and Culture Volume III*, 2nd edition with a new preface edition (Oxford; Malden: Wiley-Blackwell, 2010), p. 168.

137. Grossberg, *Cultural Studies in the Future Tense*, p. 1.

138. Ian Bogost, *How to Do Things with Videogames*, Electronic Mediations 38 (Minneapolis: University of Minnesota Press, 2011), p. xii.

139. Mary Flanagan, 'Response by Mary Flanagan to Celia Pearce, 'Towards a Game Theory of Game', in Noah Wardrip-Fruin and Pat Harrigan (eds), *First Person: New Media as Story, Performance, and Game* (Cambridge: The MIT Press, 2004), p. 145.

1 Poetics of Form and Politics of Identity; Or, Games as Cultural Palimpsests

1. Ian Bogost, 'Videogames Are a Mess: My DiGRA 2009 Keynote, on Videogames and Ontology', *Bogost.com*, 3 September 2009, http://bogost.com/writing/videogames_are_a_mess/.

2. To be clear, the franchise has demonstrated a record of diversity in regard to male protagonists: Altaïr Ibn- La'Ahad (a Syrian assassin), Ezio Auditore da Firenze (an Italian), and Ratohnhaké:ton [Connor Kenway] (a bi-racial English/Mohawk) are each of the protagonists in three primary *Assassin's Creed* titles, respectively.

3. Philip Kollar, 'Assassin's Creed 3: Liberation Review: The Price of Chains', *Polygon*, 31 October 2012, http://www.polygon.com/2012/10/31/3582448/assassins-creed-3-liberation-review (accessed 8 May 2017).

4. Hall makes mention of a 'politics of identity' and a 'politics of position' in Stuart Hall, 'Cultural Identity and Diaspora', in Jonathan Rutherford (ed.), *Identity: Community, Culture, Difference* (London: Lawrence & Wishart, 1990), p. 226. See an explication of this term in: James Procter, *Stuart Hall*, Routledge Critical Thinkers (London; New York: Routledge, 2004), pp. 117–19.

5. Stuart Hall, 'Minimal Selves', in Homi Bhabha (ed.), *Identity: The Real Me*, ICA Documents (London: Institute of Contemporary Arts, 1987), p. 45.

6. Procter, *Stuart Hall*, p. 119. See also: Stuart Hall, 'New Ethnicities', in David Morley (ed.), *Stuart Hall: Critical Dialogues in Cultural Studies* (New York: Routledge, 1996), pp. 441–9.

7. Kimberlé W. Crenshaw, 'Demarginalizing the Intersection of Race and Sex: A Black Feminist Critique of Antidiscrimination Doctrine, Feminist Theory and Antiracist Politics', *The University of Chicago Legal Forum* (1989), pp. 139–167. Kimberlé W. Crenshaw, 'Mapping the Margins: Intersectionality, Identity Politics, and Violence Against Women of Color', *Stanford Law Review*, no. 43 (July 1991), p. 1245.

8. Crenshaw, 'Mapping the Margins: Intersectionality, Identity Politics, and Violence Against Women of Color', p. 1299.

9. Stuart Hall, 'The Whites of Their Eyes', in Gail Dines and Jean McMahon Humez (eds), *Gender, Race, and Class in Media: A Critical Reader* (London: SAGE Publications, 2015), p. 104.

10. Ibid., pp. 104–105.

11. Procter, *Stuart Hall*, p. 1.

12. While I will not be discussing these essays specifically, I would like to point to key early essays on race and games: David Leonard, 'Live in Your World, Play in Ours – Race, Video Games, and Consuming the Other', *Studies in Media & Information Literacy Education* 3, no. 4 (November 2003), pp. 1–9; David Leonard, 'High Tech Blackface—Race, Sports Video Games and Becoming the Other', *Intelligent Agent* 4, no. 4.2 (2004); Dean Chan, 'Playing with Race: The Ethics of Racialized Representations in E-Games', *International Review of Information Ethics* 4 (December 2005), pp. 24–30.

13. Hall, 'The Whites of Their Eyes', p. 105.

14. Anna Everett and S.C. Watkins, 'The Power of Play: The Portrayal and Performance of Race in Video Games', in *The Ecology of Games: Connecting Youth, Games and Learning* (Cambridge: The MIT Press, 2007), pp. 141–64. See also Michel Marriott, 'Blood, Gore, Sex and Now: Race', *The New York Times*, 21 October 1999, sec. Technology, http://www.nytimes.com/1999/10/21/technology/blood-gore-sex-and-now-race.html (accessed 8 May 2017).

15. Alexander R. Galloway, 'Does the Whatever Speak?', in Lisa Nakamura and Peter Chow-White (eds), *Race After the Internet* (New York and London: Routledge, 2012), p. 119.

16. D.J. Leonard, 'Not a Hater, Just Keepin' It Real: The Importance of Race- and Gender-Based Game Studies', *Games and Culture* 1, no. 1 (1 January 2006), p. 83, doi:10.1177/1555412005281910.

17. Tara McPherson, 'U.S. Operating Systems at Mid-Century: The Intertwining of Race and UNIX', in Lisa Nakamura and Peter Chow-White (eds), *Race After the Internet* (New York and London: Routledge, 2012), p. 23.

18. Ibid., p. 24.

19. Ian G.R. Shaw and Joanne P. Sharp, 'Playing with the Future: Social Irrealism and the Politics of Aesthetics', *Social & Cultural Geography* 14, no. 3 (May 2013), p. 343, doi:10.1080/14649365.2013.765027.

20. I refer to the police killings of young black men and boys, increasingly covered in the mainstream media, such as the 'Rough Ride' van killing of Freddie Gray while in police custody (2015); Walter Scott (2015); 12-year-old Tamir Rice (2014); Michael Brown, aged 18 (2014); John Crawford III (2014); Eric Garner (2014); Jonathan Ferrell, who sought help from a nearby house after a car accident and was shot ten times by police (2013).

21. Williams, 'Assassin's Creed Unity and Rethinking the Core of Assassin's Creed.'

22. Lisa Nakamura, *Digitizing Race: Visual Cultures of the Internet*, Electronic Mediations 23 (Minneapolis: University of Minnesota Press, 2008), p. 202.

23. Ibid., pp. 207–208.

24. For more some key readings on advanced technology and race by Nakamura and others, see: Beth Kolko, Lisa Nakamura, and Gilbert Rodman (eds), *Race in Cyberspace*, 1st edition (New York: Routledge, 2000); Alicia Hedlam Hines and Alondra Nelson (ed.), *Technicolor: Race, Technology, and Everyday Life*, (New York; London: NYU Press, 2001); Lisa Nakamura, *Cybertypes: Race, Ethnicity, and Identity on the Internet* (New York: Routledge, 2002); Maria Fernandez, Faith Wilding and Michelle M. Wright (eds), *Domain Errors!: Cyberfeminist Practices* (New York: Autonomedia, 2003); Everett and Watkins, 'The Power of Play: The Portrayal and Performance of Race in Video Games'; Nakamura, *Digitizing Race*; Lisa Nakamura and Peter Chow-White (eds), *Race after the Internet* (New York: Routledge, 2012).

25. Adrienne Shaw, *Gaming at the Edge: Sexuality and Gender at the Margins of Gamer Culture* (Minneapolis: University of Minnesota Press, 2015), p. x.

26. Ibid., p. 219.

27. Ibid., pp. 218–20.

28. Ibid., pp. 225–6.

29. Matthew Thomas Payne, *Playing War: Military Video Games After 9/11* (New York: NYU Press, 2016), p. 209.

30. Bogost, 'Videogames Are a Mess: My DiGRA 2009 Keynote, on Videogames and Ontology'.

31. Statistics from 2016.

32. See for example the following reviews: Miguel Concepcion, 'Assassin's Creed III: Liberation HD Review', *GameSpot*, 23 January 2014, http://www.gamespot.com/reviews/assassin-s-creed-iii-liberation-hd-review/1900-6415643/ (accessed 8 May 2017); Vince Ingenito, 'Assassin's Creed Liberation HD Review – IGN', *IGN*, 17 January 2014, http://www.ign.com/articles/2014/01/18/assassins-creed-liberation-hd-review (accessed 8 May 2017); Kollar, 'Assassin's Creed 3'; Chris Suellentrop, 'Slavery as New Focus for a Game: Assassin's Creed: Liberation Examines Colonial Blacks', *The New York Times*, 27 January 2014, sec. C1, http://www.nytimes.com/2014/01/28/arts/video-games/assassins-creed-liberation-examines-colonial-blacks.html (accessed 8 May 2017); Nick Gillett, 'Assassin's Creed III: Liberation—Review', *Guardian*, 9 November 2012, http://www.theguardian.com/technology/2012/nov/10/assassins-creed-3-liberation-review (accessed 8 May 2017).

33. Center for Games and Playable Media, *Inventing the Future of Games [IFOG] 2011: Jordan Mechner* (UC Santa Cruz Center for Games and Playable Media, 2011), https://vimeo.com/24028511 (accessed 8 May 2017).

34. Ibid.

35. In an interview with *Assassin's Creed: Unity* (2014) Creative Director, Alex Amancio, who identified the core mechanics of the AC series: 'There are three core pillars: navigation, stealth, and combat. The combination of those three things is really unique, it's very Assassin's Creed.' See: Mike Williams, 'Assassin's Creed Unity and Rethinking the Core of Assassin's Creed', *USgamer.net*, 14 October 2014, http://www.usgamer.net/articles/assassins-creed-unity-interview-with-alex-amancio (accessed 8 May 2017).

36. Edward W. Said, *Orientalism*, 1st Vintage Books edition (New York: Vintage Books, 1979).

37. Ibid., p. 5.

38. Ibid., p. 6.

39. Vit Šisler, 'Digital Arabs: Representation in Video Games', *European Journal of Cultural Studies* 11, no. 2 (2008), pp. 203–20.

40. Ibid.

41. I would like to acknowledge and thank Wlad Godzich of the University of California at Santa Cruz for his thoughtful comments on my earlier research on *Grand Theft Auto*, regarding the playing of games as engagement with myth, during a presentation of my work in progress at the Center for Cultural Studies.

42. Said, *Orientalism*, p. 8.

243

43. Lisbeth Klastrup, 'A Poetics of Virtual Worlds', in *Proceedings of Digital Arts and Culture* (Melbourne: MelbourneDAC2003, 2003), p. 101.

44. Ibid.

45. Hall discussed this specific connection between fiction, imperialism and notions of adventure in relation to the nineteenth-century novel. However, the phrasing is very apt here, and I would extend this characterization to apply to a broader period of European colonial expansion. See: Hall, 'The Whites of Their Eyes,' p. 106.

46. There is a huge body of knowledge on blackness and issues of representation. See for example: bell hooks, *Black Looks: Race and Representation*, 1st edition (Boston: South End Press, 1992); Michael D. Harris, *Colored Pictures: Race and Visual Representation* (Chapel Hill: The University of North Carolina Press, 2006); Nicole R. Fleetwood, *Troubling Vision: Performance, Visuality, and Blackness* (Chicago: The University of Chicago Press, 2011); Alessandra Raengo, *On the Sleeve of the Visual: Race as Face Value*, 1st edition, Interfaces: Studies in Visual Culture (Hanover: Dartmouth College Press, 2013); Alexander G. Weheliye, *Habeas Viscus: Racializing Assemblages, Biopolitics, and Black Feminist Theories of the Human* (Durham: Duke University Press, 2014).

47. Derek Conrad Murray, *Queering Post-Black Art: Artists Transforming African-American Identity After Civil Rights* (London; New York: I.B.Tauris, 2016).

48. Jill Murray, 'Diverse Game Characters: Write Them Now!' (Game Developers Conference 2013, San Francisco, 29 March 2013), http://www.gdcvault.com/play/1017819/Diverse-Game-Characters-Write-Them (accessed 8 May 2017).

49. Ibid., 12:00.

50. *Plaçage* was a system of informal common-law marriage between a white man and a woman of color, which was not legally recognized – because interracial marriage was forbidden – but did grant the woman and any children produced some economic benefits and liminal security, as well as recognition of the relationship among free people of colour. See: Sybil Kein (ed.), *Creole: The History and Legacy of Louisiana's Free People of Color* (Baton Rouge: LSU Press, 2000).

51. Evan Narcisse, 'Assassin's Creed III: Liberation: The Kotaku Review', *Kotaku*, 30 October 2012, http://kotaku.com/5957502/assassins-creed-iii-liberation-the-kotaku-review (accessed 8 May 2017).

52. Dennis Scimeca, 'BioWare Developer Manveer Heir Challenges Colleagues to Combat Prejudice with Video Games', *VentureBeat*, 20 March 2014, http://venturebeat.com/2014/03/20/bioware-developer-manveer-heir-challenges-colleagues-to-combat-prejudice-with-video-games/ (accessed 8 May 2017).

53. Okwui Enwezor, *Créolité and Creolization: Documenta 11Platform3* (Distributed Art Pub Incorporated, 2003), p. 15.

54. Édouard Glissant, *Poetics of Relation*, trans. Betsy Wing (Ann Arbor: University of Michigan Press, 1997).

55. Paul Gilroy, *The Black Atlantic: Modernity and Double-Consciousness*, Reissue edition (Cambridge: Harvard University Press, 1993).

56. Catherine Clinton, *Harriet Tubman: The Road to Freedom*, 1st edition (New York: Little, Brown, 2004), p. 89.

57. Juan L. Gonzales, *Racial and Ethnic Groups in America*, 5th edition (Dubuque, Iowa: Kendall/Hunt Publishing, 2003), pp. 304–305.

58. Evan Narcisse, 'I'm Surprised By How "Black" Assassin's Creed Liberation Feels', *Kotaku*, 1 November 2012, http://kotaku.com/5957411/im-surprised-by-how-black-assassins-creed-liberation-feels (accessed 8 May 2017).

59. Jagger Gravning, 'How Major Videogames Are Slowly Readying Us for a Gay Protagonist', *Kill Screen*, 9 February 2014, http://killscreendaily.com/articles/how-major-videogames-are-slowly-readying-us-gay-protagonist/ (no longer available). See also its printing in *The Atlantic*: Jagger Gravning, 'How Video Games Are Slowly, Quietly Introducing LGBT Heroes', *The Atlantic*, 25 February 2014, http://www.theatlantic.com/entertainment/archive/2014/02/how-video-games-are-slowly-quietly-introducing-lgbt-heroes/284017/ (accessed 8 May 2017).

60. Gordon Williams, *A Dictionary of Sexual Language and Imagery in Shakespearean and Stuart Literature: Three Volume Set Volume I A-F Volume II G-P Volume III Q-Z* (A&C Black, 2001), p. 1110, p. 501.

61. Gravning, 'How Major Videogames Are Slowly Readying Us for a Gay Protagonist'.

62. Galloway, 'Does the Whatever Speak?', p. 117.

63. Ibid., p. 118.

64. D. Fox Harrell, *Phantasmal Media: An Approach to Imagination, Computation, and Expression* (Cambridge: The MIT Press, 2013).

65. D. Fox Harrell, 'Imagining Social Identities Through Computing' (Media Theater, University of California, Santa Cruz, 11 May 2015).

66. Jill Murray and Soraya Murray, 'Personal Correspondence between Jill Murray and Author', 31 May 2015.

67. This is the tagline of Abstergo Industries' advertisement for the Animus.

68. Tanine Allison, 'The World War II Video Game, Adaptation, and Postmodern History', *Literature/Film Quarterly* 38, no. 3 (2010), pp. 183–93.

69. Evan Narcisse, 'A Game That Showed Me My Own Black History', *Kotaku*, 19 December 2013, http://kotaku.com/a-game-that-showed-me-my-own-black-history-1486643518; Evan Narcisse, 'White Actress Will Voice Assassin's Creed's Black Heroine [Correction]', *Kotaku*, 29 August 2012, http://kotaku.com/5939009/white-actress-will-voice-assassins-creeds-black-heroine (accessed 8 May 2017); Narcisse, 'I'm Surprised By How "Black" Assassin's

Creed Liberation Feels'; Evan Narcisse, 'This Assassin's Creed Heroine Is a Great Black Game Character. Here's How It Happened', *Kotaku*, 27 February 2013, http://kotaku.com/5987083/this-assassins-creed-heroine-is-a-great-black-game-character-heres-how-it-happened (accessed 8 May 2017); Evan Narcisse, 'Slavery Gives Me a Weird Personal Connection to Assassin's Creed IV', *Kotaku*, 16 July 2013, http://kotaku.com/slavery-gives-me-a-weird-personal-connection-to-assassi-799210668 (accessed 8 May 2017); Evan Narcisse, 'You're An Escaped Slave In Assassin's Creed IV's Freedom's Cry DLC', *Kotaku*, 8 October 2013, http://kotaku.com/youre-an-escaped-slave-in-em-assassin-s-creed-iv-em-1442477523 (accessed 8 May 2017).

70. 'DLC' stands for downloadable content, and demarks additional content that is released after the primary title launch. While it may refer to something as simple as additional game options like clothing or weaponry, in this case, it refers to an additional storyline playable through a secondary character to the main narrative.

71. Narcisse, 'A Game That Showed Me My Own Black History'.

72. Shaun McInnis, 'Why I Keep Thinking About Assassin's Creed III: Liberation', *GameSpot*, 8 November 2012, http://www.gamespot.com/articles/why-i-keep-thinking-about-assassins-creed-iii-liberation/1100-6399671/ (accessed 8 May 2017).

73. Adrienne Shaw, 'The Tyranny of Realism: Historical Accuracy in Assassin's Creed III', *First Person Scholar*, 29 October 2014, http://www.firstperson-scholar.com/the-tyranny-of-realism/ (accessed 8 May 2017).

74. Suellentrop, 'Assassin's Creed.'

75. Ibid.

2 Aesthetics of Ambivalence and Whiteness in Crisis

1. Richard Dyer, *The Matter of Images: Essays on Representation*, 2nd edition (London: Routledge, 2002), p. 1.

2. I borrow this notion of 'meaning-producing' practice from: Stuart Hall (ed.), *Representation: Cultural Representations and Signifying Practices*, 1st edition (London; Thousand Oaks: Sage Publications & Open University, 1997), p. 29.

3. Marita Sturken and Lisa Cartwright, *Practices of Looking: An Introduction to Visual Culture*, 2nd edition (New York: Oxford University Press, 2009), pp. 21–2.

4. Wendy Hui Kyong Chun, 'On Software, Or the Persistence of Visual Knowledge', in Nicholas Mirzoeff (ed.), *The Visual Culture Reader*, 3rd edition (London; New York: Routledge, 2013), p. 79. See also: Wendy Hui Kyong Chun, *Control and Freedom:*

Power and Paranoia in the Age of Fiber Optics (Cambridge: The MIT Press, 2008). Chun cites: Louis Althusser, 'Ideology and Ideological State Apparatuses (Notes Towards an Investigation)', in *Lenin and Philosophy and Other Essays*, trans. Ben Brewster (New York: Monthly Review Press, 2001), p. 109.

5. Chun, 'On Software, Or the Persistence of Visual Knowledge', p. 80.

6. Ibid.

7. Ibid., p. 82.

8. D. Fox Harrell, *Phantasmal Media: An Approach to Imagination, Computation, and Expression* (Cambridge: The MIT Press, 2013), p. 345.

9. Harrell, *Phantasmal Media*; D. Fox Harrell, 'A Phantasmal Media Approach to Empowerment, Identity, and Computation' (Digital Inflections: Visions for the Posthuman Future, Pacific Centre for Technology and Culture, 23 January 2013), http://pactac.net/2013/01/a-phantasmal-media-approach-to-empowerment-identity-and-computation/; D. Fox Harrell, 'Imagining Social Identities Through Computing' (Media Theater, University of California, Santa Cruz, 11 May 2015).

10. Gerald Voorhees, 'Criticism and Control: Gameplay in the Space of Possibility', in *Ctrl-Alt-Play: Essays on Control in Video Gaming*, ed. Matthew Wysocki (Jefferson, N.C: McFarland & Co, 2013), p. 19.

11. Mark Berman, 'Dylann Roof, Accused Charleston Church Gunman, Indicted on Federal Hate Crime Charges', *The Washington Post*, 22 July 2015, http://www.washingtonpost.com/news/post-nation/wp/2015/07/22/dylann-roof-accused-charleston-church-gunman-has-been-indicted-on-federal-hate-crime-charges/; 'The Shootings in a Charleston Church', *The New York Times*, 18 June 2015, http://www.nytimes.com/interactive/2015/06/18/us/charleston-church-shooting-maps-and-suspect.html (accessed 8 May 2017).

12. Yoni Appelbaum, 'Why Is the Flag Still There?', *The Atlantic*, 21 June 2015, http://www.theatlantic.com/politics/archive/2015/06/why-is-the-flag-still-there/396431/ (accessed 8 May 2017).

13. Michael McLaughlin, 'Racist Manifesto Purportedly Written By Dylann Roof Surfaces Online', *The Huffington Post*, 20 June 2015, http://www.huffingtonpost.com/2015/06/20/dylann-roof-manifesto-charleston-shooting_n_7627788.html (accessed 8 May 2017).

14. Jon Swaine, 'Leader of Group Cited in "Dylann Roof Manifesto" Donated to Top Republicans', *Guardian*, 21 June 2015, http://www.theguardian.com/us-news/2015/jun/21/dylann-roof-manifesto-charlston-shootings-republicans (accessed 8 May 2017); Lindsey Bever, '"Supremacist" Earl Holt III and His Donations to Republicans', *The Washington Post*, 23 June 2015, http://www.washingtonpost.com/news/morning-mix/wp/2015/06/23/meet-earl-holt-whose-supremacist-site-influenced-alleged-charleston-church-killer-dylann-roof/ (accessed 8 May 2017).

15. CNN, *Martin Luther King Jr. III Reacts to Charleston – CNN Video*, The Michael Smerconish Program, 2015, http://www.cnn.com/videos/tv/2015/06/20/exp-smerconish-martin-luther-iii.cnn (accessed 8 May 2017).

16. To be sure, there have been many other causes asserted, including the need for gun policy reform, drug abuse, the shooting being an 'accident', madness and domestic terrorism. A board member of National Rifle Association of America (NRA), in going on the offensive in response to the public discussion of the curtailment of gun rights, blamed the slain Clementa Pinkney for his previous no-vote on a concealed-carry proposition, arguing that if others had guns at the church, they could have defended themselves. However, once Roof's manifesto was unearthed, many of these purported causes fell away from the national conversation.

17. Ruth Frankenberg, 'The Mirage of an Unmarked Whiteness', in Birgit Brander Rasmussen et al. (eds), *The Making and Unmaking of Whiteness* (Durham: Duke University Press, 2001), p. 85.

18. 'Last Rhodesian' is the web address of Dylann Roof's site, which contained the aforementioned images and nearly 2,500 word manifesto.

19. Richard Dyer, *White: Essays on Race and Culture* (London; New York: Routledge, 1997), p. 233. See note 6.

20. Tycho, 'Penny Arcade – News – Larvae', *Penny Arcade*, 24 June 2013, http://penny-arcade.com/news/post/2013/6/24/larvae1 (accessed 8 May 2017); Kirk Hamilton, 'The Last of Us: The Kotaku Review', *Kotaku*, 29 July 2014, http://kotaku.com/the-last-of-us-the-kotaku-review-511292998 (accessed 8 May 2017).

21. Hamilton, 'The Last of Us'.

22. My use of the word 'trauma' is related to discourses around art and visual culture, specifically the theorization of identity art as a form of 'trauma narrative' as set forth by art historian and theorist Hal Foster. See, particularly, his essay 'The Artist as Ethnographer' in Hal Foster, *The Return of the Real: The Avante-Garde at the End of the Century*, paperback/softback edition (Cambridge: The MIT Press, 1996), pp. 171–203. See also my criticism of this selective attribution of the term trauma narrative to forms of difference in Derek Conrad Murray and Soraya Murray, 'Uneasy Bedfellows: Canonical Art Theory and the Politics of Identity', *Art Journal* 65, no. 1 (1 March 2006), pp. 22–39, doi:10.1080/00043249.2006.10791193. However, for an excellent address of the import of trauma studies for games, see: Toby Smethurst and Stef Craps, 'Playing with Trauma: Interreactivity, Empathy, and Complicity in The Walking Dead Video Game', *Games and Culture* 10, no. 3, 1 May 2015, pp. 269–90, doi:10.1177/1555412014559306.

23. Dean Takahashi, 'The DeanBeat: The Last of Us Is This Generation's Masterpiece', *VentureBeat*, June 2013, http://venturebeat.com/2013/06/28/the-deanbeat-the-last-of-us-is-this-generations-masterpiece/ (accessed 8 May 2017); Colin Moriarty, 'Survival of the Fittest', online media and services, *IGN*

Entertainment, 5 June 2013, http://www.ign.com/articles/2013/06/05/the-last-of-us-review (accessed 8 May 2017); Samit Sarkar, 'The Last of Us Remastered Is a Stunning Visual Masterpiece', *Polygon*, 16 July 2014, http://www.polygon.com/2014/7/16/5902983/the-last-of-us-remastered-ps4-preview-graphics (accessed 8 May 2017); Daniel Nye Griffiths, ' "The Last of Us": How Game Design Shaped Naughty Dog's Masterpiece, And Transformed Its Ending', *Forbes*, 14 July 2014, http://www.forbes.com/sites/danielnyegriffiths/2014/07/14/how-game-design-transformed-the-last-of-us/ (accessed 8 May 2017).

24. Daniel Bischoff, 'The Last of Us Review', *Game Revolution*, 6 June 2013, http://www.gamerevolution.com/review/the-last-of-us (accessed 8 May 2017). See also: Moriarty, 'IGN'.

25. Chris Suellentrop, 'In the Video Game The Last of Us, Survival Favors the Man', *The New York Times*, 14 June 2013, http://www.nytimes.com/2013/06/14/arts/video-games/in-the-video-game-the-last-of-us-survival-favors-the-man.html (accessed 8 May 2017); Alexandria Neonakis, 'Game Theory: The Last of Us, Revisited', *New York Times Blog: ArtsBeat*, 30 December 2013, sec. ArtsBeat, http://artsbeat.blogs.nytimes.com/2013/12/30/game-theory-the-last-of-us-revisited/ (accessed 8 May 2017); Keith Stuart, 'The Last of Us, Bioshock: Infinite and Why All Video Game Dystopias Work the Same Way', *Guardian*, 1 July 2013, sec. Technology, http://www.theguardian.com/technology/gamesblog/2013/jul/01/last-of-us-bioshock-infinite-male-view (accessed 8 May 2017).

26. A.M. Green, 'The Reconstruction of Morality and the Evolution of Naturalism in The Last of Us', *Games and Culture* forthcoming, no. Online (7 April 2015), pp. 1–19, doi:10.1177/1555412015579489.

27. Tyler Stallings, *Whiteness, a Wayward Construction*, First Edition (Laguna Beach; Los Angeles: Fellows of Contemporary Art, 2003), p. 17.

28. Ruth Frankenberg, 'White Women, Race Matters', in Les Back and John Solomos (eds), *Theories of Race and Racism: A Reader*, Routledge Student Readers (London; New York: Routledge, 2000), p. 447. See also: Ruth Frankenberg, *White Women, Race Matters: The Social Construction of Whiteness*, 1st edition (Minneapolis: University Of Minnesota Press, 1993).

29. Frankenberg, 'White Women, Race Matters', 2000, p. 451.

30. See for example: George Lipsitz, *The Possessive Investment in Whiteness: How White People Profit from Identity Politics*, Revised and expanded edition (Philadelphia: Temple University Press, 2006).

31. Birgit Brander Rasmussen et al. (eds), 'Introduction', in *The Making and Unmaking of Whiteness* (Durham: Duke University Press, 2001), p. 6.

32. Alex Kellogg, 'Has "Whiteness Studies" Run Its Course at Colleges?', News, *inAmerica: CNN Blog*, (30 January 2012), http://inamerica.blogs.cnn.com/2012/01/30/has-whiteness-studies-run-its-course-at-colleges/ (accessed 8 May 2017).

33. Among the many notable considerations of whiteness see: Toni Morrison, *Playing in the Dark: Whiteness and the Literary Imagination*, 1st Vintage Books edition (New York: Vintage Books, 1993); Frankenberg, *White Women, Race Matters*, 1993; Ruth Frankenberg (ed.), *Displacing Whiteness: Essays in Social and Cultural Criticism* (Durham: Duke University Press, 1997); Richard Delgado and Jean Stefancic (eds), *Critical White Studies: Looking Behind the Mirror* (Philadelphia: Temple University Press, 1997); Jessie Daniels, *White Lies: Race, Class, Gender and Sexuality in White Supremacist Discourse* (New York & London: Routledge, 1997); Matt Wray and Annalee Newitz (eds), *White Trash: Race and Class in America* (New York: Routledge, 1997); Mike Hill (ed.), *Whiteness: A Critical Reader* (New York: NYU Press, 1997); Grace Elizabeth Hale, *Making Whiteness: The Culture of Segregation in the South, 1890–1940* (New York, NY: Vintage, 1999); Matthew Frye Jacobson, *Whiteness of a Different Color: European Immigrants and the Alchemy of Race* (Cambridge: Harvard University Press, 1999); Maurice Berger, *White Lies: Race and the Myths of Whiteness*, 1st edition (New York: Farrar, Straus and Giroux, 2000); Joe L. Kincheloe et al. (eds), *White Reign: Deploying Whiteness in America*, 1st St. Martin's Griffin edition (New York: St. Martin's Griffin, 2000); Birgit Brander Rasmussen et al. (eds), *The Making and Unmaking of Whiteness* (Durham: Duke University Press, 2001), http://read.dukeupress.edu/lookup/doi/10.1215/9780822381044; Ira Katznelson, *When Affirmative Action Was White: An Untold History of Racial Inequality in Twentieth-Century America*, Reprint edition (New York: W. W. Norton & Company, 2006); David R. Roediger et al., *The Wages of Whiteness: Race and the Making of the American Working Class*, New Edition (London: Verso, 2007); Nell Irvin Painter, *The History of White People*, Reprint edition (New York: W. W. Norton & Company, 2011); Tim Wise, *White Like Me: Reflections on Race from a Privileged Son*, Revised Edition (Berkeley: Soft Skull Press, 2011); Theodore Allen, *The Invention of the White Race* (London: Verso, 2012); Paula S. Rothenberg (ed.), *White Privilege: Essential Readings on the Other Side of Racism*, 4th edition (New York: Worth Publishers, 2012); Charles A. Gallagher and France Winddance Twine, *Retheorizing Race and Whiteness in the 21st Century: Changes and Challenges*, Reprint edition (London; New York: Routledge, 2013).
34. Hua Hsu, 'The End of White America?', *The Atlantic*, February 2009, http://www.theatlantic.com/magazine/archive/2009/01/the-end-of-white-america/307208/ (accessed 8 May 2017). See also: Dale Maharidge, *The Coming White Minority: California, Multiculturalism, and America's Future*, 1st Vintage Books edition (New York: Vintage Books, 1999).
35. Thomas Ross, 'Whiteness After 9/11', Washington University Journal of Law & Policy 18, no. 1 (January 2005), p. 235.

36. Ibid., pp. 238–40.
37. Ibid., p. 243.
38. Ruth Frankenberg, 'Cracks in the Façade: Whiteness and the Construction of 9/11', *Social Identities* 11, no. 6 (November 2005), p. 559, doi:10.1080/13504630500449093.
39. Ibid., p. 569.
40. Hsu cites this phrase by Pat Buchanan, a conservative thinker in his book, *Death of the West*. See: Hsu, 'The End of White America?' and also William H. Frey, *Diversity Explosion: How New Racial Demographics Are Remaking America* (Washington, DC: Brookings Institution Press, 2015).
41. This is also described in detail in the Introduction.
42. Brander Rasmussen et al., 'Introduction', p. 6.
43. Ibid.
44. Ibid., pp. 10–13.
45. Dyer, *White*.
46. Ibid., p. 11.
47. Dyer, *The Matter of Images*, p. 4.
48. Dyer, *White*, p. 3.
49. Ibid., pp. 48–57.
50. Ibid., p. 4.
51. Ibid., p. 66.
52. Ibid., p. 81.
53. Lindsey Joyce, 'An Uneven Partnership', *First Person Scholar*, 9 July 2014, http://www.firstpersonscholar.com/an-uneven-partnership/ (accessed 8 May 2017); Gerald Voorhees, 'Mourning Sex', *First Person Scholar*, 3 September 2014, http://www.firstpersonscholar.com/mourning-sex/ (accessed 8 May 2017).
54. Maddy Myers, 'Bad Dads Vs. Hyper Mode: The Father-Daughter Bond In Videogames', *Pastemagazine.com*, 30 July 2013, http://www.pastemagazine.com/articles/2013/07/hyper-mode.html (accessed 8 May 2017); Mattie Brice, 'The Dadification of Video Games Is Real', *Mattie Brice*, August 2013, http://www.mattiebrice.com/the-dadification-of-video-games-is-real/ (accessed 8 May 2017); Jess Joho, 'The Dadification of Videogames, Round Two', *Kill Screen*, 11 February 2014, http://killscreendaily.com/articles/dadification-videogames-round-two/ (no longer available); Kirk Hamilton, 'Video Gaming's Latest Breakthrough Moment', *Kotaku*, 17 February 2014, http://kotaku.com/video-gamings-latest-breakthrough-moment-1524555480 (accessed 8 May 2017).
55. From the promotional materials to the film. See: Joel Schumacher, *Falling Down* (Warner Bros., 1993); John Gabriel, 'What Do You Do When Minority Means You? *Falling Down* and the Construction of "whiteness,"' *Screen* 37, no. 2 (20 June 1996), pp. 129–51, doi:10.1093/screen/37.2.129.
56. Dyer, *White*, p. 222.

57. Ibid., p. 217.

58. Ibid., pp. 184–87.

59. Ibid., pp. 205–6.

60. Evan Watts, 'Ruin, Gender, and Digital Games', *WSQ: Women's Studies Quarterly* 39, no. 3–4 (2011), p. 248, doi:10.1353/wsq.2011.0041.

61. Ibid., pp. 255–6.

62. Giancarlo Valdes, 'In *The Last of Us*, You Have to Earn the Right to Survive (Review)', *VentureBeat*, 5 June 2013, http://venturebeat.com/2013/06/05/the-last-of-us-review/ (accessed 8 May 2017).

63. Derek A. Burrill, *Die Tryin': Videogames, Masculinity, Culture, Popular Culture and Everyday Life*, v. 18 (New York: Peter Lang, 2008), pp. 48–9.

64. Stuart, 'The Last of Us, Bioshock.'

65. Ibid.

66. Voorhees, 'Mourning Sex.'

67. Hamilton, 'Video Gaming's Latest Breakthrough Moment.'

68. Dyer, *White*, p. 208.

69. Ibid., pp. 209–11.

70. Ibid., p. 211.

71. Voorhees, 'Mourning Sex.'

72. Ibid.

73. Gregory J. Krieg, 'Freaking Out: The Best of the Worst Responses to Obama's Win', News, *ABC News*, 8 November 2012, http://abcnews.go.com/blogs/politics/2012/11/freaking-out-the-best-of-the-worst-responses-to-obamas-win/ (accessed 8 May 2017); David Horsey, 'Obama Win Brings the Great Right Wing Freak-out of 2012', *The Baltimore Sun*, 13 November 2012, http://articles.baltimoresun.com/2012-11-13/news/bs-ed-horsey-gop-20121113_1_corporate-welfare-americans-election-results (accessed 8 May 2017).

74. Soraya Murray, 'Race, Gender, and Genre in Spec Ops: The Line', *Film Quarterly* 70, no. 2 (December 2016), pp. 38–48.

75. The Metascore average of reviews for the game was 76 out of a possible 100. 'Metacritic – Movie Reviews, TV Reviews, Game Reviews, and Music Reviews', accessed 15 August 2015, http://www.metacritic.com/.

76. Miguel Sicart, *Beyond Choices: The Design of Ethical Gameplay* (Cambridge: MIT Press, 2013), pp. 111–16.

77. I will discuss only the single-player mode, although there was also a much less-favoured multiplayer mode, which the lead developer of the game, Walt Williams, also criticized as the less-optimal way to play.

78. Matt Bertz, '*Spec Ops: The Line* Review: A Descent Into Madness', Game Review, *Game Informer*, (26 June 2012), http://www.gameinformer.com/games/spec_ops_the_line/b/xbox360/archive/2012/06/26/review.aspx (accessed 8 May 2017).

79. Hollander Cooper, 'Spec Ops: The Line – Learn about the Story with Lead Writer Walt Williams', GamesRadar+, 30 March 2012, http://www.gamesradar.com/spec-ops-line-learn-about-story-lead-writer-walt-williams/ (accessed 8 May 2017); Kyle Orland, 'Spec Ops: The Line's Lead Writer on Creating an Un-Heroic War Story', Ars Technica, 19 July 2012, http://arstechnica.com/gaming/2012/07/spec-ops-the-lines-lead-writer-on-creating-an-un-heroic-war-story/ (accessed 8 May 2017); Adam Rosenberg, 'Spec Ops: The Line Post-Mortem – Finding Deeper Truths Within the Narrative With Walt Williams', G4tv.com, 17 July 2012, http://www.g4tv.com/thefeed/blog/post/726042/spec-ops-the-line-post-mortem-finding-deeper-truths-within-the-narrative-with-walt-williams/ (accessed 8 May 2017).

80. Orland, 'Spec Ops'.

81. Mitch Dyer, 'The Story Secrets of Spec Ops: The Line', IGN, 20 July 2012, http://www.ign.com/articles/2012/07/20/the-story-secrets-of-spec-ops-the-line (accessed 7 May 2017).

82. Kirk Hamilton, 'Spec Ops Writer on Violent Games: "We're Better Than That"', Games Journalism, Kotaku, (27 March 2013), http://kotaku.com/spec-ops-writer-on-violent-games-were-better-than-th-460992384 (accessed 7 May 2017).

83. Cooper, 'Spec Ops'.

84. I say 'his' because the vast majority of these types of characters are male.

85. Matthew Thomas Payne, 'War Bytes: The Critique of Militainment in Spec Ops: The Line', Critical Studies in Media Communication 31, no. 4 (8 August 2014), p. 266, doi:10.1080/15295036.2014.881518.

86. Ibid., pp. 266–8.

87. Marcus Schulzke, 'The Critical Power of Virtual Dystopias', Games and Culture 9, no. 5 (1 September 2014), p. 329, doi:10.1177/1555412014541694.

88. H. Pötzsch, 'Selective Realism: Filtering Experiences of War and Violence in First- and Third-Person Shooters', Games and Culture first published online (31 May 2015), pp. 1–23, doi:10.1177/1555412015587802.

89. H. Pötzsch, 'Selective Realism'.

90. Ibid., p. 15.

91. Rosenberg, 'Spec Ops'.

92. See my full analysis of the setting of Dubai in my analysis of game landscape as ideology in Chapter 3.

93. Anne-Marie Schleiner, 'Does Lara Croft Wear Fake Polygons? Gender and Gender-Role Subversion in Computer Adventure Games', Leonardo 34, no. 3 (1 January 2001), pp. 221–6.

94. Jon Dovey and Helen W. Kennedy, Game Cultures: Computer Games as New Media, Issues in Cultural and Media Studies (Maidenhead, Berkshire, England; New York: Open University Press, 2006), p. 93.

95. Justine Cassell and Henry Jenkins (eds), *From Barbie to Mortal Kombat: Gender and Computer Games*, p. 1. MIT Press paperback edition (Cambridge: MIT Press, 2000), p. 32.

96. Helen W. Kennedy, 'Lara Croft: Feminist Icon or Cyberbimbo?', *Game Studies: The International Journal of Computer Game Research* 2, no. 2 (December 2002).

97. Espen Aarseth, 'Genre Trouble: Narrativism and the Art of Simulation', in Noah Wardrip-Fruin and Pat Harrigan (eds), *First Person: New Media as Story, Performance, and Game*, (Cambridge: The MIT Press, 2004), p. 48.

98. Ibid., p. 46.

99. Esther MacCallum-Stewart, '"Take That, Bitches!" Refiguring Lara Croft in Feminist Game Narratives', *Game Studies* 14, no. 2 (December 2014), http://gamestudies.org/1402/articles/maccallumstewart (accessed 8 May 2017). See also: Rus McLaughlin, 'IGN Presents: The History of *Tomb Raider*', *IGN*, 29 February 2008, http://www.ign.com/articles/2008/03/01/ign-presents-the-history-of-tomb-raider (accessed 8 May 2017); Adrienne Shaw, *Gaming at the Edge: Sexuality and Gender at the Margins of Gamer Culture* (Minneapolis: University of Minnesota Press, 2015), pp. 58–63. McLaughlin writes: 'Eventually, they settled on a tough South American woman in a long braid and hot pants, willing to go to any lengths to win the greatest trophies lost to history. An Olympic-level athlete, an expert of antiquities, a born survivor. Gard named his creation Laura Cruz.'

100. An excellent analysis comparing the reimagined Lara Croft to the imperiled Greek mythological figure of Andromeda was presented by Meghan Blythe Adams, 'Andromeda on the Rocks: Retreading and Resisting Tropes of Female Sacrifice in "*Tomb Raider*"' (History of Gender in Games, Auditorium de la Grande Bibliothèque, Montréal [Québec], 26 June 2015), www.sahj.ca.

101. Dyer, *The Matter of Images*, p. 96.

102. Ibid., pp. 96–8.

103. Ibid., pp. 98–9.

104. Adams, 'Andromeda on the Rocks: Retreading and Resisting Tropes of Female Sacrifice in "*Tomb Raider*."'

105. Simon Parkin, '*Tomb Raider* – Review', *Guardian*, 1 March 2013, sec. Technology, http://www.theguardian.com/technology/gamesblog/2013/mar/01/tomb-raider-video-game-review (accessed 8 May 2017); Philip Kollar, '*Tomb Raider* Review: The Descent', *Polygon*, 25 February 2015, http://www.polygon.com/2013/2/25/4026668/tomb-raider-review (accessed 8 May 2017); Matt Miller, 'Tomb Raider Review – Old Name, Remarkable New Series', www.GameInformer.com, 25 February 2013, http://www.gameinformer.com/games/tomb_raider/b/xbox360/archive/2013/02/25/tomb-raider-review.aspx (accessed 8 May 2017); Evan Narcisse, '*Tomb Raider*: The Kotaku Review', *Kotaku*, 25 February 2013, http://kotaku.com/5986619/tomb-raider-the-kotaku-review (accessed 8 May 2017);

Becky Chambers, 'Lara Croft Is Dead, Long Live Lara Croft: Reflections On *Tomb Raider*', *The Mary Sue*, 8 March 2013, http://www.themarysue.com/tomb-raider-review/ (accessed 8 May 2017).

106. Parkin, '*Tomb Raider* – Review'.

107. This reaction to be protective toward Lara was reportedly common among play testers. See: Jason Schreier, '*Tomb Raider* Creators Say "Rape" Is Not A Word In Their Vocabulary' *Kotaku*, 29 June 2012, http://kotaku.com/5922228/tomb-raider-creators-say-rape-is-not-a-word-in-their-vocabulary (accessed 8 May 2017).

108. Ibid.

109. Dyer, *White*, p. 223.

3 The Landscapes of Games as Ideology

1. W.J.T. Mitchell, 'Imperial Landscape', in W.J.T. Mitchell (ed.), *Landscape and Power*, 2nd edition (Chicago: University of Chicago Press, 2002), p. 10.

2. Eugénie Shinkle, 'Gameworlds and Digital Gardens: Landscape and the Space of Nature in Digital Games' (World Building: Third Annual UF Games and Digital Media Conference, University of Florida, Gainesville, 1 March 2007).

3. Jordan Mechner, 'The Sands of Time: Crafting a Video Game Story', in Pat Harrigan and Noah Wardrip-Fruin (eds), *Second Person: Role Playing and Story in Games and Playable Media* (Cambridge: The MIT Press, 2007), p. 114.

4. Patrick Jagoda et al., 'Worlding through Play: Alternate Reality Games, Large-Scale Learning, and *The Source*', *American Journal of Play* 8, no. 1 (Fall 2015), pp. 74–100.

5. For some considerations of game space in earlier writings, please see: Soraya Murray, 'High Art/Low Life: The Art of Playing Grand Theft Auto', *PAJ: A Journal of Performance and Art* 27, no. 2 (1 May 2005), pp. 91–8; Soraya Murray, 'Race, Gender, and Genre in *Spec Ops: The Line*', *Film Quarterly* 70, no. 2 (December 2016), pp. 38–48.

6. Toshi Nakamura, 'Hideo Kojima: This Is What Fox Engine Is All About', *Kotaku*, 21 March 2013, http://kotaku.com/5991640/hideo-kojima-this-is-what-fox-engine-is-all-about.

7. Peter Brown, 'Metal Gear Solid V: The Phantom Pain Review', *GameSpot*, 23 August 2015, http://www.gamespot.com/reviews/metal-gear-solid-v-the-phantom-pain-review/1900-6416224/ (accessed 8 May 2017); Rich Stanton, 'Metal Gear Solid V – How Kojima Productions Is Blowing Apart the Open-World Video Game', *Guardian*, 11 June 2015, sec. Technology,

http://www.theguardian.com/technology/2015/jun/11/metal-gear-solid-v-phantom-pain-kojima-preview (accessed 8 May 2017).

8. W.J.T. Mitchell (ed.), *Landscape and Power*, 2nd edition (Chicago: University of Chicago Press, 2002), p. 1.

9. Ibid., p. 2.

10. Henry Jenkins and Kurt Squire, 'The Art of Contested Spaces', in Lucien King (ed.), *Game on: The History and Culture of Videogames* (London: Laurence King Publishing, 2002), p. 65.

11. Jon Dovey and Helen W. Kennedy, *Game Cultures: Computer Games as New Media*, Issues in Cultural and Media Studies (Maidenhead, Berkshire, England; New York: Open University Press, 2006), p. 28.

12. Dovey and Kennedy, *Game Cultures*. They in turn cite: Lev Manovich, *The Language of New Media*, Reprint edition (Cambridge: The MIT Press, 2002), pp. 246–7.

13. The second half of *The Phantom Pain* takes place in the Angola-Zaire border region. Representing Africa in this game is even more fraught, but far too complex to address in this chapter.

14. For key writings on the history and interpretation of landscape in art history and visual culture, see: Raymond Williams, *The Country and the City*, 1st issued as an Oxford University Press paperback, Reprint (New York: Oxford University Press, 1975); Jay Appleton, *Experience of Landscape* (London; New York: John Wiley & Sons Inc, 1975); Kenneth Clark, *Landscape Into Art*, 2nd Revised edition (London: John Murray Publishers Ltd, 1979); John Brinckerhoff Jackson, *The Necessity for Ruins, and Other Topics* (Amherst: University of Massachusetts Press, 1980); David H. Solkin and Richard Wilson, *Richard Wilson: The Landscape of Reaction* (London: Tate Gallery, 1982); Malcolm Andrews, *The Search for the Picturesque: Landscape Aesthetics and Tourism in Britain, 1760–1800* (Stanford: Stanford University Press, 1989); Ann Bermingham, *Landscape and Ideology: The English Rustic Tradition, 1740–1860* (Berkeley: University of California Press, 1989); William H. Truettner et al. (eds), *The West as America: Reinterpreting Images of the Frontier, 1820–1920* (Washington, DC: Published for the National Museum of American Art by the Smithsonian Institution Press, 1991); John Brinckerhoff Jackson, *A Sense of Place, a Sense of Time* (New Haven: Yale University Press, 1994); Simon Schama, *Landscape and Memory*, 1st Vintage Books edition (New York: Vintage Books, 1996); Denis E. Cosgrove, *Social Formation and Symbolic Landscape*, New edition (Madison: University of Wisconsin Press, 1998); Leo Marx, *The Machine in the Garden: Technology and the Pastoral Ideal in America* (New York: Oxford University Press, 2000); Mitchell, *Landscape and Power*; Kenneth Olwig, *Landscape, Nature, and the Body Politic: From Britain's Renaissance to America's New World* (Madison: University of Wisconsin Press, 2002); Rachel DeLue and James Elkins (eds), *Landscape Theory*, 1st edition (New York: Routledge, 2007); Denis Cosgrove

and Stephen Daniels (eds), *The Iconography of Landscape: Essays on the Symbolic Representation, Design and Use of Past Environments*, 10th printing, Cambridge Studies in Historical Geography 9 (Cambridge: Cambridge University Press, 2008); Denis E. Cosgrove, *Geography and Vision: Seeing, Imagining and Representing the World* (London; New York: I.B.Tauris, 2008); John E. Crowley, *Imperial Landscapes: Britain's Global Visual Culture, 1745–1820* (New Haven: Published for the Paul Mellon Centre for Studies in British Art by Yale University Press, 2011); Vittoria Di Palma, *Wasteland: A History* (New Haven: Yale University Press, 2014).

15. Michael McWhertor, 'Metal Gear Solid 5: The Phantom Pain Review: Future Legend', *Polygon*, 27 August 2015, http://www.polygon.com/2015/8/27/9207599/metal-gear-solid-5-the-phantom-pain-review-ps4-xbox-one-PC (accessed 8 May 2017); Sam Byford, 'Metal Gear Solid V: The One-Month Review', *The Verge*, 1 October 2015, http://www.theverge.com/2015/10/1/9431725/mgs5-review (accessed 8 May 2017).

16. Will Brooker, 'Camera-Eye, CG-Eye: Videogames and the "Cinematic"', *Cinema Journal* 48, no. 3 (2009), p. 126, doi:10.1353/cj.0.0126.

17. For an excellent overview of realism in games, both fidelity to naturalism (aesthetics), and congruence with the lived world (functional realism) see: Geoff King and Tanya Krzywinska, 'Realism, Spectacle, Sensation', in *Tomb Raiders and Space Invaders: Videogame Forms and Contexts* (London; New York: I.B.Tauris; Distributed in the U.S. by Palgrave Macmillan, 2006), pp. 124–67.

18. Payne, 'War Bytes', p. 267.

19. Jean Baudrillard, 'The Hyper-Realism of Simulation', in Mark Poster (ed.), *Jean Baudrillard: Selected Writings*, (Stanford: Stanford University Press, 1988), pp. 143–7. See also: Jean Baudrillard, *Simulacra and Simulation*, 1st edition, 17th printing edition (Ann Arbor: University of Michigan Press, 1995).

20. Chris Morris, 'Dan Houser's Very Extended Interview about Everything "Grand Theft Auto IV" and Rockstar', Blog, *Variety*, (19 April 2008), http://weblogs.variety.com/the_cut_scene/2008/04/dan-housers-ver.html (accessed 8 May 2017); Nick Cowen, 'Dan Houser Interview: Rockstar Games' Writer for GTA 4 and The Lost And Damned', *The Telegraph*, 28 January 2009, http://www.telegraph.co.uk/technology/video-games/4373632/Dan-Houser-interview-Rockstar-Gamess-writer-for-GTA-4-and-The-Lost-And-Damned.html (accessed 8 May 2017). Similarly, in regard to *Metal Gear Solid*, Derek Noon and Nick Dyer-Witheford point to the satirical critique of American imperialist tendencies: 'the ambivalences of its [*Metal Gear's*] depiction of war reflects both the encounter of Western action genres with Japan's own traditions of militarism and unabashed hyper-violence (Snake owes much to the *ronin* tradition of wandering samurai warriors), and strong strands of opposition to nuclear weapons, hostility to American global dominance, and alarm at the

mutant machine-human melds that populate the battlefields of contemporary techno-war.' See: Derek Noon and Nick Dyer-Witheford, 'Sneaking Mission: Late Imperial America and *Metal Gear Solid*', in Wright, J. Talmadge, Embrick, David G., and Lukács, András (eds.), *Utopic Dreams and Apocalyptic Fantasies: Critical Approaches to Researching Video Game Play* (Blue Ridge Summit, PA: Lexington Books, 2010), 76.

21. Janet Horowitz Murray, *Hamlet on the Holodeck: The Future of Narrative in Cyberspace* (New York: Simon and Schuster, 1997). See especially pp. 79–83.

22. Manovich, *The Language of New Media*, p. 252.

23. Espen Aarseth, 'Allegories of Space: The Question of Spatiality in Computer Games', in *Cybertext Yearbook 2000* (Jyvaskyla, Finland: Research Centre for Contemporary Culture, 2001), p. 154.

24. Henry Jenkins, 'Game Design as Narrative Architecture', in Noah Wardrip-Fruin and Pat Harrigan (eds), *First Person: New Media as Story, Performance, and Game* (Cambridge: The MIT Press, 2006), p. 121. See also: Henry Jenkins, '"Complete Freedom of Movement": Video Games as Gendered Playspace', in Justine Cassell and Henry Jenkins (eds), *From Barbie to Mortal Kombat: Gender and Computer Games*, 1st MIT Press paperback edition (Cambridge: The MIT Press, 2000), pp. 330–63; Jenkins and Squire, 'The Art of Contested Spaces'.

25. Jenkins, 'Game Design as Narrative Architecture', p. 122. See also: Jenkins, '"Complete Freedom of Movement": Video Games as Gendered Playspace'.

26. Jenkins, 'Game Design as Narrative Architecture', p. 123.

27. Ibid., pp. 124–5.

28. Michael Nitsche, *Video Game Spaces: Image, Play, and Structure in 3D Worlds* (Cambridge: The MIT Press, 2009), pp. 15–16.

29. Ibid., p. 203.

30. Ibid., p. 34.

31. Ibid., p. 182.

32. Ibid., p. 91.

33. Walter Benjamin, 'The Work of Art in the Age of Mechanical Reproduction', in Hannah Arendt (ed.), *Illuminations* (New York: Schocken Books, 1986), p. 229.

34. Ibid., p. 246. See note 10.

35. Nitsche, *Video Game Spaces*, p. 233.

36. Jonas Heide Smith et al., *Understanding Video Games: The Essential Introduction*, 2nd edition (New York: Routledge, 2013), pp. 157–92.

37. Mark J.P. Wolf, 'Worlds', in Mark J.P. Wolf and Bernard Perron (eds), *The Routledge Companion to Video Game Studies*, (New York & London: Routledge, 2014), p. 126; Mark J.P. Wolf, *Building Imaginary Worlds: The Theory and History of Subcreation* (New York: Routledge, 2012). For an excellent additional

explanation of world-building, see: Henry Jenkins, 'Building Imaginary Worlds: An Interview with Mark J.P. Wolf (Part One)', Blog, *Confessions of an Aca-Fan* (2 September 2013), http://henryjenkins.org/2013/09/building-imaginary-worlds-an-interview-with-mark-j-p-wolf-part-one.html (accessed 8 May 2017); Mark J.P. Wolf, 'Space in the Video Game', in Mark J.P. Wolf (ed.), *The Medium of the Video Game*, 1st edition (Austin: University of Texas Press, 2001), pp. 52–75.

38. Wolf, *Building Imaginary Worlds*, p. 17.

39. Ibid.

40. Henry Jenkins, 'Building Imaginary Worlds: An Interview with Mark J.P. Wolf (Part Three)', Blog, *Confessions of an Aca-Fan* (6 September 2013), http://henryjenkins.org/2013/09/building-imaginary-worlds-an-interview-with-mark-j-p-wolf-part-three.html (accessed 8 May 2017).

41. Wolf, *Building Imaginary Worlds*, p. 15.

42. James Newman, *Videogames*, 2nd edition (London; New York: Routledge, 2013), pp. 109–10.

43. Mary Fuller and Henry Jenkins, 'Nintendo and New World Travel Writing: A Dialogue', in Steven G. Jones (ed.), *Cybersociety: Computer-Mediated Communication and Community* (Sherman Oaks: SAGE Publications, 1995), p. 59, http://web.stanford.edu/class/history34q/readings/Cyberspace/Fuller Jenkins_Nintendo.html (no longer available).

44. Ibid., p. 58.

45. Ibid., p. 66.

46. Ibid., p. 67.

47. Newman, *Videogames*, p. 111.

48. Ibid., p. 109. See: Fuller and Jenkins, 'Nintendo and New World Travel Writing: A Dialogue.'

49. Newman, *Videogames*, p. 105.

50. William H. Huber, 'Epic Spatialities: The Production of Space in Final Fantasy Games', in Pat Harrigan and Noah Wardrip-Fruin (eds), *Third Person: Authoring and Exploring Vast Narratives* (Cambridge, MA: The MIT Press, 2009), p. 381.

51. Fuller and Jenkins, 'Nintendo and New World Travel Writing: A Dialogue', p. 69.

52. D. Flynn, 'Languages of Navigation within Computer Games' (Digital Art and Culture, Melbourne, Australia, 2003), http://hypertext.rmit.edu.au/dac/papers/Flynn.pdf (no longer available).

53. Geoff King and Tanya Krzywinska, 'Gamescapes: Exploration and Virtual Presence in Game-Worlds', in *Tomb Raiders and Space Invaders: Videogame Forms and Contexts* (London; New York: I.B.Tauris; Distributed in the US by Palgrave Macmillan, 2006), p. 76.

54. King and Krzywinska, *Tomb Raiders and Space Invaders*, p. 96.

55. King and Krzywinska, 'Gamescapes: Exploration and Virtual Presence in Game-Worlds', p. 101.

56. Shinkle, 'Gameworlds and Digital Gardens.'

57. Ibid.

58. King and Krzywinska, *Tomb Raiders and Space Invaders*, p. 28.

59. Johan Huizinga, *Homo Ludens: A Study of the Play-Element in Culture*, 1st edition (London: Beacon Press, 1971).

60. Mia Consalvo, 'There Is No Magic Circle', *Games and Culture* 4, no. 4 (1 October 2009), p. 415, doi:10.1177/1555412009343575.

61. Michael W. Longan, 'Playing With Landscape: Social Process and Spatial Form in Video Games', *Aether: The Journal of Media Geography* II (April 2008), p. 23.

62. Ibid., pp. 24–5.

63. Longan especially references: Cosgrove, *Social Formation and Symbolic Landscape*; Cosgrove and Daniels, *The Iconography of Landscape*.

64. Miguel Sicart, *The Ethics of Computer Games* (Cambridge; London: The MIT Press, 2011), p. 4.

65. Ibid., p. 31.

66. Ibid., p. 32.

67. In reference to 'social engineering', I am referring to it in the sense of political science (i.e., the use of mass culture to influence social attitudes), not computer security and hacking.

68. Mitchell, 'Imperial Landscape', p. 10.

69. Ibid., p. 14.

70. Appleton, *Experience of Landscape*; Clark, *Landscape Into Art*; Bermingham, *Landscape and Ideology*.

71. Mitchell, *Landscape and Power*, p. x.

72. Ibid.

73. W.J.T. Mitchell (ed.), 'Israel, Palestine, and the American Wilderness', in *Landscape and Power*, 2nd edition (Chicago: University of Chicago Press, 2002), p. 265. In his essay on Israel, Mitchell writes: 'I think of *place* and *space* in the terms made familiar by Michel de Certeau: a place is a specific location; a *"space is a practiced place"*, a site activated by movements, actions, narratives, and signs. A landscape, then, turns site into a sight, place and space into a visual image'. Mitchell cites de Certeau, p. 117. See also 'Introduction' in Mitchell, *Landscape and Power*; Michel de Certeau, *The Practice of Everyday Life*, trans. Steven Rendall, 3rd edition (Berkeley: University of California Press, 2011); Henri Lefebvre, *The Production of Space*, 1st edition (Oxford: Wiley-Blackwell, 1992).

74. Mitchell, *Landscape and Power*, p. xi.

75. Here see also Chapter 2. In mention of the technical system of code that is also a cultural system, I am making reference to: D. Fox Harrell, *Phantasmal Media:*

An Approach to Imagination, Computation, and Expression (Cambridge: The MIT Press, 2013), p. 345.

76. Mitchell, 'Imperial Landscape', p. 14.

77. Stuart Hall, 'Encoding, Decoding', in Simon During (ed.), *The Cultural Studies Reader* (London: Routledge, 1993), p. 91.

78. Ibid., p. 95.

79. Reception studies in relation to games is extremely important as well, and while the current project is more focused on ideology and representation from a cultural studies and visual studies perspective, there are excellent resources for player reception. See especially: Adrienne Shaw, *Gaming at the Edge: Sexuality and Gender at the Margins of Gamer Culture* (Minneapolis: University of Minnesota Press, 2015).

80. There are exceptions, such as games that only allow a single playthrough, or do not allow the character to regenerate once they have died. Gonzalo Frasca has discussed, for example, 'one-session games of narration', in which it is possible to play only once. See: Gonzalo Frasca, 'Don't Play It Again, Sam: One-Session and Serial Games of Narration' (Digital Arts and Culture, University of Bergen, Norway, October 1998), http://cmc.uib.no/dac98/papers/frasca.html (accessed 8 May 2017).

81. Mitchell, 'Imperial Landscape', p. 16.

82. Ibid., p. 29.

83. Mary Flanagan and Helen Nissenbaum, *Values at Play in Digital Games* (Cambridge: The MIT Press, 2014), pp. 68–9.

84. Richard Cohen, 'The Soviets' Vietnam', *The Washington Post*, 22 April 1988, http://www.washingtonpost.com/archive/opinions/1988/04/22/the-soviets-vietnam/5e7fde43-6a0c-46fb-b678-dbb89bcb720b/ (accessed 8 May 2017); Amal Hamdan, 'Afghanistan: The Soviet Union's Vietnam', News, *Al Jazeera*, (23 April 2003), http://www.aljazeera.com/archive/2003/04/2008410113842420760.html (accessed 8 May 2017); Admin, 'The Soviet Occupation of Afghanistan', *PBS NewsHour*, 10 October 2006, http://www.pbs.org/newshour/updates/asia-july-dec06-soviet_10-10/ (accessed 8 May 2017); Neda Atanasoski, 'Restoring National Faith: The Soviet-Afghan War in U.S. Media and Politics', in *Humanitarian Violence: The U.S. Deployment of Diversity*, Difference Incorporated (Minneapolis; London: University of Minnesota Press, 2013), pp. 102–27.

85. Hamdan, 'Afghanistan: The Soviet Union's Vietnam.'

86. Ibid.

87. Communications scholars Marita Sturken and Lisa Cartwright have characterized the spectacular nature of the event itself and its subsequent perpetual news media representation in the aftermath. Marita Sturken and Lisa Cartwright, *Practices of Looking: An Introduction to Visual Culture*, 2nd edition (New York: Oxford University Press, 2009), pp. 252–5.

88. Mitchell, 'Israel, Palestine, and the American Wilderness', p. 266.

89. Ibid.

90. By 'disinterested' I refer to the writings of Immanuel Kant, *Critique of the Power of Judgment*, trans. Paul Guyer and Eric Matthews (Cambridge: Cambridge University Press, 2000). In it, disinterestedness refers not to lack of interest in the subject, but lacking of the desire for something to provide a certain self-interested satisfaction.

91. Marx, *The Machine in the Garden*, p. 4.

92. Ibid., p. 370.

93. Ibid., p. 43.

94. Ibid., p. 38.

95. Ibid., p. 39.

96. Ibid., p. 43.

97. Ibid., p. 370.

98. Dan Rather, as cited in Atanasoski, 'Restoring National Faith: The Soviet-Afghan War in U.S. Media and Politics', p. 118.

99. Ibid., p. 119.

100. Ibid.

101. Neda Atanasoski, *Humanitarian Violence: The U.S. Deployment of Diversity*, Difference Incorporated (Minneapolis; London: University of Minnesota Press, 2013).

102. Atanasoski, 'Restoring National Faith: The Soviet-Afghan War in U.S. Media and Politics', pp. 103–104.

103. Ibid., p. 127.

104. Ibid., p. 102.

105. Ibid., p. 105.

106. See for example the description of *Charlie Wilson's War* (2007, dir. Mike Nichols), a film that describes the US involvement in the Soviet-Afghan War, in Atanasoski, 'Restoring National Faith: The Soviet-Afghan War in U.S. Media and Politics.' Or see the 2013 military film *Lone Survivor* (dir. Peter Berg), which relates the experience of Navy SEAL Marcus Luttrell and his team in Afghanistan in 2005 during a failed reconnaissance mission.

107. Richard Dyer, *White: Essays on Race and Culture* (London; New York: Routledge, 1997), pp. 36–7.

108. I am echoing the words here of Oscar Wilde, who in *The Decay of Lying* (New York: Brentano, 1905 [1889]) writes: 'In fact the whole of Japan is a pure invention. There is no such country, there are no such people. One of our most charming painters went recently to the Land of the Chrysanthemum in the foolish hope of seeing the Japanese. All he saw, all he had the chance of painting, were a few lanterns and some fans.'

109. Jean Baudrillard, *The Gulf War Did Not Take Place*, First Paperback edition (Bloomington: Indiana University Press, 1995), p. 16.

110. Mitchell, 'Imperial Landscape', p. 10.

111. Dudley Andrew, *Concepts in Film Theory* (Oxford; New York: Oxford University Press, 1984), p. 38.

4 The World is a Ghetto: Imaging the Global Metropolis in Playable Representation

1. Nezar AlSayyad, *Cinematic Urbanism: A History of the Modern from Reel to Real* (New York: Routledge, 2006), p. 15. AlSayyad refers in turn to Jean Baudrillard, 'Astral America' in C. Turner (trans.), *America* (London: Verso, 1988), p. 27.

2. Ibid., p. xi.

3. DONTNOD, '*Remember Me* DONTNOD Entertainment – Video Game – Jeu Vidéo', official game site, *Dontnod.com*, (2011), http://www.dont-nod.com/category/projects/rememberme-en/.

4. Rachel Hughes, 'Gameworld Geopolitics and the Genre of the Quest', in Fraser MacDonald, Rachel Hughes, and Klaus Dodds (eds), *Observant States: Geopolitics and Visual Culture*, International Library of Human Geography 16 (London; New York: I.B.Tauris, 2010), p. 123.

5. Ibid.

6. Ibid., p. 126.

7. Ibid., p. 124.

8. Ibid., pp. 139–40.

9. Ibid., p. 128. Hughes cites Frow who does not specifically discuss games. See: John Frow, *Genre* (London; New York: Routledge, 2006), p. 19.

10. Hughes, 'Gameworld Geopolitics and the Genre of the Quest', p. 128.

11. From back cover of AlSayyad, *Cinematic Urbanism*.

12. Barbara Mennel, *Cities and Cinema*, Routledge Critical Introductions to Urbanism and the City (London; New York: Routledge, 2008).

13. Ibid., p. 196.

14. From the official trailer, www.rockstargames.com/maxpayne3/videos/ (accessed 8 May 2017).

15. Dennis C. Scimeca, 'The Exhausting Violence of Max Payne 3', *The Escapist*, 3 August 2012, http://www.escapistmagazine.com/articles/view/video-games/columns/firstperson/9844-The-Exhausting-Violence-of-Max-Payne-3 (accessed 8 May).

16. Evan Narcisse, 'Max Payne 3: The Kotaku Review', *Kotaku*, 14 May 2012, http://kotaku.com/5910100/max-payne-3-the-kotaku-review (accessed 8 May).

17. Ludwig Kietzmann, 'Max Payne 3 Review: Nature of the Beast', *Engadget*, 14 May 2012, http://www.engadget.com/2012/05/14/max-payne-3-review/ (accessed 8 May); Arthur Gies, 'Max Payne 3 Review: Bullet Time Machine', *Polygon*, 14 May 2012, http://www.polygon.com/2012/10/9/3480690/max-payne-3-review-bullet-time-machine (accessed 8 May); Andrew Reiner, 'Max Payne 3 Review: The New, Same Old Payne', www.GameInformer.com, 14 May 2012, http://www.gameinformer.com/games/max_payne_3/b/xbox360/archive/2012/05/14/the-new-same-old-payne.aspx (accessed 8 May); Brian Sipple, '"Max Payne 3" Review', *Game Rant*, 2012, http://gamerant.com/max-payne-3-reviews-brian-149629/ (accessed 8 May).

18. R*A, 'Rockstar Recommends: "Elite Squad (Tropa de Elite)"', *Rockstar Games*, 10 November 2011, http://www.rockstargames.com/newswire/article/19561/rockstar-recommends-elite-squad-tropa-de-elite.html (accessed 8 May).

19. Daniel Krupa, 'Max Payne 3 Review', *IGN*, 14 May 2012, http://www.ign.com/articles/2012/05/14/max-payne-3-review (accessed 8 May 2017).

20. Keith Stuart, 'Max Payne 3 – Review', *Guardian*, 14 May 2012, sec. Technology, http://www.theguardian.com/technology/gamesblog/2012/may/14/max-payne-3-game-review (accessed 8 May 2017).

21. Brian Crecente, 'Max Payne 3 Is a Character Study Shaped by Addiction and Violence', *Polygon*, 30 April 2012, http://www.polygon.com/gaming/2012/4/30/2988059/Max-payne-3-is-a-character-study-shaped-by-addiction-and-violence (accessed 8 May 2017).

22. Ibid.

23. Keith Stuart, 'Max Payne 3 and the Problem of Narrative Dissonance', *Guardian*, 18 May 2012, sec. Technology, http://www.theguardian.com/technology/gamesblog/2012/may/18/max-payne-3-story-vs-action (accessed 8 May 2017).

24. From *Max Payne 3* gameplay, Chapter 1, entitled 'Something Rotten in the Air'

25. See Chapter 2 for my discussion of white masculinity in crisis.

26. 'Nova Esperança' means 'New Hope'

27. *Max Payne 3* gameplay, Chapter VII: A Hangover Sent Direct From Mother Nature.

28. Claire Williams, 'Ghettourism and Voyeurism, or Challenging Stereotypes and Raising Consciousness? Literary and Non-Literary Forays into the Favelas of Rio de Janeiro', *Bulletin of Latina American Research* 27, no. 4 (2008), pp. 483–500.

29. Gies, 'Max Payne 3 Review'.

30. Krupa, 'Max Payne 3 Review'.

31. One essay that briefly broaches this conversation, discusses *Max Payne 3* within the context of a post-colonial critique of games. See: S. Mukherjee,

'Playing Subaltern: Video Games and Postcolonialism', *Games and Culture*, 9 February 2016, 11, doi:10.1177/1555412015627258.

32. For more on cultural stereotypes about favelas, see: Williams, 'Ghettourism and Voyeurism, or Challenging Stereotypes and Raising Consciousness? Literary and Non-Literary Forays into the Favelas of Rio de Janeiro'; Gundo Rial y Costas, 'Spaces of Insecurity? The "favelas" of Rio de Janeiro between Stigmatization and Glorification', *Iberoamericana (2001-)* 11, no. 41 (2011). pp. 115–28; Marta Peixoto, 'Rio's Favelas in Recent Fiction and Film: Commonplaces of Urban Segregation', *PMLA* 122, no. 1 (2007), pp. 170–8.

33. This is certainly not the only game to suffer from these problematic optics. See for example, the negative press around other recent games such as *Dead Island* (2011) developed by Techland and published by Deep Silver, and *Resident Evil 5* (2009) developed and published by Capcom.

34. DONTNOD, '*Remember Me* DONTNOD Entertainment – Video Game – Jeu Vidéo'.

35. For an excellent consideration of how the stories of Philip K. Dick have been imaged in cinema after 9/11, see: Lance Rubin, 'Cultural Anxiety, Moral Clarity, and Willful Amnesia: Filming Philip K. Dick After 9/11', in Jeff Birkenstein, Anna Froula, and Karen Randell (eds), *Reframing 9/11: Film, Popular Culture and the 'War on Terror'* (New York: Continuum, 2010), pp. 183–94. For a discussion of filmic influences on *Remember Me*, see: Kirill Ulezko, 'Jean-Max Moris: "In Remember Me We Invite the Player to Join Nilin on Her Voyage of Self-Discovery"', *Gamestar*, 2013, http://gamestar.ru/english/remember_me_interview_eng.html (no longer available).

36. Esmeralda Portillo, '*Remember Me* Was Misunderstood Says Creative Director', *The Escapist*, 17 August 2014, http://www.escapistmagazine.com/news/view/136886-DONTNOD-Entertainment-Creative-Director-Says-Remember-Me-was-Misunderstood (accessed 8 May 2017).

37. Rachel Weber, 'Dontnod: Publishers Said You Can't Have a Female Character', *GamesIndustry.biz*, 19 March 2013, http://www.gamesindustry.biz/articles/2013-03-19-dontnod-publishers-said-you-cant-have-a-female-character (accessed 8 May 2017); Brenna Hillier, 'Remember Me Dev Wanted to "respect" Gamers with a Strong Female Protagonist', *VG247.com*, 16 April 2013, http://www.vg247.com/2013/04/16/remember-me-dev-wanted-to-respect-gamers-with-a-strong-female-protagonist/ (accessed 8 May 2017).

38. Hillier, 'Remember Me Dev Wanted to "respect" Gamers with a Strong Female Protagonist'.

39. Evan Narcisse, 'Remember Me: The Kotaku Review', *Kotaku*, 3 June 2013, http://kotaku.com/remember-me-the-kotaku-review-510988329 (accessed 7 May 2017).

40. Sophie Prell, 'How Facebook Inspired Remember Me to Drop Global Warming, and Why Its Protagonist Had to Be a Woman', *The Penny Arcade Report*, 18 March 2013, http://web.archive.org/web/20131211185434/http://penny-arcade.com/report/article/remember-mes-surprising-connection-to-facebook-and-why-its-protagonist-had (accessed 7 May 2017).

41. Edge, spoken to Nilin in Episode 7 of *Remember Me*.

42. Tung-Hui Hu, *A Prehistory of the Cloud* (Cambridge: The MIT Press, 2015).

43. Rubin, 'Cultural Anxiety, Moral Clarity, and Willful Amnesia: Filming Philip K. Dick After 9/11', p. 184.

44. Ibid., p. 188.

45. Manuel Castells, *The Rise of the Network Society*, 2nd edition (Oxford; Malden: Wiley-Blackwell, 2000), p. 21.

46. Ibid., pp. 442–5.

47. Manuel Castells, *End of Millennium: The Information Age: Economy, Society, and Culture Volume III*, 2nd edition with a new preface edition (Oxford; Malden: Wiley-Blackwell, 2010), p. 168.

48. See Christoph Lindner (ed.), *Globalization, Violence, and the Visual Culture of Cities* (London; New York: Routledge, 2010); Arjun Appadurai, *Modernity At Large: Cultural Dimensions of Globalization*, 1st edition (Minneapolis: University of Minnesota Press, 1996); Arjun Appadurai, *Fear of Small Numbers: An Essay on the Geography of Anger*, Public Planet Books (Durham: Duke University Press, 2006); Arjun Appadurai, *The Future as Cultural Fact: Essays on the Global Condition*, 1st edition (London: Verso, 2013); Saskia Sassen, *Expulsions: Brutality and Complexity in the Global Economy* (Cambridge: The Belknap Press of Harvard University Press, 2014).

49. Celia Pearce, 'Towards a Game Theory of Game', in Noah Wardrip-Fruin and Pat Harrigan (eds), *First Person: New Media as Story, Performance, and Game* (Cambridge: MIT Press, 2004), pp. 26–7.

50. Rowland Atkinson and Paul Willis, 'Transparent Cities: Re-shaping the Urban Experience through Interactive Video Game Simulation', *City* 13, no. 4 (December 2009), p. 404, doi:10.1080/13604810903298458.

51. Ibid., pp. 408–409.

52. Alberto Vanolo, 'The Political Geographies of Liberty City: A Critical Analysis of a Virtual Space', *City* 16, no. 3 (June 2012), p. 285, doi:10.1080/13604813.2012.662377.

53. Ibid., p. 296.

54. Marcus Schulzke, 'The Critical Power of Virtual Dystopias', *Games and Culture* 9, no. 5 (1 September 2014), pp. 315–34, doi:10.1177/1555412014541694.

55. Ibid., p. 316.

56. Oscar Moralde, 'Dimensions of the Digital City', UCLA's Journal of Cinema and Media Studies, *Mediascape* (Fall 2013), http://www.tft.ucla.edu/mediascape/Fall2013_Dimensions.html (no longer available). See also: Oscar Moralde, 'Haptic Landscapes: Dear Esther and Embodied Video Game Space', *Media Fields Journal* 8 (2014), pp. 1–15.

57. Moralde, 'Haptic Landscapes'.

58. Ulezko, 'Jean-Max Moris: "In Remember Me We Invite the Player to Join Nilin on Her Voyage of Self-Discovery"'.

59. There are several fine analyses of *Blade Runner*, which I cannot address here. See for example: Scott Bukatman, *Blade Runner*, 2nd edition, BFI Film Classics (London; New York: Palgrave Macmillan on behalf of the British Film Institute, 2012).

60. Marcus A. Doel and David B. Clarke, 'From Ramble City to the Screening of the Eye: *Blade Runner*, Death and Symbolic Exchange', in *The Cinematic City*, ed. David B. Clarke (London; New York: Routledge, 1997), p. 141. I should note that while the authors acquiesce to the film's status as a 'canonical postmodern cultural artifact' they locate its postmodernism in its formal qualities, while ultimately arguing that its vision is solidly modern.

61. Narcisse, '*Remember Me*'; Kevin VanOrd, '*Remember Me* Review', *GameSpot*, 3 June 2013, http://www.gamespot.com/reviews/remember-me-review/1900-6409150/ (accessed 8 May 2017).

62. Matt Kamen, '*Remember Me* – Review', *Guardian*, 8 June 2013, sec. Technology, http://www.theguardian.com/technology/2013/jun/09/remember-me-review (accessed 8 May 2017).

63. Ulezko, 'Jean-Max Moris: "In Remember Me We Invite the Player to Join Nilin on Her Voyage of Self-Discovery"'.

64. Tom Bramwell, 'Remember Me Review', *Eurogamer.net*, 3 June 2013, http://www.eurogamer.net/articles/2013-06-03-remember-me-review (accessed 8 May 2017).

65. A 'boss fight' or a 'boss battle' is a fight between the player-character and a major enemy, usually stronger than the rest, and usually at the end of a game's level.

66. Ulezko, 'Jean-Max Moris: "In *Remember Me* We Invite the Player to Join Nilin on Her Voyage of Self-Discovery"'.

67. David Harvey, *The Condition of Postmodernity* (Oxford: Blackwell Publishers, 1989), p. 240.

68. Ibid., pp. 247–323.

69. Ibid., p. 204.

70. Matthias Nilges, 'The Aesthetics of Destruction: Contemporary US Cinema and TV Culture', in Jeff Birkenstein, Anna Froula and Karen Randell (eds),

Reframing 9/11: Film, Popular Culture and the 'War on Terror', (New York: Continuum, 2010), p. 24.

71. Ibid.
72. Ibid., p. 29.
73. Ibid., p. 31.
74. Ibid., p. 28.
75. AlSayyad, *Cinematic Urbanism*, p. 10.
76. Ibid.
77. Ibid.
78. Mike Davis, *City of Quartz: Excavating the Future in Los Angeles*, new edition (London; New York: Verso, 2006); Edward Soja, *Thirdspace: Journeys to Los Angeles and Other Real-and-Imagined Places*, 1st edition (Cambridge: Blackwell Publishers, 1996); Fredric Jameson, *Postmodernism, Or, The Cultural Logic of Late Capitalism* (Duke University Press, 1992).
79. AlSayyad, *Cinematic Urbanism*, p. 124.
80. Davis, *City of Quartz*, p. 223. As cited by AlSayyad, *Cinematic Urbanism*, p. 125.
81. dialogue from *Max Payne 3* gameplay.
82. From the DVD cover to *Falling Down* (dir. Joel Schumacher, 1993).
83. AlSayyad, *Cinematic Urbanism*, p. 11.
84. Please see among the many fine analyses of this film: Elizabeth Mahoney, '"The People in Parentheses": Space Under Pressure in the Post-Modern City', in David B. Clarke (ed.), *The Cinematic City* (London; New York: Routledge, 1997), pp. 168–85.
85. Carl Abbott, *Imagined Frontiers: Contemporary America and Beyond* (Norman: University of Oklahoma, 2015), p. 76.
86. Ibid.
87. Ibid., p. 79.
88. Ibid., p. 85.
89. AlSayyad, *Cinematic Urbanism*, 190.
90. BBC News, 'Brazil Forces Occupy Favela ahead of World Cup', *BBC News*, 31 March 2014, http://www.bbc.com/news/world-latin-america-26809732 (accessed 8 May 2017); Shasta Darlington, 'Brazilian Army Occupies Rio Shantytown ahead of World Cup', News, *CNN*, 24 April 2014, http://edition.cnn.com/2014/04/24/sport/football/brazil-world-cup-favela-slums/index.html (accessed 8 May 2017); Lucy Westcott, 'Brazilian Police Invade Rio's Slum Ahead of This Summer's World Cup', News, *The Wire: News From the Atlantic*, 31 March 2014, http://www.thewire.com/global/2014/03/police-swarm-brazilian-slum-to-clean-up-before-world-cup/359916/ (accessed 8 May 2017); Matt Sandy, 'World Cup Showdown in Rio', News, *Al Jazeera America*, 18

May 2014, http://projects.aljazeera.com/2014/world-cup-favelas/index.html (accessed 8 May 2017); Owen Gibson and Jonathan Watts, 'World Cup: Rio Favelas Being "Socially Cleansed" in Runup to Sporting Events', *Guardian*, 5 December 2013, sec. World news, http://www.theguardian.com/world/2013/dec/05/world-cup-favelas-socially-cleansed-olympics (accessed 8 May 2017).

91. 'Mean Streets, Revisited', *The Economist*, 17 November 2012, http://www.economist.com/news/americas/21566653-brazils-biggest-city-becoming-more-dangerous-mean-streets-revisited (accessed 8 May 2017).

92. Gibson and Watts, 'World Cup'.

93. Ibid.

94. Westcott, 'Brazilian Police Invade Rio's Slum Ahead of This Summer's World Cup'.

95. BBC Two Documentary, *Welcome to Rio*, TV, vol. Episode 01, Welcome to Rio, 2014, https://www.youtube.com/watch?v=8CIhhfhMCjI (accessed 8 May 2017); Nicole Froio, 'Meet the Elite Cops Cleaning Up Rio's Favelas', *VICE News*, 1 May 2014, https://news.vice.com/article/meet-the-elite-cops-cleaning-up-rios-favelas (accessed 8 May 2017); Sandy, 'World Cup Showdown in Rio'.

96. Evan Watts, 'Ruin, Gender, and Digital Games', *WSQ: Women's Studies Quarterly* 39, no. 3–4 (2011), pp. 247–65, doi:10.1353/wsq.2011.0041.

97. AlSayyad, *Cinematic Urbanism*, p. 27.

Bibliography

Aarseth, Espen, 'Genre Trouble: Narrativism and the Art of Simulation', in Noah Wardrip-Fruin and Pat Harrigan (eds), *First Person: New Media as Story, Performance, and Game* (Cambridge: The MIT Press, 2004), pp. 45–55.

——, 'Allegories of Space: The Question of Spatiality in Computer Games', in *Cybertext Yearbook 2000* (Jyvaskyla, Finland: Research Centre for Contemporary Culture, 2001), pp. 152–71.

——, 'Computer Game Studies, Year One', *Game Studies: The International Journal of Computer Game Research* 1, no. 1 (July 2001). http://gamestudies.org/0101/editorial.html.

Abbott, Carl, *Imagined Frontiers: Contemporary America and Beyond* (Norman: University of Oklahoma, 2015).

Adams, Ernest, 'Single-Player, Multiplayer, MMOG: Design Psychologies for Different Social Contexts', presented at the Game Developers Conference, San Francisco, CA, March 2010. http://www.gdcvault.com/play/1012332/Single-Player-Multiplayer-MMOG-Design.

Adams, Meghan Blythe, 'Andromeda on the Rocks: Retreading and Resisting Tropes of Female Sacrifice in "Tomb Raider"', presented at the History of Gender in Games, Auditorium de la Grande Bibliothèque, Montréal [Québec], 26 June 2015. www.sahj.ca.

Admin, 'The Soviet Occupation of Afghanistan', *PBS NewsHour*, 10 October 2006. http://www.pbs.org/newshour/updates/asia-july-dec06-soviet_10-10/.

Alexander, Leigh, 'Sexism, Lies and Video Games: The Culture War Nobody Is Winning', *Time*, 5 September 2014. http://time.com/3274247/video-game-culture-war/.

——, '"Gamers" Don't Have to Be Your Audience. "Gamers" Are Over', *Gamasutra*, 28 August 2014. http://www.gamasutra.com/view/news/224400/Gamers_dont_have_to_be_your_audience_Gamers_are_over.php.

Allen, Theodore, *The Invention of the White Race* (London: Verso, 2012).

Allison, Tanine, 'The World War II Video Game, Adaptation, and Postmodern History', *Literature/Film Quarterly* 38, no. 3 (2010), pp. 183–93.

AlSayyad, Nezar, *Cinematic Urbanism: A History of the Modern from Reel to Real* (New York: Routledge, 2006).

Althusser, Louis, 'Ideology and Ideological State Apparatuses (Notes Towards an Investigation)', in *Lenin and Philosophy and Other Essays*, translated by Ben Brewster (New York: Monthly Review Press, 2001).

Bibliography

American Psychological Association, 'APA Review Confirms Link Between Playing Violent Video Games and Aggression', http://www.apa.org, 13 August 2015. http://www.apa.org/news/press/releases/2015/08/violent-video-games.aspx.

Anderson, Monica, 'Views on Gaming Differ by Race, Ethnicity', *Pew Research Center*, 17 December 2015. http://www.pewresearch.org/fact-tank/2015/12/17/views-on-gaming-differ-by-race-ethnicity/.

Andrew, Dudley, *Concepts in Film Theory* (Oxford; New York: Oxford University Press, 1984).

Andrews, Malcolm, *The Search for the Picturesque: Landscape Aesthetics and Tourism in Britain, 1760–1800* (Stanford: Stanford University Press, 1989).

Anthropy, Anna, *Rise of the Videogame Zinesters: How Freaks, Normals, Amateurs, Artists, Dreamers, Dropouts, Queers, Housewives, and People like You Are Taking Back an Art Form*, Seven Stories Press 1st edition (New York: Seven Stories Press, 2012).

Appadurai, Arjun, *The Future as Cultural Fact: Essays on the Global Condition*, 1st edition (London: Verso, 2013).

——, *Fear of Small Numbers: An Essay on the Geography of Anger*, Public Planet Books (Durham: Duke University Press, 2006).

——, *Modernity at Large: Cultural Dimensions of Globalization*, 1st edition (Minneapolis: University of Minnesota Press, 1996).

Appelbaum, Yoni, 'Why Is the Flag Still There?', *The Atlantic*, 21 June 2015. http://www.theatlantic.com/politics/archive/2015/06/why-is-the-flag-still-there/396431/.

Appleton, Jay, *Experience of Landscape* (London, New York: John Wiley & Sons Inc., 1975).

Atanasoski, Neda, *Humanitarian Violence: The U.S. Deployment of Diversity*, Difference Incorporated (Minneapolis; London: University of Minnesota Press, 2013).

Atkinson, Rowland, and Paul Willis, 'Transparent Cities: Re-shaping the Urban Experience through Interactive Video Game Simulation', *City* 13, no. 4 (December 2009), pp. 403–17. doi:10.1080/13604810903298458.

Baker, Houston A., Manthia Diawara, and Ruth H. Lindeborg (eds), *Black British Cultural Studies: A Reader*, Black Literature and Culture (Chicago: University of Chicago Press, 1996).

Bal, Mieke, 'From Cultural Studies to Cultural Analysis: A Controlled Reflection on the Formation of Method', in Paul Bowman (ed.), *Interrogating Cultural Studies: Theory, Politics and Practice* (London; Sterling: Pluto Press, 2003), pp. 30–40.

——, 'Responses to Mieke Bal's "Visual Essentialism and the Object of Visual Culture" (2003): Mieke Bal's Reply to the Responses', *Journal of Visual Culture* 2, no. 2 (1 August 2003), pp. 260–8. doi:10.1177/14704129030022012.

——, 'Visual Essentialism and the Object of Visual Culture', *Journal of Visual Culture* 2, no. 1 (1 April 2003), pp. 5–32. doi:10.1177/147041290300200101.

Balsamo, Anne, 'Feminism and Cultural Studies', *The Journal of the Midwest Modern Language Association* 24, no. 1 (1 April 1991), pp. 50–73. doi:10.2307/1315025.

Baudrillard, Jean, *Simulacra and Simulation*, 1st edition, 17th printing edition (Ann Arbor: University of Michigan Press, 1995).

——, *The Gulf War Did Not Take Place*, 1st paperback edition (Bloomington: Indiana University Press, 1995).

——, 'The Hyper-Realism of Simulation', in Mark Poster (ed.), *Jean Baudrillard: Selected Writings* (Stanford: Stanford University Press, 1988), pp. 143–7.

BBC News, 'Brazil Forces Occupy Favela ahead of World Cup', *BBC News*, 31 March 2014. http://www.bbc.com/news/world-latin-america-26809732.

——, 'Blog Death Threats Spark Debate', *BBC*, 27 March 2007, sec. Technology. http://news.bbc.co.uk/2/hi/technology/6499095.stm.

BBC Two Documentary, *Welcome to Rio*, TV. Vol. Episode 01, Welcome to Rio, 2014. https://www.youtube.com/watch?v=8CIhhfhMCjI.

Benjamin, Walter, 'The Work of Art in the Age of Mechanical Reproduction' in Hannah Arendt (ed.), *Illuminations* (New York: Schocken Books, 1986), pp. 217–43.

Berger, John, *Ways of Seeing*, Reprint edition (London: Penguin Books, 1990).

Berger, Maurice, *White Lies: Race and the Myths of Whiteness*, 1st edition (New York: Farrar, Straus and Giroux, 2000).

Berman, Mark, 'Dylann Roof, Accused Charleston Church Gunman, Indicted on Federal Hate Crime Charges', *The Washington Post*, 22 July 2015. http://www.washingtonpost.com/news/post-nation/wp/2015/07/22/dylann-roof-accused-charleston-church-gunman-has-been-indicted-on-federal-hate-crime-charges/.

Bermingham, Ann, *Landscape and Ideology: The English Rustic Tradition, 1740–1860* (Berkeley: University of California Press, 1989).

Bertz, Matt, 'Spec Ops: The Line Review: A Descent Into Madness', Game Review, *Game Informer*, 26 June 2012. http://www.gameinformer.com/games/spec_ops_the_line/b/xbox360/archive/2012/06/26/review.aspx.

Bever, Lindsey, '"Supremacist" Earl Holt III and His Donations to Republicans', *The Washington Post*, 23 June 2015. http://www.washingtonpost.com/news/morning-mix/wp/2015/06/23/meet-earl-holt-whose-supremacist-site-influenced-alleged-charleston-church-killer-dylann-roof/.

Biddle, Sam, 'The Psychopaths of GamerGate Are All That's Left, and They're Terrifying', *Gawker*, 2 February 2015. http://internet.gawker.com/the-psychopaths-of-gamergate-are-all-thats-left-and-th-1683271908.

Birmingham, University of, *Women Take Issue: Aspects of Women's Subordination* (London: Hutchinson, 1978).

Bischoff, Daniel, 'The Last of Us Review', *Game Revoution*, 6 June 2013. http://www.gamerevolution.com/review/the-last-of-us.

Blodgett, Bridget and Anastasia Salter, '#1ReasonWhy: Game Communities and the Invisible Woman', in *Proceedings of the 9th International Conference on the Foundations of Digital Games*, Society for the Advancement of the Science of Digital Games, 2014. http://www.fdg2014.org/proceedings.html.

Bogost, Ian, *How to Talk about Videogames* (Minneapolis: University of Minnesota Press, 2015).

———, *How to Do Things with Videogames*, Electronic Mediations 38 (Minneapolis: University of Minnesota Press, 2011).

———, *Persuasive Games: The Expressive Power of Videogames* (Cambridge: The MIT Press, 2010).

———, 'Videogames Are a Mess: My DiGRA 2009 Keynote, on Videogames and Ontology', *Bogost.com*, 3 September 2009. http://bogost.com/writing/videogames_are_a_mess/.

———, *Unit Operations: An Approach to Videogame Criticism*, 1st edition (Cambridge: The MIT Press, 2006).

Bolter, Jay David, and Richard Grusin, *Remediation: Understanding New Media* (Cambridge: The MIT Press, 2003).

Bramwell, Tom, 'Remember Me Review', *Eurogamer.net*, 3 June 2013. http://www.eurogamer.net/articles/2013-06-03-remember-me-review.

Brander Rasmussen, Birgit, Eric Klinenberg, Irene J. Nexica, and Matt Wray (eds), 'Introduction', in *The Making and Unmaking of Whiteness* (Durham: Duke University Press, 2001), pp. 1–24.

——— (eds), *The Making and Unmaking of Whiteness* (Durham: Duke University Press, 2001). http://read.dukeupress.edu/lookup/doi/10.1215/9780822381044.

Bray, Hiawatha, 'Brianna Wu Appears at PAX East Videogame Convention', *BostonGlobe.com*, 8 March 2015. https://www.bostonglobe.com/metro/2015/03/08/brianna-appears-pax-east-videogame-convention/hEzlyb5ggIf03vKyc-Ua2aL/story.html.

Brice, Mattie, 'The Dadification of Video Games Is Real', *Mattie Brice*, August 2013. http://www.mattiebrice.com/the-dadification-of-video-games-is-real/.

Brown, Peter, 'Metal Gear Solid V: The Phantom Pain Review', *GameSpot*, 23 August 2015. http://www.gamespot.com/reviews/metal-gear-solid-v-the-phantom-pain-review/1900-6416224/.

Brown, Wendy, *Regulating Aversion: Tolerance in the Age of Identity and Empire*, 3rd printing, 1st paperback printing edition (Princeton: Princeton University Press, 2008).

Bryson, Norman, Michael Ann Holly and Keith Moxey (eds), *Visual Culture: Images and Interpretations* (Wesleyan, 2013).

Bukatman, Scott, *Blade Runner*, 2nd edition, BFI Film Classics (London; New York: Palgrave Macmillan on behalf of the British Film Institute, 2012).

Burrill, Derek A., *Die Tryin': Videogames, Masculinity, Culture*. Popular Culture and Everyday Life (New York: Peter Lang, 2008).

Byford, Sam, 'Metal Gear Solid V: The One-Month Review', *The Verge*, 1 October 2015. http://www.theverge.com/2015/10/1/9431725/mgs5-review.

Cassell, Justine, and Henry Jenkins (eds), *From Barbie to Mortal Kombat: Gender and Computer Games*. 1st MIT Press paperback edition (Cambridge: The MIT Press, 2000).

Castells, Manuel, *End of Millennium: The Information Age: Economy, Society, and Culture Volume III*. 2nd edition with a New Preface edition (Oxford; Malden: Wiley-Blackwell, 2010).

——, *The Rise of the Network Society*, 2nd edition (Oxford; Malden: Wiley-Blackwell, 2000).

Center for Games and Playable Media, *Inventing the Future of Games [IFOG] 2011: Jordan Mechner*. UC Santa Cruz Center for Games and Playable Media, 2011. https://vimeo.com/24028511.

Certeau, Michel de, *The Practice of Everyday Life*, translated by Steven Rendall, 3rd edition (Berkeley: University of California Press, 2011).

Chambers, Becky, 'Lara Croft Is Dead, Long Live Lara Croft: Reflections On Tomb Raider', *The Mary Sue*, 8 March 2013. http://www.themarysue.com/tomb-raider-review/.

Chan, Dean, 'Playing with Race: The Ethics of Racialized Representations in E-Games', *International Review of Information Ethics* 4 (December 2005), pp. 24–30.

Chang, Alenda Y., 'Games as Environmental Texts', *Qui Parle: Critical Humanities and Social Sciences* 19, no. 2 (Spring/Summer 2011), pp. 57–84.

Chess, Shira, and Adrienne Shaw, 'A Conspiracy of Fishes, Or, How We Learned to Stop Worrying About #GamerGate and Embrace Hegemonic Masculinity', *Journal of Broadcasting & Electronic Media* 59, no. 1 (2 January 2015), pp. 208–20. doi:10.1080/08838151.2014.999917.

Chomsky, Noam, and Robert W. McChesney, *Profit Over People: Neoliberalism & Global Order*, 1st edition (New York: Seven Stories Press, 1999).

Chun, Wendy Hui Kyong, 'On Software, Or the Persistence of Visual Knowledge', in Nicholas Mirzoeff (ed.), *The Visual Culture Reader*, 3rd edition (London; New York: Routledge, 2013), pp. 65–85.

——, *Control and Freedom: Power and Paranoia in the Age of Fiber Optics* (Cambridge: The MIT Press, 2008).

Clark, Kenneth, *Landscape Into Art*, 2nd Revised edition (London: John Murray Publishers Ltd, 1979).

Clinton, Catherine, *Harriet Tubman: The Road to Freedom*, 1st edition (New York: Little, Brown, 2004).

CNN, *Martin Luther King Jr. III Reacts to Charleston – CNN Video*, The Michael Smerconish Program, 2015. http://www.cnn.com/videos/tv/2015/06/20/exp-smerconish-martin-luther-iii.cnn.

Cohen, Richard, 'The Soviets' Vietnam', *The Washington Post*, 22 April 1988. http://www.washingtonpost.com/archive/opinions/1988/04/22/the-soviets-vietnam/5e7fde43-6a0c-46fb-b678-dbb89bcb720b/.

Concepcion, Miguel, Assassin's Creed III: Liberation HD Review', *GameSpot*, 23 January 2014. http://www.gamespot.com/reviews/assassin-s-creed-iii-liberation-hd-review/1900-6415643/.

Consalvo, Mia, 'There Is No Magic Circle', *Games and Culture* 4, no. 4 (1 October 2009), pp. 408–17. doi:10.1177/1555412009343575.

Cooper, Hollander, 'Spec Ops: The Line – Learn about the Story with Lead Writer Walt Williams', *GamesRadar+*, 30 March 2012. http://www.gamesradar.com/spec-ops-line-learn-about-story-lead-writer-walt-williams/.

Cosgrove, Denis, and Stephen Daniels (eds), *The Iconography of Landscape: Essays on the Symbolic Representation, Design and Use of Past Environments*, 10th printing, Cambridge Studies in Historical Geography 9 (Cambridge: Cambridge University Press, 2008).

Cosgrove, Denis E., *Geography and Vision: Seeing, Imagining and Representing the World* (London; New York: I.B.Tauris, 2008).

——, *Social Formation and Symbolic Landscape*, New edition (Madison: University of Wisconsin Press, 1998).

Coughlan, Sean, 'Violent Video Games Leave Teens "Morally Immature"', *BBC News*, 6 February 2014. http://www.bbc.com/news/education-26049333.

Cowen, Nick, 'Dan Houser Interview: Rockstar Games's Writer for GTA 4 and The Lost And Damned', *The Telegraph*, 28 January 2009. http://www.telegraph.co.uk/technology/video-games/4373632/Dan-Houser-interview-Rockstar-Gamess-writer-for-GTA-4-and-The-Lost-And-Damned.html.

Crecente, Brian, 'Max Payne 3 Is a Character Study Shaped by Addiction and Violence', *Polygon*, 30 April 2012. http://www.polygon.com/gaming/2012/4/30/2988059/Max-payne-3-is-a-character-study-shaped-by-addiction-and-violence.

Crenshaw, Kimberlé W., 'Mapping the Margins: Intersectionality, Identity Politics, and Violence Against Women of Color', *Stanford Law Review* 43 (July 1991), pp. 1241–99.

——, 'Demarginalizing the Intersection of Race and Sex: A Black Feminist Critique of Antidiscrimination Doctrine, Feminist Theory and Antiracist Politics', *University of Chicago Legal Forum*, 1989, pp. 139–67.

Cross, Katherine, 'We Will Force Gaming to Be Free', *First Person Scholar*, 8 October 2014. http://www.firstpersonscholar.com/we-will-force-gaming-to-be-free/.

Crowley, John E., *Imperial Landscapes: Britain's Global Visual Culture, 1745–1820* (New Haven: Published for the Paul Mellon Centre for Studies in British Art by Yale University Press, 2011).

Daniels, Jessie, *White Lies: Race, Class, Gender and Sexuality in White Supremacist Discourse* (New York; London: Routledge, 1997).

Darlington, Shasta, 'Brazilian Army Occupies Rio Shantytown ahead of World Cup', News. *CNN*, 24 April 2014. http://edition.cnn.com/2014/04/24/sport/football/brazil-world-cup-favela-slums/index.html.

Davies, Bronwyn and Peter Bansel, 'Neoliberalism and Education', *International Journal of Qualitative Studies in Education* 20, no. 3 (May 2007), pp. 247–59. doi:10.1080/09518390701281751.

Davis, Helen, *Understanding Stuart Hall* (London; Thousand Oaks, Calif: SAGE Publications, 2004).

Davis, Mike, *City of Quartz: Excavating the Future in Los Angeles*, New edition (London; New York: Verso, 2006).

Delgado, Richard and Jean Stefancic (eds), *Critical White Studies: Looking Behind the Mirror* (Philadelphia: Temple University Press, 1997).

DeLue, Rachel and James Elkins (eds), *Landscape Theory*, 1st edition (New York: Routledge, 2007).

Di Palma, Vittoria, *Wasteland: A History* (New Haven: Yale University Press, 2014).

Doel, Marcus A. and David B. Clarke, 'From Ramble City to the Screening of the Eye: Blade Runner, Death and Symbolic Exchange', in David B. Clarke (ed.), *The Cinematic City* (London; New York: Routledge, 1997), pp. 140–67.

DONTNOD, 'Remember Me DONTNOD Entertainment – Video Game – Jeu Vidéo', Official game site. *Dontnod.com*, 2011. http://www.dont-nod.com/category/projects/rememberme-en/.

Dovey, Jon and Helen W. Kennedy, *Game Cultures: Computer Games as New Media*, Issues in Cultural and Media Studies (Maidenhead, Berkshire, England; New York: Open University Press, 2006).

During, Simon, *Cultural Studies: A Critical Introduction* (London; New York: Routledge, 2005).

Dyer, Mitch, 'The Story Secrets of Spec Ops: The Line', *IGN*, 20 July 2012. http://www.ign.com/articles/2012/07/20/the-story-secrets-of-spec-ops-the-line.

Dyer, Richard, *The Matter of Images: Essays on Representation*, 2nd edition (London: Routledge, 2002).

———, *White: Essays on Race and Culture* (London; New York: Routledge, 1997).

Dyer-Witheford, Nick and Greig de Peuter, *Games of Empire: Global Capitalism and Video Games*, Electronic Mediations 29 (Minneapolis: University of Minnesota Press, 2009).

Edwards, Jim, 'Gamergate FBI file shows no charges brought despite confessions', *Business Insider*, 16 February 2017. http://www.businessinsider.com/gamergate-fbi-file-2017-2.

Elkins, James, *The Object Stares Back: On the Nature of Seeing* (San Diego: Mariner Books, 1997).

Entertainment Software Association, 'U.S. Video Game Industry Generates $23.5 Billion in Revenue for 2015', Press Release, Washington, DC: Entertainment Software Association, 16 February 2016. http://www.theesa.com/article/u-s-video-game-industry-generates-23-5-billion-in-revenue-for-2015/.

———, '2015 Annual Report: A Year of Innovation and Achievement', Annual Report, Entertainment Software Association, 2015. http://www.theesa.com/article/2015-esa-annual-report/.

———, 'Games: Improving the Economy', Entertainment Software Association, 4 November 2014.

Enwezor, Okwui, *Créolité and Creolization: Documenta 11_Platform3*, Distributed Art Pub Incorporated, 2003.

Eördögh, Fruzsina, 'The Anti-Feminist Internet Targets "Depression Quest" Game Creator Zoe Quinn', *Motherboard*, 19 August 2014. http://motherboard.vice.com/blog/zoe-quinn-slut-shaming-the-feminist-conspiracy-and-depression-quest.

Evans, Jessica, and Stuart Hall (eds), *Visual Culture: The Reader* (London; Thousand Oaks: SAGE Publications in association with the Open University, 1999).

Everett, Anna, Alex Champlin and John Vanderhoef, 'Race, Space, and Digital Games: An Interview with Anna Everett', *Media Fields Journal* 8 (2014), pp. 1–11.

Everett, Anna and S.C. Watkins, 'The Power of Play: The Portrayal and Performance of Race in Video Games', in *The Ecology of Games: Connecting Youth, Games and Learning* (Cambridge: The MIT Press, 2007), pp. 141–64.

Fernández, María, Faith Wilding and Michelle M. Wright (eds), *Domain Errors!: Cyberfeminist Practices* (New York: Autonomedia, 2003).

Fernández-Vara, Clara, *Introduction to Game Analysis* (New York: Routledge, 2014).

Fish, Stanley, 'Neoliberalism and Higher Education', *Opinionator* (accessed 22 April 2015). http://opinionator.blogs.nytimes.com/2009/03/08/neoliberalism-and-higher-education/.

——, 'Aim Low', *The Chronicle of Higher Education*, 16 May 2003. http://chronicle.com/article/Aim-Low/45210.

Flanagan, Mary, *Critical Play: Radical Game Design* (Cambridge: The MIT Press, 2009).

——, 'Response by Mary Flanagan to Celia Pearce, "Towards a Game Theory of Game"', in Noah Wardrip-Fruin and Pat Harrigan (eds), *First Person: New Media as Story, Performance, and Game* (Cambridge: The MIT Press, 2004), pp. 143–6.

Flanagan, Mary and Helen Nissenbaum, *Values at Play in Digital Games* (Cambridge: The MIT Press, 2014).

Fleetwood, Nicole R. *Troubling Vision: Performance, Visuality, and Blackness* (Chicago: The University of Chicago Press, 2011).

Flynn, D., 'Languages of Navigation within Computer Games', presented at the Digital Art and Culture, Melbourne, Australia, 2003. http://hypertext.rmit.edu.au/dac/papers/Flynn.pdf.

Foster, Hal, *The Return of the Real: The Avante-Garde at the End of the Century*, Paperback/softback edition (Cambridge: The MIT Press, 1996).

Frank, Jenn, 'How to Attack a Woman Who Works in Video Gaming', *Guardian*, 1 September 2014. http://www.theguardian.com/technology/2014/sep/01/how-to-attack-a-woman-who-works-in-video-games.

Frankenberg, Ruth, 'Cracks in the Façade: Whiteness and the Construction of 9/11', *Social Identities* 11, no. 6 (November 2005), pp. 553–71. doi:10.1080/13504630500449093.

——, 'The Mirage of an Unmarked Whiteness', in Birgit Brander Rasmussen, Eric Klinenberg, Irene J. Nexica and Matt Wray (eds), *The Making and Unmaking of Whiteness* (Durham: Duke University Press, 2001), pp. 72–96.

——, 'White Women, Race Matters', in Les Back and John Solomos (eds), *Theories of Race and Racism: A Reader*, Routledge Student Reader (London; New York: Routledge, 2000), pp. 447–61.

—— (ed.), *Displacing Whiteness: Essays in Social and Cultural Criticism* (Durham, NC: Duke University Press, 1997).

——, *White Women, Race Matters: The Social Construction of Whiteness*, 1st edition (Minneapolis: University of Minnesota Press, 1993).

Frasca, Gonzalo, 'Don't Play It Again, Sam: One-Session and Serial Games of Narration', presented at the Digital Arts and Culture, University of Bergen, Norway, October 1998. http://cmc.uib.no/dac98/papers/frasca.html.

Freire-Medeiros, Bianca, '"I Went to the City of God": Gringos, Guns and the Touristic Favela', *Journal of Latin American Cultural Studies* 20, no. 1 (1 March 2011), pp. 21–34. doi:10.1080/13569325.2011.562631.

Frey, William H., *Diversity Explosion: How New Racial Demographics Are Remaking America* (Washington, DC: Brookings Institution Press, 2015).

Froio, Nicole, 'Meet the Elite Cops Cleaning Up Rio's Favelas', *VICE News*, 1 May 2014. https://news.vice.com/article/meet-the-elite-cops-cleaning-up-rios-favelas.

Frow, John, *Genre* (London; New York: Routledge, 2006).

Fuller, Mary and Henry Jenkins, 'Nintendo and New World Travel Writing: A Dialogue' in Steven G. Jones (ed.), *Cybersociety: Computer-Mediated Communication and Community* (Sherman Oaks: SAGE Publications, 1995), pp. 57–72. http://web.stanford.edu/class/history34q/readings/Cyberspace/FullerJenkins_Nintendo.html.

Gabriel, John, 'What Do You Do When Minority Means You? *Falling Down* and the Construction of "whiteness"', *Screen* 37, no. 2 (20 June 1996), pp. 129–51. doi:10.1093/screen/37.2.129.

Gallagher, Charles A. and France Winddance Twine, *Retheorizing Race and Whiteness in the 21st Century: Changes and Challenges*, Reprint edition (London; New York: Routledge, 2013).

Galloway, Alexander R., 'Does the Whatever Speak?', in Lisa Nakamura and Peter Chow-White (eds), *Race After the Internet* (New York and London: Routledge, 2012), pp. 111–27.

——, *The Interface Effect* (Cambridge; Malden: Polity, 2012).

——, *Gaming: Essays on Algorithmic Culture*, Electronic Mediations 18 (Minneapolis: University of Minnesota Press, 2006).

Gibson, Owen and Jonathan Watts, 'World Cup: Rio Favelas Being "Socially Cleansed" in Runup to Sporting Events', *Guardian*, 5 December 2013, sec. World news. http://www.theguardian.com/world/2013/dec/05/world-cup-favelas-socially-cleansed-olympics.

Gies, Arthur, 'Max Payne 3 Review: Bullet Time Machine', *Polygon*, 14 May 2012. http://www.polygon.com/2012/10/9/3480690/max-payne-3-review-bullet-time-machine.

Gillett, Nick, 'Assassin's Creed III: Liberation – Review', *Guardian*, 9 November 2012. http://www.theguardian.com/technology/2012/nov/10/assassins-creed-3-liberation-review.

Gilroy, Paul, *The Black Atlantic: Modernity and Double-Consciousness*, Reissue edition (Cambridge, Mass: Harvard University Press, 1993).

Giroux, Henry, 'Academic Unfreedom in America: Rethinking the University as a Democratic Public Sphere', *WORKS AND DAYS* 51/52, 53/54, no. 26 & 27 (September 2008), pp. 45–71.

Giroux, Henry, and Susan Searls Giroux, *Take Back Higher Education: Race, Youth, and the Crisis of Democracy in the Post-Civil Rights* (New York: Palgrave Macmillan, 2004).

Glissant, Edouard, *Poetics of Relation*, translated by Betsy Wing (Ann Arbor: University of Michigan Press, 1997).

Gonzales, Juan L, *Racial and Ethnic Groups in America*, 5th edition (Dubuque, Iowa: Kendall/Hunt Publishing, 2003).

Gravning, Jagger, 'How Video Games Are Slowly, Quietly Introducing LGBT Heroes', *The Atlantic*, 25 February 2014. http://www.theatlantic.com/entertainment/archive/2014/02/how-video-games-are-slowly-quietly-introducing-lgbt-heroes/284017/.

——, 'How Major Videogames Are Slowly Readying Us for a Gay Protagonist', *Kill Screen*, 9 February 2014. http://killscreendaily.com/articles/how-major-videogames-are-slowly-readying-us-gay-protagonist/.

Grayson, Nathan, 'Why Aren't We Discussing Videogame Violence?' *Rock, Paper, Shotgun*, 28 December 2012. http://www.rockpapershotgun.com/2012/12/28/why-arent-we-discussing-videogame-violence/.

Green, A. M., 'The Reconstruction of Morality and the Evolution of Naturalism in The Last of Us', *Games and Culture* forthcoming, no. Online (7 April 2015), pp. 1–19. doi:10.1177/1555412015579489.

Griffiths, Daniel Nye. '"The Last of Us": How Game Design Shaped Naughty Dog's Masterpiece, And Transformed Its Ending', *Forbes*, 14 July 2014. http://www.forbes.com/sites/danielnyegriffiths/2014/07/14/how-game-design-transformed-the-last-of-us/.

Grossberg, Lawrence, *Cultural Studies in the Future Tense* (Durham: Duke University Press, 2010).

——, *Bringing It All Back Home: Essays on Cultural Studies* (Durham: Duke University Press, 1997).

Grossberg, Lawrence, Cary Nelson, and Paula A. Treichler (eds), *Cultural Studies* (New York: Routledge, 1992).

Guins, Raiford, *Game After: A Cultural Study of Video Game Afterlife* (Cambridge: The MIT Press, 2014).

Hale, Grace Elizabeth, *Making Whiteness: The Culture of Segregation in the South, 1890–1940* (New York: Vintage, 1999).

Hall, Stuart, 'The Whites of Their Eyes:', in Gail Dines and Jean McMahon Humez (eds), *Gender, Race, and Class in Media: A Critical Reader* (London: SAGE Publications, 2015), pp. 104–107.

——, 'Notes on Deconstructing "the Popular"', in John Storey (ed.), *Cultural Theory and Popular Culture: A Reader* (New Jersey: Pearson / Prentice Hall, 1998), pp. 442–53.

—— (ed.), *Representation: Cultural Representations and Signifying Practices*, 1st edition (London; Thousand Oaks: Sage Publications & Open University, 1997).

——, 'New Ethnicities', in David Morley (ed.), *Stuart Hall: Critical Dialogues in Cultural Studies* (New York: Routledge, 1996), pp. 441–9.

——, 'Encoding, Decoding', in Simon During (ed.), *The Cultural Studies Reader* (London: Routledge, 1993), pp. 90–103.

——, 'Cultural Studies and Its Theoretical Legacies', in Lawrence Grossberg, Cary Nelson and Paula A. Treichler (eds), *Cultural Studies* (New York: Routledge, 1992), pp. 277–94.

——, 'Cultural Identity and Diaspora', in Jonathan Rutherford (ed.), *Identity: Community, Culture, Difference* (London: Lawrence & Wishart, 1990), pp. 222–37.

——, 'Minimal Selves', in Homi Bhabha (ed.), *Identity: The Real Me*, ICA Documents (London: Institute of Contemporary Arts, 1987), pp. 44–6.

—— (ed.), *Culture, Media, Language: Working Papers in Cultural Studies, 1972–79* (London: [Birmingham, West Midlands]: Hutchinson; Centre for Contemporary Cultural Studies, University of Birmingham, 1980).

Hall, Stuart, Paul Gilroy, Lawrence Grossberg and Angela McRobbie (eds), *Without Guarantees: In Honour of Stuart Hall* (London; New York: Verso, 2000).

Hall, Stuart, Sut Jhally and Media Education Foundation, *The Origins of Cultural Studies a Lecture* (Northampton: Media Education Foundation, 2006).

Hall, Stuart, David Morley and Kuan-Hsing Chen (eds), *Stuart Hall: Critical Dialogues in Cultural Studies*, Comedia (London; New York: Routledge, 1996).

Hamdan, Amal, 'Afghanistan: The Soviet Union's Vietnam', News, *Al Jazeera*, 23 April 2003. http://www.aljazeera.com/archive/2003/04/2008410113842420760.html.

Hamilton, Kirk, 'The Last of Us: The Kotaku Review', *Kotaku*, 29 July 2014. http://kotaku.com/the-last-of-us-the-kotaku-review-511292998.

——, 'Video Gaming's Latest Breakthrough Moment', *Kotaku*, 17 February 2014. http://kotaku.com/video-gamings-latest-breakthrough-moment-1524555480.

——, 'Spec Ops Writer on Violent Games: "We're Better Than That"', Games Journalism, *Kotaku*, 27 March 2013. http://kotaku.com/spec-ops-writer-on-violent-games-were-better-than-th-460992384.

Hardt, Michael and Antonio Negri, *Empire* (Cambridge: Harvard University Press, 2001).

Harrell, D. Fox, 'Imagining Social Identities Through Computing', Media Theater, University of California, Santa Cruz, 11 May 2015.

——, 'A Phantasmal Media Approach to Empowerment, Identity, and Computation', presented at the Digital Inflections: Visions for the Posthuman Future, Pacific Centre for Technology and Culture, 23 January 2013. http://pactac.net/2013/01/a-phantasmal-media-approach-to-empowerment-identity-and-computation/.

——, *Phantasmal Media: An Approach to Imagination, Computation, and Expression* (Cambridge: The MIT Press, 2013).

Bibliography

Harrigan, Pat, and Noah Wardrip-Fruin (eds), *Third Person: Authoring and Exploring Vast Narratives*. (Cambridge: The MIT Press, 2009).

Harris, Michael D., *Colored Pictures: Race and Visual Representation* (Chapel Hill: The University of North Carolina Press, 2006).

Harvey, David, *A Brief History of Neoliberalism* (Oxford: Oxford University Press, 2007).

———, *The Condition of Postmodernity* (Oxford: Blackwell Publishers, 1989).

Hern, Alex, 'Battlefield 1 Halts '#justWWIthings' Campaign before Remembrance Sunday', *Guardian*, 31 October 2016, sec. Technology. https://www.theguardian.com/technology/2016/oct/31/battlefield-1-justwwithings-campaign-remembrance-sunday.

Hill, Mike (ed.), *Whiteness: A Critical Reader* (New York: NYU Press, 1997).

Hillier, Brenna, 'Remember Me Dev Wanted to "respect" Gamers with a Strong Female Protagonist', *VG247.com*, 16 April 2013. http://www.vg247.com/2013/04/16/remember-me-dev-wanted-to-respect-gamers-with-a-strong-female-protagonist/.

Hines, Alicia Hedlam, *Technicolor: Race, Technology, and Everyday Life*, Thuy Linh N. Tu and Alondra Nelson (eds), (New York; London: NYU Press, 2001).

Honneth, Axel, *The Struggle for Recognition: The Moral Grammar of Social Conflict*, Reprint edition (Cambridge: Polity Press, 2004).

hooks, bell, *Black Looks: Race and Representation*, 1st edition (Boston: South End Press, 1992).

Horsey, David, 'Obama Win Brings the Great Right Wing Freak-out of 2012', *The Baltimore Sun*. 13 November 2012. http://articles.baltimoresun.com/2012-11-13/news/bs-ed-horsey-gop-20121113_1_corporate-welfare-americans-election-results.

Howells, Richard, and Joaquim Negreiros, *Visual Culture*, 2nd edition (Cambridge: Polity, 2012).

Hsu, Hua, 'The End of White America?', *The Atlantic*, February 2009. http://www.theatlantic.com/magazine/archive/2009/01/the-end-of-white-america/307208/.

Hu, Tung-Hui, *A Prehistory of the Cloud* (Cambridge: The MIT Press, 2015).

Huber, William H., 'Epic Spatialities: The Production of Space in Final Fantasy Games', in Pat Harrigan and Noah Wardrip-Fruin (eds), *Third Person: Authoring and Exploring Vast Narratives* (Cambridge: The MIT Press, 2009), pp. 373–84.

Hughes, Rachel, 'Gameworld Geopolitics and the Genre of the Quest', in Fraser MacDonald, Rachel Hughes, and Klaus Dodds (eds), *Observant States: Geopolitics and Visual Culture*, International Library of Human Geography 16 (London; New York: I.B.Tauris, 2010), pp. 123–42.

Huizinga, Johan, *Homo Ludens: A Study of the Play-Element in Culture*, 1st edition (London: Beacon Press, 1971).

Ingenito, Vince, 'Assassin's Creed Liberation HD Review – IGN', *IGN*, 17 January 2014. http://www.ign.com/articles/2014/01/18/assassins-creed-liberation-hd-review.

Isbister, Katherine, *How Games Move Us: Emotion by Design*, *Playful Thinking* (Cambridge: The MIT Press, 2016).

Jackson, John Brinckerhoff, *A Sense of Place, a Sense of Time* (New Haven: Yale University Press, 1994).

——, *The Necessity for Ruins, and Other Topics* (Amherst: University of Massachusetts Press, 1980).

Jacobson, Matthew Frye, *Whiteness of a Different Color: European Immigrants and the Alchemy of Race* (Cambridge: Harvard University Press, 1999).

Jagoda, Patrick, Melissa Gilliam, Peter McDonald and Peter Russell, 'Worlding through Play: Alternate Reality Games, Large-Scale Learning, and *The Source*', *American Journal of Play* 8, no. 1 (Fall 2015), pp. 74–100.

Jameson, Fredric, *Postmodernism, Or, The Cultural Logic of Late Capitalism* (Duke University Press, 1992).

Jenkins, Henry, 'Building Imaginary Worlds: An Interview with Mark J.P. Wolf (Part Three)', Blog. *Confessions of an Aca-Fan*, 6 September 2013. http://henryjenkins.org/2013/09/building-imaginary-worlds-an-interview-with-mark-j-p-wolf-part-three.html.

——, 'Building Imaginary Worlds: An Interview with Mark J.P. Wolf (Part One)', Blog. *Confessions of an Aca-Fan*, 2 September 2013. http://henryjenkins.org/2013/09/building-imaginary-worlds-an-interview-with-mark-j-p-wolf-part-one.html.

——, 'Game Design as Narrative Architecture', in Noah Wardrip-Fruin and Pat Harrigan (eds), *First Person: New Media as Story, Performance, and Game* (Cambridge: The MIT Press, 2006), pp. 118–30.

——, '"Complete Freedom of Movement": Video Games as Gendered Playspace', in Justine Cassell and Henry Jenkins (eds), *From Barbie to Mortal Kombat: Gender and Computer Games*, 1st MIT Press paperback edition (Cambridge: MIT Press, 2000), pp. 330–63.

Jenkins, Henry, and Kurt Squire, 'The Art of Contested Spaces', in Lucien King (ed.), *Game on: The History and Culture of Videogames* (London: Laurence King Publishing, 2002), pp. 65–75. http://web.mit.edu/21fms/People/henry3/contestedspaces.html.

Joho, Jess, 'The Dadification of Videogames, Round Two', *Kill Screen*, 11 February 2014. http://killscreendaily.com/articles/dadification-videogames-round-two/.

Jones, Amelia (ed.), *The Feminism and Visual Culture Reader*, 2nd edition (London: Routledge, 2010).

Jones, Steven E., *The Meaning of Video Games: Gaming and Textual Strategies* (New York: Routledge, 2008).

Joyce, Lindsey, 'An Uneven Partnership: Representations of Gender in *The Last of Us*', *First Person Scholar*, 9 July 2014. http://www.firstpersonscholar.com/an-uneven-partnership/.

Kamen, Matt, 'Remember Me – Review', *Guardian*, 8 June 2013, sec. Technology. http://www.theguardian.com/technology/2013/jun/09/remember-me-review.

Kant, Immanuel, *Critique of the Power of Judgment*, translated by Paul Guyer and Eric Matthews (Cambridge: Cambridge University Press, 2000).

Katznelson, Ira, *When Affirmative Action Was White: An Untold History of Racial Inequality in Twentieth-Century America*, Reprint edition (New York: W. W. Norton & Company, 2006).

Kein, Sybil (ed.), *Creole: The History and Legacy of Louisiana's Free People of Color* (Baton Rouge: LSU Press, 2000).

Kelion, Leo, 'EA Boss Denies Video Games Encourage Violent Attacks', *BBC News*, 21 January 2013. http://www.bbc.com/news/technology-21274482.

Kellogg, Alex, 'Has "Whiteness Studies" Run Its Course at Colleges?' News, *inAmerica: CNN Blog*, 30 January 2012. http://inamerica.blogs.cnn.com/2012/01/30/has-whiteness-studies-run-its-course-at-colleges/.

Kennedy, Helen W., 'Lara Croft: Feminist Icon or Cyberbimbo?' *Game Studies: The International Journal of Computer Game Research* 2, no. 2 (December 2002).

Keogh, Brendan, 'Across Worlds and Bodies: Criticism in the Age of Video Games', *Journal of Games Criticism* 1, no. 1 (22 January 2014), pp. 1–26.

Kietzmann, Ludwig, 'Max Payne 3 Review: Nature of the Beast', *Engadget*, 14 May 2012. http://www.engadget.com/2012/05/14/max-payne-3-review/.

Kincheloe, Joe L., Shirley R. Steinberg, Nelson M. Rodriguez and Ronald Chennault (eds), *White Reign: Deploying Whiteness in America*, 1st St. Martin's Griffin edition (New York: St. Martin's Griffin, 2000).

King, Geoff, and Tanya Krzywinska, *Tomb Raiders and Space Invaders: Videogame Forms and Contexts* (London; New York: I.B.Tauris; Distributed in the U.S. by Palgrave Macmillan, 2006)

Klastrup, Lisbeth. 'A Poetics of Virtual Worlds', in *Proceedings of Digital Arts and Culture* (Melbourne: MelbourneDAC2003, 2003), pp. 100–109.

Kolko, Beth, Lisa Nakamura, and Gilbert Rodman (eds), *Race in Cyberspace*, 1st edition (New York: Routledge, 2000).

Kollar, Philip, 'Tomb Raider Review: The Descent', *Polygon*, 25 February 2015. http://www.polygon.com/2013/2/25/4026668/tomb-raider-review.

———, 'Assassin's Creed 3: Liberation Review: The Price of Chains', *Polygon*, 31 October 2012. http://www.polygon.com/2012/10/31/3582448/assassins-creed-3-liberation-review.

Krieg, Gregory J., 'Freaking Out: The Best of the Worst Responses to Obama's Win', News, *ABC News*, 8 November 2012. http://abcnews.go.com/blogs/politics/2012/11/freaking-out-the-best-of-the-worst-responses-to-obamas-win/.

Krupa, Daniel, 'Max Payne 3 Review', *IGN*, 14 May 2012. http://www.ign.com/articles/2012/05/14/max-payne-3-review.

Lefebvre, Henri, *The Production of Space*, 1st edition (Oxford: Wiley-Blackwell, 1992).

Leonard, D.J., 'Not a Hater, Just Keepin' It Real: The Importance of Race- and Gender-Based Game Studies', *Games and Culture* 1, no. 1 (1 January 2006), pp. 83–88. doi:10.1177/1555412005281910.

Leonard, David, 'High Tech Blackface – Race, Sports Video Games and Becoming the Other', *Intelligent Agent* 4, no. 4.2 (2004).

———, 'Live in Your World, Play in Ours' – Race, Video Games, and Consuming the Other', *Studies in Media & Information Literacy Education* 3, no. 4 (November 2003), p. 1–9.

Lewis, Helen, 'Gamergate: A Brief History of a Computer-Age War', *Guardian*, 11 January 2015. http://www.theguardian.com/technology/2015/jan/11/gamergate-a-brief-history-of-a-computer-age-war.

Lien, Tracey, 'Why Are Women Leaving the Tech Industry in Droves?' *Los Angeles Times*, 22 February 2015. http://www.latimes.com/business/la-fi-women-tech-20150222-story.html#page=1.

Lindner, Christoph (ed.), *Globalization, Violence, and the Visual Culture of Cities* (London; New York: Routledge, 2010).

Lipsitz, George, *The Possessive Investment in Whiteness: How White People Profit from Identity Politics*. Revised and expanded edition (Philadelphia: Temple University Press, 2006).

Longan, Michael W., 'Playing With Landscape: Social Process and Spatial Form in Video Games', *Aether: The Journal of Media Geography* II (April 2008), pp. 23–40.

MacCallum-Stewart, Esther, '"Take That, Bitches!" Refiguring Lara Croft in Feminist Game Narratives', *Game Studies* 14, no. 2 (December 2014). http://gamestudies.org/1402/articles/maccallumstewart.

Maharidge, Dale, *The Coming White Minority: California, Multiculturalism, and America's Future*, 1st Vintage Books edition (New York: Vintage Books, 1999).

Mahoney, Elizabeth, '"The People in Parentheses": Space Under Pressure in the Post-Modern City', in David B. Clarke (ed.), *The Cinematic City* (London; New York: Routledge, 1997), pp. 168–85.

Malkowski, Jennifer, and TreaAndrea M. Russworm (eds), *Gaming Representation: Race, Gender, and Sexuality in Video Game Studies* (Bloomington: Indiana University Press, 2017).

Manovich, Lev, *The Language of New Media*, Reprint edition (Cambridge: The MIT Press, 2002).

Marriott, Michel, 'Blood, Gore, Sex and Now: Race', *The New York Times*, 21 October 1999, sec. Technology. http://www.nytimes.com/1999/10/21/technology/blood-gore-sex-and-now-race.html.

Martinez, Elizabeth, Arnoldo Garcia and National Network for Immigrant and Refugee Rights. 'CorpWatch: What Is Neoliberalism?', *CorpWatch*, 1 January 1997. http://www.corpwatch.org/article.php?id=376.

Marx, Leo, *The Machine in the Garden: Technology and the Pastoral Ideal in America* (New York: Oxford University Press, 2000).

Masao, Miyoshi, 'Ivory Tower in Escrow', in Miyoshi Masao and H.D. Harootunian (eds), *Learning Places: The Afterlives of Area Studies* (Durham: Duke University Press, 2002), pp. 19–60.

McElroy, Griffin, 'IGDA Draws Backlash, Member Resignations over Female Dancers at GDC Party (Update: IGDA Responds)', *Polygon*, 28 March 2013. http://www.polygon.com/2013/3/28/4157266/igda-gdc-party-brenda-romero-resignation.

McGonigal, Jane, *SuperBetter: A Revolutionary Approach to Getting Stronger, Happier, Braver, and More Resilient** (New York: Penguin Books, 2015).

McInnis, Shaun, 'Why I Keep Thinking About Assassin's Creed III: Liberation', *GameSpot*, 8 November 2012. http://www.gamespot.com/articles/why-i-keep-thinking-about-assassins-creed-iii-liberation/1100-6399671/.

McLaughlin, Michael, 'Racist Manifesto Purportedly Written By Dylann Roof Surfaces Online', *The Huffington Post*, 20 June 2015. http://www.huffingtonpost.com/2015/06/20/dylann-roof-manifesto-charleston-shooting_n_7627788.html.

McLaughlin, Rus, 'IGN Presents: The History of Tomb Raider', *IGN*, 29 February 2008. http://www.ign.com/articles/2008/03/01/ign-presents-the-history-of-tomb-raider.

McLennen, Sophia, 'Neoliberalism and the Crisis of Intellectual Engagement', *Works and Days* 26–27 (2009, 2008), pp. 259–470.

McPherson, Tara, 'U.S. Operating Systems at Mid-Century: The Intertwining of Race and UNIX', in Lisa Nakamura and Peter Chow-White (eds), *Race After the Internet* (New York and London: Routledge, 2012), pp. 21–37.

McRobbie, Angela, *The Uses of Cultural Studies: A Textbook* (London; Thousand Oaks, Calif: SAGE, 2005).

McWhertor, Michael, 'Metal Gear Solid 5: The Phantom Pain Review: Future Legend', *Polygon*, 27 August 2015. http://www.polygon.com/2015/8/27/9207599/metal-gear-solid-5-the-phantom-pain-review-ps4-xbox-one-PC.

Mead, Corey, *War Play: Video Games and the Future of Armed Conflict* (Boston: Eamon Dolan/Houghton Mifflin Harcourt, 2013).

'Mean Streets, Revisited', *The Economist*, 17 November 2012. http://www.economist.com/news/americas/21566653-brazils-biggest-city-becoming-more-dangerous-mean-streets-revisited.

Mechner, Jordan, 'The Sands of Time: Crafting a Video Game Story', in Pat Harrigan and Noah Wardrip-Fruin (eds), *Second Person: Role Playing and Story in Games and Playable Media* (Cambridge: The MIT Press, 2007), pp. 111–20.

Mennel, Barbara, *Cities and Cinema*, Routledge Critical Introductions to Urbanism and the City (London; New York: Routledge, 2008).

'Metacritic – Movie Reviews, TV Reviews, Game Reviews, and Music Reviews' (accessed 15 August 2015). http://www.metacritic.com/.

Miller, Matt, 'Tomb Raider Review – Old Name, Remarkable New Series', www. GameInformer.com, 25 February 2013. http://www.gameinformer.com/ games/tomb_raider/b/xbox360/archive/2013/02/25/tomb-raider-review. aspx.

Mirzoeff, Nicholas (ed.), *The Visual Culture Reader*, 3rd edition (London; New York: Routledge, 2013).

——, *An Introduction to Visual Culture*, 2nd edition (London; New York: Routledge, 2009).

Mitchell, W.J.T., 'Imperial Landscape', in W.J.T. Mitchell (ed.), *Landscape and Power*, 2nd edition (Chicago: University of Chicago Press, 2002), pp. 5–34.

——, *What Do Pictures Want?: The Lives and Loves of Images* (Chicago: University of Chicago Press, 2005).

—— (ed.), 'Israel, Palestine, and the American Wilderness', in W.J.T. Mitchell (ed.), *Landscape and Power*, 2nd edition (Chicago: University of Chicago Press, 2002), pp. 261–90.

—— (ed.), *Landscape and Power*, 2nd edition (Chicago: University of Chicago Press, 2002)

Moralde, Oscar, 'Haptic Landscapes: Dear Esther and Embodied Video Game Space', *Media Fields Journal* 8 (2014), pp. 1–15.

——, 'Dimensions of the Digital City', UCLA's Journal of Cinema and Media Studies, *Mediascape*, Fall 2013. http://www.tft.ucla.edu/mediascape/Fall2013_ Dimensions.html.

Moriarty, Colin, 'Survival of the Fittest', online media and services, *IGN Entertainment*, 5 June 2013. http://www.ign.com/articles/2013/06/05/the-last-of-us-review.

Morris, Chris, 'Dan Houser's Very Extended Interview about Everything 'Grand Theft Auto IV' and Rockstar', Blog. *Variety*, 19 April 2008. http://weblogs.variety.com/the_cut_scene/2008/04/dan-housers-ver.html.

Morrison, Toni, *Playing in the Dark: Whiteness and the Literary Imagination*, 1st Vintage Books edition (New York: Vintage Books, 1993).

Mukherjee, Souvik, 'Playing Subaltern: Video Games and Postcolonialism', *Games and Culture*, 9 February 2016. doi:10.1177/1555412015627258.

Murray, Derek Conrad, *Queering Post-Black Art: Artists Transforming African-American Identity After Civil Rights* (London; New York: I.B.Tauris, 2016).

Murray, Derek Conrad, and Soraya Murray, 'Uneasy Bedfellows: Canonical Art Theory and the Politics of Identity', *Art Journal* 65, no. 1 (1 March 2006), pp. 22–39. doi:10.1080/00043249.2006.10791193.

Murray, Janet Horowitz, *Hamlet on the Holodeck: The Future of Narrative in Cyberspace* (New York: Simon and Schuster, 1997).

Murray, Jill, 'Diverse Game Characters: Write Them Now!' presented at the Game Developers Conference 2013, San Francisco, 29 March 2013. http://www.gdcvault.com/play/1017819/Diverse-Game-Characters-Write-Them.

Murray, Jill, and Soraya Murray, 'Personal Correspondence between Jill Murray and Author', 31 May 2015.

Murray, Soraya, 'Race, Gender, and Genre in *Spec Ops: The Line*', *Film Quarterly* 70, no. 2 (December 2016), pp. 38–48.

———, 'High Art/Low Life: The Art of Playing Grand Theft Auto', *PAJ: A Journal of Performance and Art* 27, no. 2 (1 May 2005), pp. 91–8.

Myers, Maddy, 'Bad Dads Vs. Hyper Mode: The Father-Daughter Bond In Videogames', *Pastemagazine.com*, 30 July 2013. http://www.pastemagazine.com/articles/2013/07/hyper-mode.html.

Nakamura, Lisa, 'Racism, Sexism, and Gaming's Cruel Optimism', in Malkowski, Jennifer, and TreaAndrea M. Russworm (eds), *Gaming Representation: Race, Gender, and Sexuality in Video Game Studies* (Bloomington: Indiana University Press, 2017), pp. 245–50.

———, *Digitizing Race: Visual Cultures of the Internet*, Electronic Mediations 23 (Minneapolis: University of Minnesota Press, 2008).

———, *Cybertypes: Race, Ethnicity, and Identity on the Internet* (New York: Routledge, 2002).

Nakamura, Lisa, and Peter Chow-White (eds), *Race after the Internet* (New York: Routledge, 2012).

Nakamura, Toshi, 'Hideo Kojima: This Is What Fox Engine Is All About', *Kotaku*, 21 March 21 2013. http://kotaku.com/5991640/hideo-kojima-this-is-what-fox-engine-is-all-about.

Narcisse, Evan, 'A Game That Showed Me My Own Black History', *Kotaku*, 19 December 2013. http://kotaku.com/a-game-that-showed-me-my-own-black-history-1486643518.

———, 'You're An Escaped Slave In Assassin's Creed IV's Freedom's Cry DLC', *Kotaku*, 8 October 2013. http://kotaku.com/youre-an-escaped-slave-in-em-assassin-s-creed-iv-em-1442477523.

———, 'Slavery Gives Me a Weird Personal Connection to Assassin's Creed IV', *Kotaku*, 16 July 2013. http://kotaku.com/slavery-gives-me-a-weird-personal-connection-to-assassi-799210668.

———, 'Remember Me: The Kotaku Review', *Kotaku*, 3 June 2013. http://kotaku.com/remember-me-the-kotaku-review-510988329.

——, 'This Assassin's Creed Heroine Is a Great Black Game Character. Here's How It Happened', *Kotaku*, 27 February 2013. http://kotaku.com/5987083/this-assassins-creed-heroine-is-a-great-black-game-character-heres-how-it-happened.

——, 'Tomb Raider: The Kotaku Review', *Kotaku*, 25 February 2013. http://kotaku.com/5986619/tomb-raider-the-kotaku-review.

——, 'I'm Surprised By How "Black" Assassin's Creed Liberation Feels', *Kotaku*, 1 November 2012. http://kotaku.com/5957411/im-surprised-by-how-black-assassins-creed-liberation-feels.

——, 'Assassin's Creed III: Liberation: The Kotaku Review', *Kotaku*, 30 October 2012. http://kotaku.com/5957502/assassins-creed-iii-liberation-the-kotaku-review.

——, 'White Actress Will Voice Assassin's Creed's Black Heroine [Correction]', *Kotaku*, 29 August 2012. http://kotaku.com/5939009/white-actress-will-voice-assassins-creeds-black-heroine.

——, 'Max Payne 3: The Kotaku Review', *Kotaku*, 14 May 2012. http://kotaku.com/5910100/max-payne-3-the-kotaku-review.

Neonakis, Alexandria, 'Game Theory: The Last of Us, Revisited', *New York Times Blog: ArtsBeat*, 30 December 2013, sec. ArtsBeat. http://artsbeat.blogs.nytimes.com/2013/12/30/game-theory-the-last-of-us-revisited/.

Newman, James, *Videogames*, 2nd edition (London; New York: Routledge, 2013).

Nielsen Company, 'Gaming Gone Global: Keeping Tabs on Worldwide Trends', *Nielsen*, 31 May 2016. http://www.nielsen.com/us/en/insights/news/2016/gaming-gone-global-keeping-tabs-on-worldwide-trends.html.

Nilges, Matthias, 'The Aesthetics of Destruction: Contemporary US Cinema and TV Culture', in Jeff Birkenstein, Anna Froula and Karen Randell (eds), *Reframing 9/11: Film, Popular Culture and the 'War on Terror'* (New York: Continuum, 2010), pp. 23–33.

Nitsche, Michael, *Video Game Spaces: Image, Play, and Structure in 3D Worlds* (Cambridge: The MIT Press, 2009).

Noon, Derek and Nick Dyer-Witheford, 'Sneaking Mission: Late Imperial America and *Metal Gear Solid*', in J. Talmadge Wright, David G. Embrick, and András Lukács (eds), *Utopic Dreams and Apocalyptic Fantasies: Critical Approaches to Researching Video Game Play* (Blue Ridge Summit, PA: Lexington Books, 2010), pp. 73–95.

October, 'Questionnaire on Visual Culture', *October* 77, Summer (1996), pp. 25–70.

Olwig, Kenneth, *Landscape, Nature, and the Body Politic: From Britain's Renaissance to America's New World* (Madison: University of Wisconsin Press, 2002).

Orland, Kyle, 'Spec Ops: The Line's Lead Writer on Creating an Un-Heroic War Story', *Ars Technica*, 19 July 2012. http://arstechnica.com/gaming/2012/07/spec-ops-the-lines-lead-writer-on-creating-an-un-heroic-war-story/.

Painter, Nell Irvin, *The History of White People*, Reprint edition (New York: W. W. Norton & Company, 2011).

Parkin, Simon, 'Zoe Quinn's Depression Quest', *The New Yorker*, 9 September 2014. http://www.newyorker.com/tech/elements/zoe-quinns-depression-quest.

——, 'Tomb Raider – Review', *Guardian*, 1 March 2013, sec. Technology. http://www.theguardian.com/technology/gamesblog/2013/mar/01/tomb-raider-video-game-review.

Payne, Matthew Thomas, *Playing War: Military Video Games After 9/11* (New York: NYU Press, 2016).

——, 'War Bytes: The Critique of Militainment in *Spec Ops: The Line*', *Critical Studies in Media Communication* 31, no. 4 (8 August 2014), pp. 265–82. doi:10.1080/15295036.2014.881518.

Pearce, Celia, 'Towards a Game Theory of Game', in Noah Wardrip-Fruin and Pat Harrigan (eds), *First Person: New Media as Story, Performance, and Game* (Cambridge: The MIT Press, 2004), pp. 143–53.

Peixoto, Marta, 'Rio's Favelas in Recent Fiction and Film: Commonplaces of Urban Segregation' *PMLA* 122, no. 1 (2007), pp. 170–8.

Petit, Carolyn, 'Why Political Engagement Is Critical to Games Journalism' *A Game of Me*, 23 August 2014. http://agameofme.tumblr.com/post/95611752882/why-political-engagement-is-critical-to-games.

Plante, Chris, 'An Awful Week to Care about Video Games' *Polygon*, 29 August 2014. http://www.polygon.com/2014/8/28/6078391/video-games-awful-week.

Pollock, Griselda, 'Becoming Cultural Studies: The Daydream of the Political' in Paul Bowman (ed.), *Interrogating Cultural Studies: Theory, Politics and Practice* (London; Sterling, 2003), pp. 125–41.

Pollock, Griselda, James Elkins, Nicholas Mirzoeff, Michael Ann Holly, W.J.T. Mitchell, Norman Bryson and Peter Leech, 'Responses to Mieke Bal's "Visual Essentialism and the Object of Visual Culture" (2003)', *Journal of Visual Culture* 2, no. 2 (1 August 2003). doi:10.1177/14704129030022012.

Portillo, Esmeralda, 'Remember Me Was Misunderstood Says Creative Director', *The Escapist*, 17 August 2014. http://www.escapistmagazine.com/news/view/136886-DONTNOD-Entertainment-Creative-Director-Says-Remember-Me-was-Misunderstood.

Pötzsch, Holger, 'Selective Realism: Filtering Experiences of War and Violence in First- and Third-Person Shooters', *Games and Culture*, first published online (31 May 2015), pp. 1–23. doi:10.1177/1555412015587802.

Prell, Sophie, 'How Facebook Inspired Remember Me to Drop Global Warming, and Why Its Protagonist Had to Be a Woman', *The Penny Arcade Report*, 18 March 2013. http://web.archive.org/web/20131211185434/http://penny-arcade.com/report/article/remember-mes-surprising-connection-to-facebook-and-why-its-protagonist-had.

Procter, James, *Stuart Hall*, Routledge Critical Thinkers (London; New York: Routledge, 2004).

R*A, 'Rockstar Recommends: "Elite Squad (Tropa de Elite)"', *Rockstar Games*, 10 November 2011. http://www.rockstargames.com/newswire/article/19561/rockstar-recommends-elite-squad-tropa-de-elite.html.

Rabin, Roni Caryn, 'Video Games and the Depressed Teenager', *The New York Times*, 18 January 2011. http://well.blogs.nytimes.com/2011/01/18/video-games-and-the-depressed-teenager/.

Raengo, Alessandra, *On the Sleeve of the Visual: Race as Face Value*, 1st edition, Interfaces: Studies in Visual Culture (Hanover: Dartmouth College Press, 2013).

Reiner, Andrew, 'Max Payne 3 Review: The New, Same Old Payne', *GameInformer*, 14 May 2012. http://www.gameinformer.com/games/max_payne_3/b/xbox360/archive/2012/05/14/the-new-same-old-payne.aspx.

Rial y Costas, Gundo, 'Spaces of Insecurity? The "favelas" of Rio de Janeiro between Stigmatization and Glorification', *Iberoamericana (2001-)* 11, no. 41 (2011), pp. 115–28.

Rodman, Gilbert B., *Why Cultural Studies?* (Hoboken: Wiley, 2014).

Roediger, David R., Mike Davis, Michael Sprinker, and Kathleen Cleaver, *The Wages of Whiteness: Race and the Making of the American Working Class*, New edition (London: Verso, 2007).

Rojek, Chris, *Stuart Hall*, Key Contemporary Thinkers (Cambridge: Polity, 2003).

Romero, Brenda and Leigh Alexander, 'GDC Vault – #1ReasonToBe', *GDC Vault*, 2014. http://www.gdcvault.com/play/1020593/.

Rose, Gillian. *Visual Methodologies: An Introduction to Researching with Visual Materials*, 3rd edition (London; Thousand Oaks: SAGE Publications Ltd, 2011).

Rosenberg, Adam, 'Spec Ops: The Line Post-Mortem – Finding Deeper Truths Within the Narrative With Walt Williams', *G4tv.com*, 17 July 2012. http://www.g4tv.com/thefeed/blog/post/726042/spec-ops-the-line-post-mortem-finding-deeper-truths-within-the-narrative-with-walt-williams/.

Ross, Thomas, 'Whiteness After 9/11', *Washington University Journal of Law & Policy* 18, no. 1 [Whiteness: Some Critical Perspectives] (January 2005), pp. 223–43.

Rothenberg, Paula S. (ed.), *White Privilege: Essential Readings on the Other Side of Racism*, 4th edition (New York: Worth Publishers, 2012).

Rubin, Lance, 'Cultural Anxiety, Moral Clarity, and Willful Amnesia: Filming Philip K. Dick After 9/11', in Jeff Birkenstein, Anna Froula and Karen Randell (eds), *Reframing 9/11: Film, Popular Culture and the 'War on Terror'* (New York: Continuum, 2010), pp. 183–94.

Russworm, TreaAndrea, *Blackness Is Burning: Civil Rights, Popular Culture, and the Problem of Recognition* (Detroit: Wayne State University Press, 2016).

Bibliography

Ryan, Michael, and Hanna Musiol (eds), *Cultural Studies: An Anthology* (Malden; Oxford: Blackwell Pub, 2008).

Ryerson, Liz, 'On "Gamers" and Identity', *First Person Scholar*, 10 September 2014. http://www.firstpersonscholar.com/on-gamers-and-identity/.

Said, Edward W., *Orientalism*, 1st Vintage Books edition (New York: Vintage Books, 1979).

Salter, Anastasia, and Bridget Blodgett, 'Hypermasculinity & Dickwolves: The Contentious Role of Women in the New Gaming Public', *Journal of Broadcasting & Electronic Media* 56, no. 3 (July 2012), pp. 401–16. doi:10.1080/08838151.2012.705199.

Sandy, Matt, 'World Cup Showdown in Rio', News, *Al Jazeera America*, 18 May 2014. http://projects.aljazeera.com/2014/world-cup-favelas/index.html.

Sarkar, Samit, 'The Last of Us Remastered Is a Stunning Visual Masterpiece', *Polygon*, 16 July 2014. http://www.polygon.com/2014/7/16/5902983/the-last-of-us-remastered-ps4-preview-graphics.

Sarkeesian, Anita, 'One Week of Harassment on Twitter', *Feminist Frequency*, 20 January 2015. http://femfreq.tumblr.com/post/109319269825/one-week-of-harassment-on-twitter.

Sassen, Saskia, *Expulsions: Brutality and Complexity in the Global Economy* (Cambridge: The Belknap Press of Harvard University Press, 2014).

Schama, Simon, *Landscape and Memory*, 1st Vintage Books edition (New York: Vintage Books, 1996).

Schleiner, Anne-Marie, 'Does Lara Croft Wear Fake Polygons? Gender and Gender-Role Subversion in Computer Adventure Games', *Leonardo* 34, no. 3 (1 January 2001), pp. 221–6.

Schrank, Brian, and Jay David Bolter, *Avant-Garde Videogames: Playing with Technoculture* (Cambridge: The MIT Press, 2014).

Schreier, Jason, 'Tomb Raider Creators Say "Rape" Is Not A Word In Their Vocabulary', *Kotaku*, 29 June 2012. http://kotaku.com/5922228/tomb-raider-creators-say-rape-is-not-a-word-in-their-vocabulary.

Schulman, Norma, 'Conditions of their Own Making: An Intellectual History of the Centre for Contemporary Cultural Studies at the University of Birmingham', *Canadian Journal of Communication* 18, no. 1 (1 January 1993). http://www.cjc-online.ca/index.php/journal/article/view/717.

Schulzke, Marcus, 'The Critical Power of Virtual Dystopias', *Games and Culture* 9, no. 5 (1 September 2014), pp. 315–34. doi:10.1177/1555412014541694.

Scimeca, Dennis, 'BioWare Developer Manveer Heir Challenges Colleagues to Combat Prejudice with Video Games', *VentureBeat*, 20 March 2014. http://venturebeat.com/2014/03/20/bioware-developer-manveer-heir-challenges-colleagues-to-combat-prejudice-with-video-games/.

Scimeca, Dennis C., 'The Exhausting Violence of Max Payne 3', *The Escapist*, 3 August 2012. http://www.escapistmagazine.com/articles/view/video-games/columns/firstperson/9844-The-Exhausting-Violence-of-Max-Payne-3.

Shaw, Adrienne, *Gaming at the Edge: Sexuality and Gender at the Margins of Gamer Culture* (Minneapolis: University of Minnesota Press, 2015).

———, 'The Tyranny of Realism: Historical Accuracy in Assassin's Creed III', *First Person Scholar*, 29 October 2014. http://www.firstpersonscholar.com/the-tyranny-of-realism/.

———, 'What Is Video Game Culture? Cultural Studies and Game Studies', *Games and Culture* 5, no. 4 (1 October 2010), pp. 403–24. doi:10.1177/155541 2009360414.

Shaw, Ian G.R. and Joanne P. Sharp, 'Playing with the Future: Social Irrealism and the Politics of Aesthetics', *Social & Cultural Geography* 14, no. 3 (May 2013), pp. 341–59. doi:10.1080/14649365.2013.765027.

Shinkle, Eugénie, 'Gameworlds and Digital Gardens: Landscape and the Space of Nature in Digital Games', presented at the World Building: Third Annual UF Games and Digital Media Conference, University of Florida, Gainesville, 1 March 2007.

Sicart, Miguel, *Play Matters* (Cambridge: The MIT Press, 2014).

———, *Beyond Choices: The Design of Ethical Gameplay* (Cambridge: The MIT Press, 2013).

———, *The Ethics of Computer Games* (Cambridge; London: The MIT Press, 2011).

Sipple, Brian, '"Max Payne 3" Review', *Game Rant*, 2012. http://gamerant.com/max-payne-3-reviews-brian-149629/.

Šisler, Vit, 'Digital Arabs: Representation in Video Games', *European Journal of Cultural Studies* 11, no. 2 (2008), pp. 203–20.

Smethurst, Toby and Stef Craps, 'Playing with Trauma: Interreactivity, Empathy, and Complicity in The Walking Dead Video Game', *Games and Culture* 10, no. 3 (1 May 2015), pp. 269–90. doi:10.1177/1555412014559306.

Smith, Jonas Heide, Simon Egenfeldt-Nielsen, Susana Pajares Tosca and Simon Egenfeldt-Nielsen, *Understanding Video Games: The Essential Introduction*, 2nd edition (New York: Routledge, 2013).

Soja, Edward, *Thirdspace: Journeys to Los Angeles and Other Real-and-Imagined Places*, 1st edition (Cambridge: Blackwell Publishers, 1996).

Solkin, David H. and Richard Wilson, *Richard Wilson: The Landscape of Reaction* (London: Tate Gallery, 1982).

Sreenivasan, Hari, '#Gamergate Leads to Death Threats against Women', *PBS NewsHour*, 16 October 2014. http://www.pbs.org/newshour/bb/gamergate-leads-death-threats-women-gaming-industry/.

St. George, Donna, 'Study Links Violent Video Games, Hostility', *The Washington Post*, 3 November 2008, sec. Technology. http://www.washingtonpost.com/wp-dyn/content/article/2008/11/02/AR2008110202392.html.

Stafford, Patrick, 'How to End Video Games' Bullying Problem: Change the Games', *The Atlantic*, 22 May 2014. http://www.theatlantic.com/entertainment/archive/2014/05/how-to-fix-video-games-bullying-problem/371344/.

Stallings, Tyler, *Whiteness, a Wayward Construction*, 1st edition (Laguna Beach; Los Angeles: Fellows of Contemporary Art, 2003).

Stanton, Rich, 'Metal Gear Solid V – How Kojima Productions Is Blowing Apart the Open-World Video Game', *Guardian*, 11 June 2015, sec. Technology. http://www.theguardian.com/technology/2015/jun/11/metal-gear-solid-v-phantom-pain-kojima-preview.

Stewart, Keith, 'Gamergate: The Community Is Eating Itself but There Should Be Room for All', *Guardian*, 3 September 2014. http://www.theguardian.com/technology/2014/sep/03/gamergate-corruption-games-anita-sarkeesian-zoe-quinn.

Storey, John, *Cultural Studies and the Study of Popular Culture*, 3rd. edition (Edinburgh: Edinburgh University Press, 2010).

———, *What Is Cultural Studies?: A Reader* (Bloomsbury, USA, 1996).

Stuart, Keith, 'The Last of Us, Bioshock: Infinite and Why All Video Game Dystopias Work the Same Way', *Guardian*, 1 July 2013, sec. Technology. http://www.theguardian.com/technology/gamesblog/2013/jul/01/last-of-us-bioshock-infinite-male-view.

———, 'Max Payne 3 and the Problem of Narrative Dissonance', *Guardian*, 18 May 2012, sec. Technology. http://www.theguardian.com/technology/gamesblog/2012/may/18/max-payne-3-story-vs-action.

———, 'Max Payne 3 – Review', *Guardian*, 14 May 2012, sec. Technology. http://www.theguardian.com/technology/gamesblog/2012/may/14/max-payne-3-game-review.

Sturken, Marita, and Lisa Cartwright, *Practices of Looking: An Introduction to Visual Culture*, 2nd edition (New York: Oxford University Press, 2009).

Sudnow, David, *Pilgrim in the Microworld* (New York: Warner Books, 1983).

Suellentrop, Chris, 'Slavery as New Focus for a Game: Assassin's Creed: Liberation Examines Colonial Blacks', *The New York Times*, 27 January 2014, sec. C1. http://www.nytimes.com/2014/01/28/arts/video-games/assassins-creed-liberation-examines-colonial-blacks.html.

———, 'In the Video Game The Last of Us, Survival Favors the Man', *The New York Times*, 14 June 2013. http://www.nytimes.com/2013/06/14/arts/video-games/in-the-video-game-the-last-of-us-survival-favors-the-man.html.

Swaine, Jon, 'Leader of Group Cited in "Dylann Roof Manifesto" Donated to Top Republicans', *Guardian*, 21 June 2015. http://www.theguardian.com/us-news/2015/jun/21/dylann-roof-manifesto-charlston-shootings-republicans.

Takahashi, Dean, 'The DeanBeat: The Last of Us Is This Generation's Masterpiece', *VentureBeat*, June 2013. http://venturebeat.com/2013/06/28/the-deanbeat-the-last-of-us-is-this-generations-masterpiece/.

Tavernise, Sabrina, 'Numbers of Children of Whites Falling Fast', *The New York Times*, 6 April 2011. http://www.nytimes.com/2011/04/06/us/06census.html.

The Princeton Review, 'Top Graduate Schools for Video Game Design – College Rankings', Natick: IAC/InterActive Unit, 2015. http://www.princetonreview.com/college-rankings/game-design/top-graduate-schools-for-video-game-design.

'The Shootings in a Charleston Church', *The New York Times*, 18 June 2015. http://www.nytimes.com/interactive/2015/06/18/us/charleston-church-shooting-maps-and-suspect.html.

Truettner, William H., Nancy K. Anderson, National Museum of American Art (US), Denver Art Museum and St. Louis Art Museum (eds), *The West as America: Reinterpreting Images of the Frontier, 1820–1920* (Washington: Published for the National Museum of American Art by the Smithsonian Institution Press, 1991).

Turner, Graeme, *British Cultural Studies: An Introduction*, 3rd edition (London; New York: Routledge, 2003).

Tycho, 'Penny Arcade – News – Larvae', *Penny Arcade*, 24 June 2013. http://penny-arcade.com/news/post/2013/6/24/larvae1.

Ulezko, Kirill, 'Jean-Max Moris: "In Remember Me We Invite the Player to Join Nilin on Her Voyage of Self-Discovery"', *Gamestar*, 2013. http://gamestar.ru/english/remember_me_interview_eng.html.

Valdes, Giancarlo, 'In The Last of Us, You Have to Earn the Right to Survive (Review)', *VentureBeat*, 5 June 2013. http://venturebeat.com/2013/06/05/the-last-of-us-review/.

Vanolo, Alberto, 'The Political Geographies of Liberty City: A Critical Analysis of a Virtual Space', *City* 16, no. 3 (June 2012), pp. 284–98. doi:10.1080/13604813.2012.662377.

VanOrd, Kevin, 'Remember Me Review', *GameSpot*, 3 June 2013. http://www.gamespot.com/reviews/remember-me-review/1900-6409150/.

Voorhees, Gerald, 'Mourning Sex', *First Person Scholar*, 3 September 2014. http://www.firstpersonscholar.com/mourning-sex/.

——, 'Criticism and Control: Gameplay in the Space of Possibility', in Matthew Wysocki (ed.), *Ctrl-Alt-Play: Essays on Control in Video Gaming* (Jefferson, NC: McFarland & Co, 2013), pp. 9–20.

Wardrip-Fruin, Noah, *Expressive Processing: Digital Fictions, Computer Games, and Software Studies* (Cambridge: The MIT Press, 2009).

——, 'Playable Media and Textual Instruments', *Dichtung Digital*, 2005. http://www.dichtung-digital.de/2005/1/Wardrip-Fruin/index.htm.

Watts, Evan, 'Ruin, Gender, and Digital Games', *WSQ: Women's Studies Quarterly* 39, no. 3–4 (2011), pp. 247–65. doi:10.1353/wsq.2011.0041.

Weber, Rachel, 'Dontnod: Publishers Said You Can't Have a Female Character', *GamesIndustry.biz*, 19 March 2013. http://www.gamesindustry.biz/articles/2013-03-19-dontnod-publishers-said-you-cant-have-a-female-character.

Weheliye, Alexander G., *Habeas Viscus: Racializing Assemblages, Biopolitics, and Black Feminist Theories of the Human* (Durham: Duke University Press, 2014).

Westcott, Lucy, 'Brazilian Police Invade Rio's Slum Ahead of This Summer's World Cup', News, *The Wire: News From the Atlantic*, 31 March 2014. http://www.thewire.com/global/2014/03/police-swarm-brazilian-slum-to-clean-up-before-world-cup/359916/.

Will, Brooker, 'Camera-Eye, CG-Eye: Videogames and the "Cinematic"', *Cinema Journal* 48, no. 3 (2009), pp. 122–8. doi:10.1353/cj.0.0126.

Williams, Claire, 'Ghettourism and Voyeurism, or Challenging Stereotypes and Raising Consciousness? Literary and Non-Literary Forays into the Favelas of Rio de Janeiro', *Bulletin of Latina American Research* 27, no. 4 (2008), pp. 483–500.

Williams, Gordon, *A Dictionary of Sexual Language and Imagery in Shakespearean and Stuart Literature: Three Volume Set Volume I A-F Volume II G-P Volume III Q-Z* (London: A&C Black, 2001).

Williams, Jeffrey J., 'The Pedagogy of Debt', *College Literature* 33, no. 4 (2006), pp. 155–69.

——, 'The Post-Welfare State University', *American Literary History* 18, no. 1 (Spring) (2006), pp. 190–216.

Williams, Mike, 'Assassin's Creed Unity and Rethinking the Core of Assassin's Creed', *USgamer.net*, 14 October 2014. http://www.usgamer.net/articles/assassins-creed-unity-interview-with-alex-amancio.

Williams, Raymond, *The Country and the City*, 1st issued as an Oxford University Press paperback, Reprint edition (New York: Oxford University Press, 1975).

Wise, Tim, *White Like Me: Reflections on Race from a Privileged Son*, Revised edition (Berkeley: Soft Skull Press, 2011).

Wofford, Taylor, 'APA Says Video Games Make You Violent, but Critics Cry Bias', *Newsweek*, 20 August 2015. http://www.newsweek.com/apa-video-games-violence-364394.

Wolf, Mark J.P., 'Worlds', in Mark J.P. Wolf and Bernard Perron (eds), *The Routledge Companion to Video Game Studies* (New York; London: Routledge, 2014), pp. 125–31.

——, *Building Imaginary Worlds: The Theory and History of Subcreation* (New York: Routledge, 2012).

——, 'Space in the Video Game', in Mark J.P. Wolf (ed.), *The Medium of the Video Game*, 1st edition (Austin: University of Texas Press, 2001), pp. 52–75.

Wolf, Mark J.P., and Bernard Perron (eds), *The Routledge Companion to Video Game Studies*, Routledge Companions (New York: Routledge, 2014).

Woolley, Emma M., 'Don't Believe the "conspiracy," Gaming Has Bigger Problems than "corruption"', *The Globe and Mail*, 27 August 2014. http://www.theglobeandmail.com/technology/digital-culture/dont-believe-the-conspiracy-gaming-has-bigger-problems-than-corruption/article20230850/.

Wray, Matt, and Annalee Newitz (eds), *White Trash: Race and Class in America* (New York: Routledge, 1997).

Wu, Brianna, 'Rape and Death Threats Are Terrorizing Female Gamers. Why Haven't Men in Tech Spoken Out?' *The Washington Post*, 20 October 2014. http://www.washingtonpost.com/posteverything/wp/2014/10/20/rape-and-death-threats-are-terrorizing-female-gamers-why-havent-men-in-tech-spoken-out/.

Žižek, Slavoj, 'Tolerance as an Ideological Category', *Critical Inquiry* 34, no. 4 (2008), pp. 660–82. doi:10.1086/592539.

Index

Index

Index

Index

Index

Index

Index

Index

Index

Index